An Introduction to Sociology

For Eirene

AN INTRODUCTION TO SOCIOLOGY

Ken Browne

Polity Press

The right of Ken Browne to be identified as author of this work
has been asserted in accordance with the Copyright, Designs and
Patents Act 1988.

First published 1992 by Polity Press
in association with Blackwell Publishers Ltd.
Reprinted 1992, 1993, 1994, 1995, 1996

Editorial office:
Polity Press
65 Bridge Street
Cambridge CB2 1UR, UK

Marketing and production:
Blackwell Publishers Ltd
108 Cowley Road
Oxford OX4 1JF, UK

Blackwell Publishers Inc.
238 Main Street,
Cambridge, MA 02142, USA

A CIP catalogue record for this book is available from the British Library.

Library of Congress Cataloging in Publication Data
Browne, Ken. 1951–
    An introduction to sociology / Ken Browne.
        p.   cm.
    Includes index.
    ISBN 0–7456–0921–X. — ISBN 0–7456–0922–8 (pbk.)
    1. Sociology.   2. Great Britain—Social conditions.   I. Title.
    HM51.B884   1992   91–41059
    301—dc20   CIP

Typeset in 11 on 13 pt Sabon
by TecSet Ltd, Wallington, Surrey
Printed in Great Britain by T.J. Press (Padstow) Ltd,
Padstow, Cornwall.

This book is printed on acid-free paper.

Contents

Contents

Acknowledgements

Writing a book is, like any other productive enterprise, very much a social process. Particular thanks go to my students at North Warwickshire College who, over several years, were unwittingly used as guinea-pigs for much of the material in the pages that follow. I must also thank Eirene Mitsos, who has read the book more times than anyone will probably ever do again. Robert Rowell and Denam Whitehead did fine work in producing the illustrations, making excellent interpretations of often quite vague suggestions. They have made a great contribution to the final product. Tony Giddens showed great confidence in the book, and his early comments gave me the spur to make many qualitative improvements in the text. Many thanks are owed to Laurie Taylor for his willingness and generosity in writing the preface. Thanks must also go to Heather Lynn of the Centre for Research in Ethnic Relations at Warwick University for providing contemporary data. Kevin Bonnet, Gareth Gillespie, and John Sanderson provided very useful and full critiques which helped to improve the quality of the book. Avril Leigh and Cecil Browne were very helpful and supportive in reading the typescript for poor grammar and construction, and made many useful suggestions. I'd like to thank Debbie Seymour and Pam Thomas for their support and encouragement, Fiona Sewell for her informed and dazzlingly professional copy-editing, and all the other staff at Polity Press.

I am grateful to all those who gave permission to reproduce copyright material, particularly The Controller of Her Majesty's Stationery Office for permission to reproduce data from Crown Copyright publications. Other thanks must go to Blackwell Publishers, British Gas, The Commission for Racial Equality, The Equal Opportunities Commission, Phil Evans, Michael Dyer, David Haldane, R. R. C. Penfold, Ken Pyne, Clara Vulliamy, The Family Policy Studies Centre, Gower Publishing, HarperCollins Publishers, London Weekend Television, Macmillan, the NSPCC, Penguin Books, Barrie

Percival and Loughborough Grammar School, The Labour Party, Peugeot-Talbot, Philip Allan Publishers, *Punch*, Routledge, Rover Group, The Child Poverty Action Group, *The Guardian*, *The Independent on Sunday*, and JBP/House of Viz. The source of copyright material is acknowledged in the text. Should any copyright holder have been inadvertently overlooked, the author and publishers will be glad to make suitable arrangements at the first possible opportunity.

Preface

For years I've found it almost impossible to give a straight answer to a question which I must have been asked a thousand times: 'What book would you recommend to someone who wanted to find out what sociology was all about?' My problem was that although I knew the names of several texts which described themselves as 'introductory', there was hardly one amongst them which genuinely started from 'scratch', or which managed to bring together the nuts and bolts of the subject and at the same time do justice to its imaginative appeal.

Ken Browne's book succeeds in all these respects. It is genuinely introductory, moving gently from common-sense ideas towards sociological explanations in a language which is refreshingly free from jargon, academic references and lengthy quotations, and which is regularly complemented by diagrams, charts, cartoons and exercises. Nothing is taken for granted. If Browne is going to tell you that a certain social practice is equivalent to re-arranging the deck chairs on the Titanic, he'll remember to tell younger readers about the fate of the Titanic.

This careful step-by-step approach does not mean that the book is in any way simplistic. It tackles the full range of sociological topics and maintains an excellent balance between data, concepts, theories and methods. What's more, it's up to date. Proper attention is given to the 'founding fathers', but it is good to find an introductory sociology text which can call on examples from a post-Thatcher Britain and a post-communist Eastern Europe.

But what pleases me most about this book is its author's ability to convey the sense that it all matters, that sociology's capacity to unmask and de-mystify our taken-for-granted social and cultural arrangements, makes it not only an exciting and challenging subject but one which might even help make the world a better place. And in case any readers want to get started straightaway there is practical help on research methods and quite enough tantalizing proposals for research projects to ensure that our institutions and communities are soon bustling with a whole new generation of inquisitive sociologists.

It can't have been an easy task. A great deal of planning and organization has obviously gone into the production of what on the face of it looks such a straightforward text. I was not at all surprised to learn that it had all been thoroughly road-tested by Browne at North Warwickshire College, where, for several years, his own students were used (by his own admission) as 'guinea-pigs for much of the material in the pages that follow'. They are lucky to have had such a conscientious teacher.

I suspect that the future of sociology in this country is far more dependent upon the quality of introductory textbooks than it is upon some of the more esoteric debates about the nature of the subject which fill the pages of the journals. All those who are just beginning to ask what sociology is all about – people in schools, colleges, evening classes, as well as people who at the moment would never think of going near an educational institution – will only want to go on towards the cutting edge of the subject if the answer which they now receive to their enquiry is lucid, intelligent and provocative. That is exactly the type of response provided by Ken Browne in these pages.

Laurie Taylor
Professor of Sociology,
University of York

Introduction

This book is intended as an elementary introduction to sociology for both the general reader and those studying at GCSE level. No previous knowledge of sociology is assumed. All the key issues and areas included in GCSE and other introductory sociology courses are covered, with each chapter closely modelled on the syllabus content of the major GCSE examining boards.

The book is particularly suited to further education students studying for GCSE on one-year courses, who require a clear and concise account of each topic area. It is also suitable for use by students on other introductory courses which have a sociological component, such as nursing, social work, and community care courses in further education. This book will enable the content of such courses to be covered easily and thoroughly, and allow time for students and teachers or tutors to discuss, pursue the acquisition of skills, and carry out the coursework assignments which are often important aspects of such courses. Students studying at home or on other distance-learning courses will find the book a valuable companion to their studies. Those who are contemplating an 'A' level sociology course and wish to get some idea of the areas covered will find the book useful as preparatory reading.

Reading about sociology is no substitute for getting involved in the fascination and difficulties of doing an actual piece of research. Chapter 16 provides a comprehensive guide to sociological research methods and the way to tackle project work. Suggestions on appropriate research topics are included at the end of every chapter except chapters 1 and 16.

How to Use this Book

Most chapters in this book are fairly self-contained, and it is not necessary to read them in any particular order or to read all of them. Select chapters according to the course you are studying. Those not familiar with the interpretation of statistical data will find it useful to study the appendix fairly early on. Those doing research projects of various kinds should read chapter 16. When issues are discussed in more than one chapter, cross-references are made in the text.

Throughout the book, a range of activities and discussion topics is included. These provide valuable exercises to develop your skills and understanding, and should be attempted whenever possible, though they are not essential for understanding each chapter. Important terms are printed in **bold type** when they first appear. These are normally explained in the text, and listed at the end of the chapter. They are also included in a comprehensive glossary at the end of the book. Unfamiliar terms should be checked in the glossary or index for further clarification or explanation. The detailed contents pages or the index should be used to find particular themes or references.

Chapter summaries outline the key points that should have been learnt after reading each chapter. These should be used as checklists for revision – if you cannot do what is asked, then refer back to the chapter to refresh your memory. The glossary at the end of the book also provides both a valuable reference source and a revision aid, as you can check the meaning of terms.

A last word: do not look on this book as your final and absolute source of authority. Much of sociology is controversial and the subject of intense and heated debate. Discuss with others what you read in this book, and bring to your studies a questioning mind and an unwillingness to accept uncritically statements or assertions that are frequently advanced. Take nothing for granted and do not accept things at face value. Above all, enjoy sociology.

1 Introducing Sociology

Newcomers to sociology often have only a vague idea as to what the subject is about, though they frequently have an interest in people. This interest is a good start, because the focus of sociology is on the influences from society which mould the behaviour of people, their experiences, and their interpretations of the world around them. To learn sociology is to learn about how human societies are constructed, and where our beliefs and daily routines come from; it is to re-examine in a new light many of the taken-for-granted assumptions which we all hold, and which influence the way we think about ourselves and others. Sociology is above all about developing a critical understanding of society. In developing this, sociology can itself contribute to changes in society, for example by highlighting and explaining social problems like divorce, crime, and poverty. The study of sociology can provide the essential tools for a better understanding of the world we live in, and therefore the means for improving it.

What is Sociology?

Sociology is the systematic (or planned and organized) study of human groups and social life in modern societies. It is concerned with the study of **social institutions.** These are the various organized social arrangements which are found in all societies. For example, the family is an institution which is concerned with arrangements for marriage, such as at what age people can marry, who they can marry and how many partners they can have, and the upbringing of children. The education system establishes ways of passing on attitudes, knowledge, and skills from one generation to the next. Work and the economic system organize the way the production of goods will be carried out, and religious institutions are concerned with people's relations with the supernatural.

Sociology tries to understand how these various social institutions operate, and how they relate to one another, such as the influence the family might have on how well children perform in the education system. Sociology is also concerned with describing and explaining the patterns of inequality, deprivation, and conflict which are a feature of nearly all societies.

Sociology and Common Sense

Sociology is concerned with studying many things which most people already know something about. Everyone will have some knowledge and understanding of family life, the education system, work, the mass media, and religion simply by living as a member of society. This leads many people to assume that the topics studied by sociologists and the explanations sociologists produce are really just common sense: what 'everyone knows'.

This is a very mistaken assumption. Sociological research has shown many widely held 'common-sense' ideas and explanations to be false. Ideas such as that there is no real poverty left in modern Britain; that the poor and unemployed are inadequate and lazy; that everyone has equal chances in life; that the rich are rich because they work harder; that men are 'naturally' superior to women; that it is obvious that men and women will fall in love and live together; these have all been questioned by sociological research. The re-examination of such common-sense views is very much the concern of sociology.

A further problem with common-sense explanations is that they are tightly bound up with the beliefs of a particular society at particular periods of time. Different societies have differing common-sense ideas. The Hopi Indians' common-sense view of why it rains is very different from our own – they do a rain dance to encourage the rain gods. Common-sense ideas also change over time in one society. In Britain, for example, we no longer burn witches when the crops fail, but seek scientific explanations for such events.

Not all the findings of sociologists undermine common-sense, and the work of sociologists has made important contributions to the common-sense understandings of members of society. For example, the knowledge which most people have about the changing family in Britain, with rising rates of divorce and growing numbers of single parents, is largely due to the work of sociologists. However, sociology differs from common-sense in two important ways:

- Sociologists use a sociological imagination. This means that, while they study the familiar routines of daily life, sociologists look at them in unfamiliar ways or from a different angle. They ask if things really are as common-sense says they are. Sociologists re-examine existing assumptions, by studying how things were in the past, how they've changed, how they differ between societies, and how they might change in the future.

- Sociologists look at evidence on issues before making up their minds. The explanations and conclusions of sociologists are based on precise evidence which has been collected through painstaking research using established research procedures.

Sociology and Naturalistic Explanations

Naturalistic explanations are those which assume that various kinds of human behaviour are natural or based on innate (in-born) biological characteristics. If this were the case, then one would expect human behaviour to be the same in all societies, as people's biological make-up doesn't change between societies. In fact, by comparing different societies, sociologists have discovered that there are very wide differences between societies in customs, values, beliefs, and social behaviour. For example, there are wide differences between societies in the roles of men and women and what is considered appropriate 'masculine' and 'feminine' behaviour. This can only be because people learn to behave in different ways in different societies. Sociological explanations recognize that most human behaviour is learnt by individuals as members of society, rather than being something with which they are born. Individuals learn how to behave from a wide range of social institutions right throughout their lives. Sociologists call this process of learning **socialization**.

Sociology and Science

Sociology is one of a group of subjects, including economics, psychology, and politics, which are known as the social sciences. The idea that sociology might be considered a science poses a number of problems. This is because the term 'science' is usually associated with the study of the natural world, in subjects like physics, chemistry, and biology which make up the natural sciences.

However, the study of society by sociologists presents a range of problems which do not exist in the natural sciences, as the following comparison suggests.

Natural science   Social science

Photos: Michael Dyer LRPS.

Natural science
- Experiments can be carried out to test and prove ideas and it is possible to isolate causes in laboratory conditions.

- As a result of experiments, natural scientists can accurately predict what will happen in the same circumstances in the future. For example, the chemist can predict with certainty, as a result of experiments in laboratory condi-

Sociology
- Human beings have rights, and might well object to being experimented upon. For example, the idea of removing children from their parents and raising them in isolation to test the influence of society on human behaviour would be regarded by most people as outrageous. Sociology also wants to study society in its normal state, not in the artificial conditions of an experiment.
- Human behaviour cannot be predicted with such certainty: in two similar situations, people may react differently, and people can change their minds.

tions, that some combinations of chemicals will cause explosions.

- In the natural sciences, the presence of the scientist doesn't affect the behaviour of chemicals or objects.

- Sociologists studying people may change the behaviour of those being studied, who may become embarrassed, be more defensive and careful about what they say, or act differently because they have been selected for study. If this happens, then the results obtained will not give a true picture of how people behave normally.

- The natural scientist does not have to persuade objects, chemicals, or, usually, animals to cooperate in research.

- People may refuse to answer questions or otherwise cooperate, making sociological research difficult or impossible. They can lie or otherwise distort and conceal the truth when they are being researched, making the findings of research suspect.

Is Sociology Scientific?

The differences between the natural sciences and sociology mean that sociologists cannot follow exactly the same procedures nor produce such precise findings as those in the natural sciences. Despite this, sociology might still be regarded as adopting a scientific approach to the study of society because it has the following features:

- **Value freedom** – the personal beliefs and prejudices of the sociologist should not be allowed to influence the way research is carried out and evidence interpreted. Obviously the personal interests and beliefs of the sociologist will influence the choice of topic he or she studies, but the research itself should not be distorted by these beliefs. In other words, sociologists should not 'cook the books' to make their point.
- **Objectivity** – the sociologist should approach topics with an open mind, and be prepared to consider all the evidence in a detached way.
- The use of systematic research methods – sociologists collect evidence about topics using planned and organized methods. These are discussed fully in chapter 16.
- The use of evidence – sociological descriptions of social life, and the explanations and conclusions drawn, are based on carefully collected evidence.

- The capacity for being checked – the findings and conclusions of sociological research are open to inspection, criticism, and testing by other researchers. 'Bad' sociology, using inadequate evidence to reach unjustifiable conclusions, is likely to be torn to shreds by others interested in the topic.

Some Key Introductory Ideas

Socialization and Culture

Socialization is the life-long process of learning the **culture** of any society. The term 'culture' refers to the language, beliefs, **values** and **norms, customs, roles,** knowledge, and skills which combine to make up the 'way of life' of any society. This culture is socially transmitted (passed on through socialization) from one generation to the next.

Roles and Role Conflict

Roles are the patterns of behaviour which are expected from people in different positions in society – they are very much like the roles actors play in a television series. People in society play many different roles in their lifetimes, such as those of a boy or girl, a child and an adult, a student, a parent, a friend, and work roles like factory worker, police officer, or teacher. People in these roles are expected by society to behave in particular ways. The police officer who steals, or the teacher who is drunk in the classroom, shows what these expectations of behaviour are!

One person plays many roles at the same time. For example, a woman may play the roles of woman, mother, worker, sister, and wife at the same time. This may lead to **role conflict**, where the successful performance of two or more roles at the same time may come into conflict with one another, such as the conflict between the roles of full-time worker and mother which some women experience.

Activity

1. List all the roles you play, and briefly outline what others expect of you in each of these roles. For example, how are you expected to

behave as a student, and what activities are you expected to carry out which you wouldn't have to if you were not a student?
2. From your list of roles, try to pick out those which conflict with each other, as suggested in the cartoon below.

Role conflict for working women

Values and Norms

Values are ideas and beliefs about what is 'right' and 'wrong', and the important standards which are worth maintaining and achieving in any society. They provide general guidelines for behaviour. In Britain, values include beliefs about respect for human life, privacy, and private property, about the importance of marriage and the importance of money and success. There are often strong pressures on people to conform to a society's values, which are frequently written down as **laws**. These are official legal rules which are formally enforced by the police, courts, and prison, and involve legal punishment if they are broken. Laws against murder, for example, enforce the value attached to human life in our society.

Norms are social rules which define correct and acceptable behaviour in a society or social group to which people are expected to conform. Norms are much more specific than values: they put values (general guidelines) into practice in particular situations. The rule that someone should not generally enter rooms without knocking reflects the value of privacy, and rules about not drinking and driving reflect the value of respect for human life. Norms exist in all areas of social life. In Britain, those who are late for work, jump queues in supermarkets, laugh during funerals, walk through the streets naked, or never say hello to friends are likely to be seen as annoying, rude, or odd because they are not following the norms of accepted behaviour. Norms are mainly informally enforced – by the disapproval of other people, embarrassment, or a 'telling off' from parents.

Customs are norms which have existed for a long time and have become a part of society's traditions – kissing under the mistletoe at Christmas, buying Easter eggs, or lighting candles at Divali are typical customs found in Britain.

Values and norms are part of the culture of a society, and are learned and passed on through socialization. They differ between societies – the values and norms of an African tribe are very different from those of people in modern Britain. They may also change over time and vary between social groups in the same society. In Britain, living together without being married is much more accepted today than it was in the past, and wearing turbans – which is seen as normal dress among Sikh men – would be seen as a bit weird among white teenagers.

Social Control

Social control is the term given to the various methods used to persuade or force individuals to conform to those social values and norms which have been learnt through socialization, and to prevent **deviance** – a failure to conform to social norms.

Sanctions are the rewards and punishments by which social control is achieved and conformity to norms and values enforced. These may be either *positive sanctions*, rewards of various kinds, or *negative sanctions*, various types of punishment. The type of sanction will depend on the seriousness of the norm: positive sanctions may range from gifts of sweets from parents to children, to merits and prizes at school, to knighthoods and medals; negative sanctions may range from a feeling of embarrassment, to being ridiculed or gossiped about or regarded as a bit eccentric/'a bit odd', to being fined or imprisoned.

Discussion

Discuss the various positive and negative sanctions which affect the way you behave in your daily life.

Chapter Summary

After studying this chapter, you should be able to:

- Explain why sociology is different from common-sense and naturalistic explanations.
- Explain some of the problems sociologists face compared to those working in the natural sciences.
- Explain why sociology is scientific.
- Define the meaning of socialization, culture, roles, role conflict, values, laws, norms, social control, deviance, and positive and negative sanctions, and explain their importance in understanding human behaviour in human society.

Key Terms

culture
customs
deviance
laws
norms
objectivity
role conflict
roles
sanctions
social control
social institutions
socialization
sociology
value freedom
values

2 Social Stratification

Social Stratification

Most people would agree that few societies are really equal. The study of social stratification is of central concern to sociologists, because modern societies display such a wide range of inequalities. These include inequalities between rich and poor, between social classes, between men and women, and between black and white. Inequalities exist in a wide range of areas of social life, such as in job security, leisure opportunities, health, housing, income, and the power to influence events in society. Much of this book is concerned with describing and explaining these inequalities, so an understanding of social stratification provides a necessary starting point for the newcomer to sociology.

The word 'stratification' comes from 'strata' or layers, as in the way different types of rock are piled on top of one another to form rock strata. **Social stratification** refers to the division of society into a pattern of layers or strata made up of a hierarchy of unequal social groups. These stand in relations of advantage and disadvantage to one another in terms of features such as income, wealth, occupational status, race, or sex, depending on the stratification system. Those at the top of the stratification hierarchy will generally have more power in society than those at the bottom.

Activity

Make a list of what you consider to be the most important inequalities in society today. Explain in all cases why you think they are important in people's lives and how they affect the chances they get in life.

Key Terms Used in the Study of Social Stratification

- *Economic inequality* refers to all those material things which affect the lives of individuals, such as their wealth, their income, and the hours they work. These inequalities can be measured, and continue to exist regardless of whether people recognize them as important or not.
- **Life chances** are the chances of obtaining those things defined as desirable and of avoiding those things defined as undesirable in any society. Life chances include the chances of obtaining things like good-quality housing, good health, holidays, job security, and educational success, and avoiding things like ill-health and unemployment.
- **Status** refers to the differing amounts of prestige or respect given to different positions in a group or society by other members of that group or society. Status involves people's social standing in the eyes of others. Status inequalities only exist so long as other people in a group or society continue to recognize them. For example, a vicar in a Christian society is generally given high status, but is unlikely to be given such status in a society practising witchcraft or voodoo.
- **Status groups** are groups of people sharing a similar status. For example, teachers generally share the same status.
- *Ascribed status* is status which is given to an individual at birth and usually can't be changed. Examples of such status include a person's age, race, sex, or place or family of birth. Members of the Royal Family in Britain have ascribed status.
- *Achieved status* refers to status that individuals have achieved through their own efforts, such as in education, skill, or promotion at work and career success.
- *Status symbols* are things that 'show off' people's status to others, such as the kind of job they have, the way they spend their money, the sort of house they live in, the car they drive, and their general lifestyle. All these things may be highly or lowly rated by other members of society.

- **Social mobility** is the term used to describe the movement up or down the social hierarchy between levels of a stratification system. For example, a person who came from a working-class family but became a middle-class doctor would have achieved upward social mobility. An **open society** is one where social mobility is possible; a **closed society** is one where no social mobility is possible.

Systems of Stratification

Sociologists have identified three major types of stratification system, which have important differences between them: the caste system, feudal estates, and social class.

The Caste System

The **caste system** is the most rigid system of stratification and is associated with India. The levels of the social hierarchy are called castes, and this hierarchy is fixed and clearly defined. The social position of individuals is ascribed at birth in accordance with Hindu religious beliefs and customs. Hindus believe in reincarnation – that people are born again after death. Hinduism suggests that people's behaviour in their previous life will decide the caste they are born into after rebirth. Since people believe the social position they are born into (their caste) is god-given, they generally accept their ascribed caste position.

A caste society is a closed society, with no social mobility possible from one caste to another. Each caste is completely closed off from others by religious rules and restrictions, which ensure that very little social contact occurs between members of different castes. The purity of each caste is maintained by **endogamy**. This means that marriage is only permitted to a person of the same caste. Besides the choice of marriage partner, caste membership also determines social status and occupation.

In the Indian system, the Hindu religion divides the population into five major castes:

1. Brahmins – the highest caste of priests and religious people.
2. Kshatriya – rulers and administrators.
3. Vaisya – merchants and farmers.
4. Sudras – manual workers.
5. The 'Untouchables' – literally, a group without a caste: social outcasts.

Despite recent attempts by the Indian government to remove the inequalities of the caste system, the system still continues, as many people still accept the Hindu religious beliefs on which it is based.

It has been suggested that the apartheid regime in South Africa shows some similarities with the caste system. Here people are stratified according to ascribed racial characteristics (white, coloured, and Bantu or black populations), with legal restrictions on mixing/marriage between different races, and with an almost 'religious' ideology of white supremacy. However, changes in the late 1980s in South Africa weakened some of the traditional features of the apartheid regime, and the system may be abolished in the 1990s.

Feudal Estates

Feudalism was typically found in medieval Europe. The levels of the social hierarchy were called estates, and based on ownership of land. There was no legal equality between estates, and people in higher estates had more legal rights and privileges than those in lower ones. The lower estates had obligations and duties to those higher up the hierarchy, which were backed up by laws. For example, there was an obligation for serfs to work one day a week on the master's land. Membership of any estate was determined largely by birth, with social position, power, and status all ascribed at birth.

Feudalism was, like the caste system, a closed society, with social mobility from one estate to another extremely limited. However, some upward mobility to a higher estate was possible, for example through gifts of land as a reward for outstanding military service. In general, estates were preserved by endogamy, and inter-marriage was only rarely allowed between individuals of different estates.

The feudal system of stratification looked something like the diagram below:

The Feudal Hierarchy

| First estate | → The king
Aristocracy and gentry (knights, barons and earls) |

| Second estate | → The Church (bishops, abbots, and clergy) |

| Third estate | → Merchants, artisans, free peasants and serfs |

Social Class

Social class is the form of stratification found in industrial societies, like modern Britain. Social classes can be defined as broad groups of people who share a similar economic situation, such as occupation, income, and ownership of wealth. Often, these criteria are closely related to each other and to other aspects of individuals' lives, such as their level of education, their status and lifestyle (for example, housing, car ownership, and leisure activities), and how much power and influence they have in society.

The main differences between the social class system and the caste and feudal systems are:

- Social class is not based on religion or law, but mainly on economic criteria such as occupation, wealth, and income.
- The levels of the social hierarchy (social classes) are not clearly separated from one another: the divisions between social classes are frequently quite vague – it is hard to say, for example, where the working class ends and the middle class begins.
- Social class differences are not backed up by legal differences. All members of society in theory have equal legal rights, and those in higher social classes do not have legal authority over those in lower classes.
- There are no legal or religious restrictions on inter-marriage between people of different social classes. In theory people can marry whom they like; in practice people tend to marry someone in their own social class.
- Social class societies are open societies. There are no legal or religious restrictions on the movement of individuals from one social class to another, and social mobility is possible.
- The social class system is generally meritocratic. A **meritocracy** is a society where social positions are generally achieved by merit, such as educational qualifications, talent, and skill, rather than ascribed from birth. However, the social class of the family into which a child is born can have an important effect on his or her life chances. Entry into the propertied upper class is still mainly through inherited wealth, and therefore social positions here remain mainly ascribed rather than achieved.

Social class and status

An individual's social class and status are often closely linked, and a member of a high social class will usually have high status as well. This is because the amount of social respect individuals get is often influenced by the same factors as their social class – their wealth, their income, and their occupation.

'Look. Don't judge me by the clothes I wear, the car I drive, the books I read, the food I eat, the music I like, the friends I see, the money I earn, the place I live, the job I have, the things I say or the way I act. OK?'

Reproduced by permission of *Punch*.

However, while an individual can only belong to one social class, he or she may have several statuses. For example, a person with a low-status working-class job such as a refuse collector may achieve high status as a local councillor. Similarly, it is quite possible for two people to share the same social class but to have different statuses. For example, a white semi-skilled manual worker will find it easier to achieve status in a group of racially prejudiced white workers than a black or Asian immigrant, who may be given lower status simply because of his or her race, even if he or she has the same occupation and income as the white worker.

Activity

1. If you were trying to decide a person's social class, what features would you take into account? Think about issues such as her or his job, speech, dress, housing, leisure activities, level of education, and car ownership. List all the features you can think of.
2. Now put your list into order of importance, with the most important features first. Explain why you have put them in that order.

Two Views of Social Class

In the last activity, you listed the most important features that you would take into account in deciding a person's social class. The features you think important, though, may not be the same as those chosen by others. A similar dispute exists among sociologists. While most sociologists would agree that social classes consist of groups of people who share a similar economic situation, there are different views regarding exactly which aspect of that economic situation is the most important in defining a person's social class. The following discussion deals with two of the most common definitions of social class which are used by sociologists: the Marxist view of class, and the definition of class by a person's occupation.

The Marxist Theory of Social Class

Much sociological discussion about social class has been influenced by the writings of Karl Marx (1818–83), who based his ideas on industrial capitalism in nineteenth-century England.

Karl Marx, 1818–83

Ownership of the means of production

For Marx, an individual's social class was defined by whether or not she or he owned the **means of production**. By this Marx meant factories and land – the key resources necessary for producing society's goods, whose ownership brought to their owners an unearned income in the form of profit.

Bourgeoisie and proletariat

Marx argued there were two basic social classes in capitalist industrial society: the class of owners of the means of production (whom he called the **bourgeoisie** or capitalists) and the class of non-owners (whom he called the **proletariat** or working class). The proletariat, since they owned no means of production, had no alternative means of livelihood but to work for the bourgeoisie. The bourgeoisie exploited the proletariat, making profits out of them by keeping wages low and paying them as little as possible instead of giving them the full payment for their work.

The ruling class

The class of owners was also a ruling class, according to Marx. For example, because they owned the means of production, the bourgeoisie could decide where factories should be located and whether they should be opened or closed down, and they could control the workforce through hiring and firing. Democratically-elected governments could not afford to ignore the power of the bourgeoisie, otherwise they might face rising unemployment and other social problems if the bourgeoisie decided not to invest its money.

The ruling ideas

The ruling ideas in society – what Marx called the 'dominant ideology' – were those of the owning class, and the major institutions in society reflected these ideas. For example, the laws protected the owning class rather than the workers; religion acted as the 'opium of the people', persuading the proletariat to accept their position as just and natural (rather than rebelling against it), by promising future rewards in heaven for putting up with their present suffering; the bourgeoisie's ownership of the mass media meant only their ideas were put forward. In this way, the working class were almost brainwashed into accepting their position. They failed to recognize they were being exploited and therefore did not rebel against the bourgeoisie, because they thought their position was 'natural' and they could see no alternative to it. Marx called this lack of awareness by the proletariat of their own interests **false consciousness**.

Exploitation, class conflict, and revolution

Marx predicted the working class would become poorer and poorer and society would become divided into two major social classes: a small, wealthy, and powerful bourgeoisie and a large, poverty-stricken proletariat. The exploitation of the proletariat by the bourgeoisie, Marx believed, would eventually lead to major class conflict between the poverty-stricken proletariat and the bourgeoisie. The proletariat would struggle against the bourgeoisie through strikes, demonstrations, and other forms of protest. The proletariat would then develop **class consciousness** – an awareness of their common working-class interests and their exploitation – until eventually they would make a socialist revolution and overthrow the bourgeoisie.

Marxist views of false consciousness and class consciousness

Communism

After the revolution, the proletariat would nationalize the means of production (which were formerly the private property of the bourgeoisie) by putting them in the hands of the state. The means of production would therefore be collectively owned and run in the interests of everyone, not just of the bourgeoisie. Capitalism would be destroyed and a new type of society would be created, which would be without exploitation, without classes, and without class conflict. This equal, classless society Marx called **Communism**.

A summary of Marx's theory of class

Marx's theory of social class is based on a model of two social classes, defined by whether or not they own the means of production. The bourgeoisie (the owning class) is a ruling class which exploits the proletariat (the non-owning class). This exploitation gives rise to class conflict between these two major classes. The proletariat will eventually overthrow the bourgeoisie in the socialist revolution, and create an equal, classless society called Communism.

The strengths and weaknesses of Marx's theory of class

There has been much discussion of the Marxist view of social class, particularly whether it can still be applied in modern industrial societies like Britain. One of the more obvious criticisms of Marx is that the revolution he predicted has not happened in Britain or any of the Western industrialized societies. While many of the class inequalities and conflicts which Marx identified remain in modern capitalist industrial societies, the communist solutions he proposed do not seem to be working in the way he foresaw. In those countries where revolutions have occurred, like the countries of Eastern Europe, the Soviet Union, and China, Communism did not succeed in creating an equal society, and there emerged a new 'ruling class' of people who were better off than the majority. In 1989–91, a major wave of popular revolts shook Eastern Europe and the Soviet Union, and swept away the former Communist regimes. In Russia, where the first successful socialist revolution took place, the Communist Party was even banned in 1991. Some other competing arguments over Marx's theory of social class in relation to Britain are shown below:

Strengths
- The means of production remain mostly privately owned in the hands of a small minority of the population. There are still great inequalities of wealth and income in modern Britain, and widespread poverty: 10 per cent of the population own 53 per cent of the

Weaknesses
- While great inequalities in wealth and income continue to exist, the working class has not got poorer as Marx predicted. Living standards have improved vastly since Marx's day, and the welfare state and compulsory state education have given the working class a

Strengths	*Weaknesses*
wealth, and an estimated 30 per cent of people are living in relative poverty.	better lifestyle than Marx predicted.
• There remains much evidence of major social class inequalities in life chances, such as in health, housing, and levels of educational achievement and job security.	• Compulsory education has given the working class more chances of upward social mobility, and the welfare state provides a safety net guaranteeing a minimum income for all. Housing, health, and educational standards are much improved compared to the nineteenth century.
• Unemployment is an on-going problem, and affects most severely those in working-class occupations.	• Unemployment benefits help to reduce the more severe hardships which were associated with unemployment in Marx's day.
• The owners of the means of production still have much more power and influence than the majority. For example, the major positions in the state, industry, and banking are held by the privileged rich who have attended public schools, and they own the mass media.	• Voting rights and the formation of trade unions have given the working class more power and influence in society than when Marx was writing.
• The laws still favour the bourgeoisie, such as those which try to weaken trade unions and make it difficult to take legal strike action against employers. In a *Guardian* ICM survey in 1991, 67 per cent of the population agreed that there was 'one law for the rich and one for the poor'.	• The laws are passed by a democratically elected Parliament, chosen in free elections. The laws therefore may be said to represent the will of the majority.
• There is still evidence of opposing class interests and class conflict, such as strikes and industrial sabotage in the workplace. The 1989 British Social Attitudes Survey reported that over half of the population of modern Britain still believe there are strong conflicts	• Marx suggested only the two opposing classes of bourgeoisie and proletariat would emerge. In fact, the past century has seen the emergence of a new middle class of professionals, managers, and office workers between the bourgeoisie and proletariat. While

between rich and poor and between managers and workers.

these groups do not own the means of production, they benefit from exercising authority on behalf of the bourgeoisie and have higher status and better income and life chances than the working class. They generally have no interest in overthrowing the bourgeoisie. Trade unions are basically concerned with improving pay within the system rather than promoting revolution.

Discussion

1. Discuss the strengths and weaknesses of Marx's theory of class given above. Do you think Marx's ideas are still relevant in any way in the modern world, or do you think they are basically old-fashioned and out of date? Try to think of other evidence and examples to back up your viewpoint besides those given above.
2. To what extent do you think there are conflicts between groups of people in modern Britain, such as conflicts between rich and poor, managers and workers, and the unemployed and people with jobs? Why do you think these conflicts might exist? How might society be made more equal, with reduced conflicts between people?

Defining Class by Occupation

Max Weber, who lived between 1864 and 1920, was opposed to the Marxist theory of social class. He argued that the most important factors defining social class were the skills and qualifications which people possessed when competing for work in the job market. Employers were willing to give some people higher pay and status than others because they possessed the scarce skills and qualifications necessary for some occupations. This meant there were many social classes, consisting of people in different occupations requiring different types of skill and qualification. This view of Weber's has been generally accepted by most sociologists, and occupation has become a widely-used definition of class.

Occupation is certainly the most common definition of social class used by governments, by advertising agencies when doing market research, and by sociologists when doing surveys. This is because a person's occupation is an easy piece of information to obtain, and people's occupation is generally a good guide to their skills and qualifications, their income, their life chances, and other important aspects of their lives. Occupation is also a major factor influencing status in society, and most people judge the social standing of themselves and others by the jobs they do.

Activity

List all the ways you can think of that a person's occupation might affect other aspects of his or her life, such as family life, status in society, housing, health, leisure activities, beliefs and values, future planning, and so on. Make sure you explain precisely how the effects you mention are linked to a person's job.

The Registrar-General's Scale

There is a wide range of occupational scales in use, but one of the best known and widely used definitions of class by occupation is that of the Registrar-General. The Registrar-General is in charge of the government statistical department, and is responsible for carrying out the census and registering births, marriages, and deaths, among other things.

The Registrar-General's Scale divides the population into five social classes based upon occupation and employment status, with a division of class III into manual and non-manual workers (the division between working class and middle class). Non-manual (middle-class) occupations are those of people who work primarily in offices, doing mainly mental rather than physical work. The manual (working-class) occupations are those of people who work mainly with their hands (sometimes called **blue-collar workers**). The term **white-collar workers** refers to non-manual clerical workers and sales personnel in Class III.

Manual work

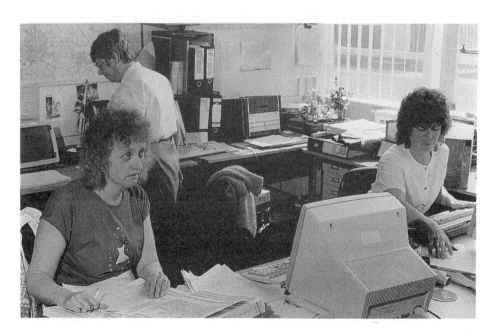

Non-manual work
Photo: Michael Dyer LRPS.

The Registrar-General's Scale

	Social class	*Examples of occupations*
	Class I Professional	Accountants, architects, doctors, dentists, solicitors, surveyors
Middle class	Class II Intermediate	Managers, teachers, nurses, pilots, farmers, members of parliament
	Class III (Non-manual) Skilled Non-manual	Clerical workers, estate agents, secretaries, typists, shop assistants
	Class III (Manual) Skilled Manual	Bus drivers, bricklayers, electricians, hairdressers, police constables, cooks
Working class	Class IV Semi-Skilled Manual	Bartenders, bus con- ductors, agricultural workers, postal workers
	Class V Unskilled Manual	Road sweepers, labourers refuse collectors, window cleaners

The Standard Occupational Classification

The Registrar-General's Scale is to be replaced in the 1990s by the Standard Occupational Classification, which contains a wider range of occupational groups. There are nine major groups of occupations, classified according to their similarity of qualification, training, skills, and experience.

The Standard Occupational Classification

Social class	Examples of occupations
Class 1 Managers and Administrators	Police inspectors and above, managers and administrators in national and local government and large companies
Class 2 Professional	Teachers, solicitors, architects, vicars, social workers, librarians
Class 3 Associate Professional and Technical	Surveyors, computer programmers, nurses, youth workers, journalists
Class 4 Clerical and Secretarial	Clerical workers, secretaries, typists, receptionists
Class 5 Craft and Related	Bricklayers, electricians, plumbers, car mechanics, butchers, bakers
Class 6 Personal and Protective Services	Traffic wardens, police officers (sergeant and below), hairdressers, nursery nurses, waiters/waitresses
Class 7 Sales	Sales reps, sales assistants, supermarket check-out operators
Class 8 Plant and Machine Operatives	Assembly-line workers, packers, bus conductors, bus/lorry/taxi drivers
Class 9 Other Occupations	Coal miners, farm workers, refuse collectors, postal workers, road sweepers, cleaners, hospital porters

Activity

The Registrar-General's Scale ranks occupations according to the status of the job (employment status), while the Standard Occupational Classification ranks occupations according to their similarity of qualification, training, skills and experience. Examine some of the occupations listed in the two scales. Do you agree with the categories they are placed in? Do you think some should be placed in higher or lower classes? Give reasons for your answers.

The problems of defining class by occupation

While occupation is very commonly used to define social class, the use of occupation and occupational scales presents a number of problems for the sociologist:

- The use of occupation excludes the wealthy upper class, who own property and have a great deal of power but often don't have an occupation. Occupational scales therefore do not reveal major differences in wealth and income within and between social classes.
- Groups outside paid employment are excluded, such as housewives and the never-employed unemployed. Housework is not recognized as an occupation.
- Social class is based primarily on the occupation of the 'head' of the household – this is usually assumed to be the man. While this makes such scales blatantly sexist, it is also out of date now that so many households have both male and female partners as major breadwinners.
- The use of a single head of household ignores dual-worker families, where both partners are working. Such families have much better life chances than single-income households in the same class. Their combined incomes might even give them the lifestyle of a higher social class.
- The classes on occupational scales tend to be very broad, and disguise major differences within each class. For example, professionals (Class I on the Registrar-General's Scale and Class 2 on the Standard Occupational Classification) include both poorly-paid junior NHS doctors and rich Harley Street private specialists. Similarly, teachers, architects, and solicitors are all put in Class 2 on the Standard Occupational Classification. There are major differences in income and life chances between such people, yet they are placed in the same class.

The Class Structure of Britain

Often, when talking of social class, sociologists will refer to terms quite loosely. Figure 2.1 illustrates which groups of occupations are generally being referred to when particular social classes in modern Britain are mentioned. Note that the main division between working class and middle class is generally accepted as being that between manual and non-manual occupations.

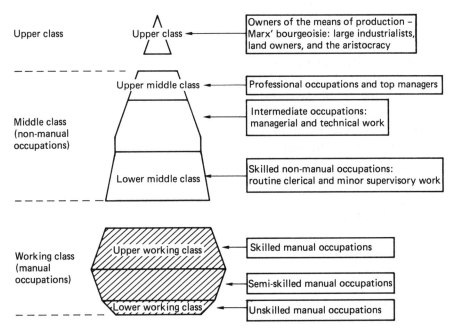

Figure 2.1 The class structure

Chapter Summary

After studying this chapter, you should be able to:

- Explain what is meant by social stratification.
- Describe the main features of the caste, estate, and class systems, and the differences between them.
- Explain what is meant by the term 'status'.
- Define the term 'social class'.
- Describe the main features of the Marxist theory of class, and discuss some of its strengths and weaknesses.

- Explain why sociologists often use occupation as an indicator of social class, and explain the problems in the use of occupation and occupational scales.
- Outline the five classes on the Registrar-General's Scale, and briefly describe the Standard Occupational Classification.
- Outline the main social classes in Britain today.

Project Suggestions

1. Ask a sample of people about their attitudes to social class – what they think it is, what is the most important factor defining it, whether it is still important, whether everyone has the same chances in life. Ask them to describe themselves as middle or working class, and to say why.
2. Make a list of occupations drawn from all classes on the Registrar-General's Scale and ask a sample of people to put them into order of importance. Ask them how they decided the order. Do your results coincide with the Registrar-General's Scale?

Key Terms

blue-collar workers
bourgeoisie
caste system
class consciousness
closed society
Communism
endogamy
false consciousness
feudalism
life chances
means of production
meritocracy
open society
proletariat
social class
social mobility
social stratification
status
status groups
white-collar workers

3 Social Class in Modern Britain

Many people assume that social class is not really very important today, often blaming sociologists for highlighting class inequalities which don't really have much impact on people's lives. However, pretending that social classes don't exist will not make them go away, any more than not being able to see a plate glass door will stop you from hurting yourself when you walk into it. Ask yourself why you don't buy expensive clothes, houses, and cars, or travel first class by train. Why don't you go to exotic foreign countries three times a year? Why don't you eat out at restaurants all the time instead of cooking? Why don't you try to skip National Health Service waiting lists by paying for private medicine?

The point is that social classes do not exist merely in the mind of the sociologist: there are wide, measurable differences in life chances between social classes. The higher the social class of an individual, the more access she or he will have to society's resources – such as better housing, cars, food, holidays, income, and job security – and the more influence he or she will have in society. The following section examines some examples of these class differences, and further examples are discussed in other parts of this book (see particularly chapter 12 on inequality in education).

Activity

Think of all the differences you can between social classes in modern Britain. How would you explain the class differences you have identified?

Class Inequalities

Wealth and Income

In 1988, 5 per cent of the population owned 38 per cent of the UK's wealth, and 10 per cent of the population owned 53 per cent of the wealth. The poorest 50 per cent of the population owned only 6 per cent of the UK's wealth. The top 20 per cent of income earners got roughly the same share as the bottom 60 per cent, and in 1991, there was a wider gap between the high-paid and the low-paid than at any time since records began in 1886. Poverty remains widespread, with 30 per cent of the population of Britain living in or on the margins of poverty in 1987. These issues are discussed in the next chapter.

Health and Life Expectation

Despite the welfare state and the National Health Service, major differences in health continue to exist between social classes. A man from social Class I on average lives seven years longer than a man from social Class V. As shown in figure 3.1, two-thirds more babies die at birth or in the first week of life (a **perinatal death**) or in the first year of life (**infant mortality**) in social Class V than in social Class I. Figure 3.2 shows how chronic sickness and acute sickness rise as one moves down the social class hierarchy (chronic sickness is long-standing illness or disability; acute sickness refers to restriction of normal activity due to illness or injury in the previous two weeks before interview). In 1991, a survey showed the death rate from heart disease was about one half higher than average for people in social Class V, compared to one half lower than average for those in social Class I. This is just part of a mass of evidence which shows that lower working-class people suffer more from almost all diseases than those in the upper middle class.

Activity

Study figures 3.1 and 3.2 and then answer the following questions:
1. Which social class has the highest level of infant mortality?
2. Which social class has about 9.5 perinatal deaths per thousand births?
3. Which social class has the lowest level of infant mortality?

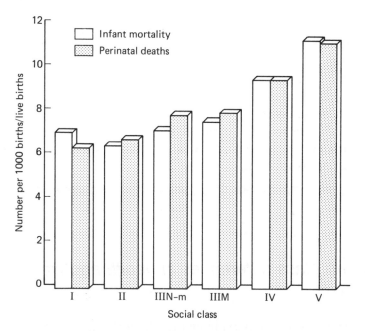

Figure 3.1 Perinatal deaths and infant mortality (for births within marriage only): by social class of father, England and Wales, 1988

Source: OPCS, Mortality statistics 1988, HMSO, 1991.

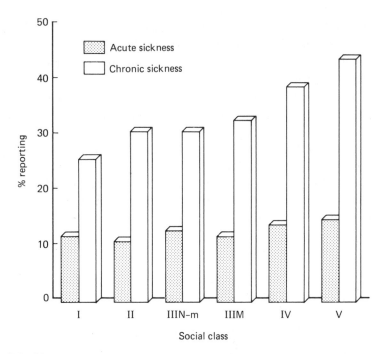

Figure 3.2 Chronic and acute sickness: by social class, Great Britain, 1988

Source: Calculated from General Household Survey, 1988.

4. What is the approximate difference between the number per thousand of perinatal deaths in Class I and in Class V?
5. What is the difference between the percentage of people reporting chronic sickness in Class I and in Class V?
6. In which social classes were those who reported the same levels of chronic sickness?
7. Figure 3.1 shows more babies dying within the first week or within the first year of life in social Class V than in social Class I. Suggest explanations for this.

Explaining class differences in health and life expectation

These differences are often explained by the following features of working-class life which are less likely to be experienced by those in middle-class occupations:

- Longer working hours, with shiftwork and overtime.
- Poorer conditions at work, with more risks to health and safety through accidents and industrial diseases.
- Less time off work with pay to visit the doctor.
- Lower income, leading to poorer diets and housing.
- More likelihood of working-class areas being at risk through industrial and traffic pollution.
- Poorer medical care in working-class areas, with long hospital waiting lists and overworked GPs, and lack of enough income to make use of private medicine.
- Lower levels of education, which often mean less awareness of health and the services which are available.
- Poverty in old age, due to the lack of an occupational pension and inadequate earnings while working to save for old age.
- Smoking, which tends to be more common in the working class.

Class Differences in Employment

The different status of occupations is backed up by different terms and conditions of employment under which people work. These improve with movement upward through the social class hierarchy.

Even the lowest level of non-manual workers, routine clerical workers, have better terms and conditions of employment than manual workers, although they don't always earn more. Manual workers, compared to the non-manual middle class:

- Get lower pay, despite working longer hours with shiftwork and overtime (see table 3.1).
- Have shorter holidays.
- Work in more dangerous and less hygienic working conditions, with greater risks of accident and disease.
- Are more supervised at work, having to clock in, getting pay 'docked' for lateness, and not being allowed time off with pay for personal reasons.
- Are less likely to receive full pay during sickness, or to belong to an employer's pension scheme.
- Have much less job security: the risk of unemployment is seven times greater for an unskilled manual worker than for someone in social Class I.

Table 3.1 Levels of average pay and hours in April 1990 (full-time employees

	Males		Females	
	Manual	Non-manual	Manual	Non-manual
Average gross weekly earnings (£)	237.2	354.9	148.0	215.5
of which (%):				
Overtime payments	16%	3%	6%	2%
PBR payments	7%	4%	7%	2%
Shift premium etc. payments	3%	0.5%	3%	1%
Average total weekly hours	45.2	38.7	39.8	36.9
Of which overtime hours(%)	13%	4%	5%	2%

PBR = payment by result.

Source: Adapted from *Employment Gazette*, November, 1990, p. 572, table 1.

Discussion

How might the terms and conditions of employment of manual workers affect their attitudes to work, their leisure activities, and their plans for the future?

Activity

Refer to table 3.1.
1. Which occupational group worked the shortest hours?
2. Which occupational group worked the most overtime?
3. Which groups had the largest percentage of their pay made up of payments by result?
4. Which group had the lowest percentage of pay made up of payments for working shifts?
5. What differences does the table show between male and female full-time employees? Suggest possible explanations for the differences you identify.

Explaining class differences in employment

Class differences in employment are often explained or justified by the higher education, training, and increased management responsibility of many non-manual workers, and the need to retain their commitment and loyalty to the firm and thus protect the firm's interests and investment. Even routine office workers often have some knowledge of the firm's 'secrets', such as profit levels, accounts, sales, and orders, and the management might want to conceal these 'secrets' from manual workers, particularly if they are submitting a pay claim. It is therefore in the firm's interest to try to retain the loyalty and commitment of non-manual staff. The tighter control and poorer conditions of work of manual workers suggest they are not trusted by management, are considered more dispensable, and can be more easily replaced. The generally poorer pay of women, whether manual or non-manual, compared to males (illustrated in table 3.1) is fully discussed in chapter 6.

Changes in the Class Structure

The Changing Occupational Structure

In nineteenth-century Britain, the majority of people were working in manual working-class occupations, with less than a quarter being considered upper or middle class. However, in the last hundred years, changes in the economy have occurred which have changed the occupational structure. These changes include:

- A growth in the tertiary sector of the economy, which is concerned with the provision of services, such as administration, sales, finance and insurance, transport, distribution, and the running of government services (like the welfare state and education).
- A decline in semi-skilled and unskilled manual work, as technology takes over these tasks, and creates more skilled jobs.
- A steady increase in the percentage of the workforce engaged in non-manual occupations, especially white-collar occupations such as routine clerical work.
- An increase in lower professional occupations, like teachers and social workers.

These developments have led to a change in the shape of the social structure, with unskilled and semi-skilled manual occupations getting smaller and skilled manual and lower middle-class occupations getting larger. As shown in figure 3.3, the social structure has changed from the pyramid shape that existed in the nineteenth century to the shape of a diamond.

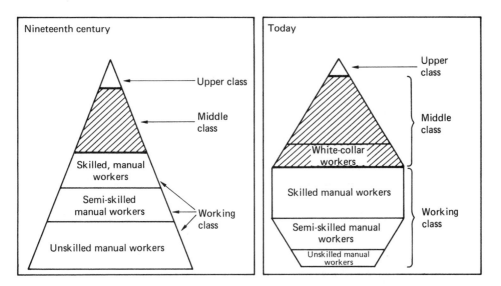

Figure 3.3 The changing shape of the class structure in Great Britain

Embourgeoisement and the Growth of the New Working Class

> **Embourgeoisement** is the idea that the differences between the middle class and working class are disappearing, with well-paid manual workers merging into the middle class.

In the 1960s, the wages and living standards of skilled manual workers improved greatly, often exceeding those of some of the middle class. These highly-paid manual workers were known as **affluent workers**. They could afford to buy their own homes and live in middle-class areas, and to buy the consumer goods like cars which previously only the middle class could afford. This gave rise to the idea of embourgeoisement.

The embourgeoisement thesis was tested by Goldthorpe, Lockwood et al. in 1969 among highly-paid manual workers in three firms in Luton, including the Vauxhall car factory, in a piece of research called *The Affluent Worker in the Class Structure*. This research found that many differences still separated manual workers from the middle class, and that embourgeoisement was not occurring.

They found the following differences still separated affluent manual workers from the middle class:

- Their high wages were only obtained at the cost of overtime and shift-working – working conditions which were rarely experienced by non-manual workers.
- They lacked 'fringe benefits' which non-manual workers received, such as employers' pension and sick pay schemes.
- They had more limited promotion opportunities and less job security than non-manual workers.
- They had an instrumental attitude to work. This means their main concern was with money. The purpose of work was not to achieve status, promotion, or job satisfaction (as in the middle class), but to get money to enjoy life outside work.
- Even though they lived on the same estates as non-manual workers, manual workers did not mix with them, preferring the company of other manual workers like themselves.

The Changing Working Class: The 'Traditional' and 'New' Working Classes

While the Luton research suggested well-paid manual workers were not merging into the middle class, Goldthorpe and Lockwood did consider affluent workers to be part of a new working class, because they had a much more affluent lifestyle and a more privatized family life than the traditional working class. There was also evidence to suggest they had an instrumental attitude to the Labour Party and trade unions, only supporting them for selfish motives of personal gain rather than out of a sense of loyalty to their workmates. In the 1980s, many of these affluent workers in fact switched to voting Conservative because they thought the Conservatives offered them more personal benefits than the Labour Party.

In the 1970s and 1980s, the 'new' working class that Lockwood and Goldthorpe discussed expanded, and the traditional working class grew smaller. The main features of these two sections of the working class are summarized in figure 3.4.

The Changing Nature of Clerical Work: The Proletarianization of White-Collar Workers

Proletarianization is the opposite of embourgeoisement. It is the suggestion that, rather than affluent workers becoming middle class, the lower middle class (mainly clerical workers) are descending into the working class.

The proletarianization of clerical work can only really be understood by examining the changing position of clerical workers (sometimes referred to as 'clerks', white-collar workers, or even, for the old-fashioned, as black-coated workers) since the last century.

Clerical work in the nineteenth century

In the nineteenth century, clerks were closely associated with management decision-making, and were often left to work on their own initiative and responsibility. They generally received higher pay than factory workers, had

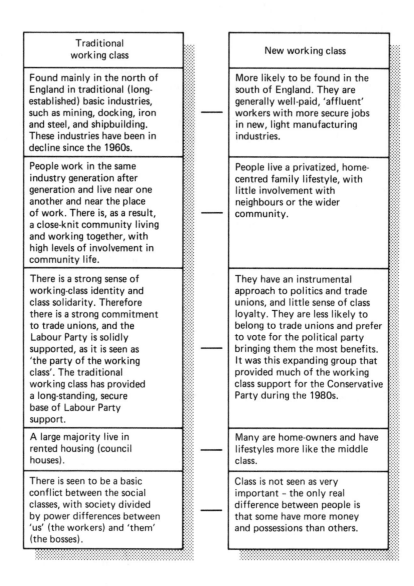

Traditional working class	New working class
Found mainly in the north of England in traditional (long-established) basic industries, such as mining, docking, iron and steel, and shipbuilding. These industries have been in decline since the 1960s.	More likely to be found in the south of England. They are generally well-paid, 'affluent' workers with more secure jobs in new, light manufacturing industries.
People work in the same industry generation after generation and live near one another and near the place of work. There is, as a result, a close-knit community living and working together, with high levels of involvement in community life.	People live a privatized, home-centred family lifestyle, with little involvement with neighbours or the wider community.
There is a strong sense of working-class identity and class solidarity. Therefore there is a strong commitment to trade unions, and the Labour Party is solidly supported, as it is seen as 'the party of the working class'. The traditional working class has provided a long-standing, secure base of Labour Party support.	They have an instrumental approach to politics and trade unions, and little sense of class loyalty. They are less likely to belong to trade unions and prefer to vote for the political party bringing them the most benefits. It was this expanding group that provided much of the working class support for the Conservative Party during the 1980s.
A large majority live in rented housing (council houses).	Many are home-owners and have lifestyles more like the middle class.
There is seen to be a basic conflict between the social classes, with society divided by power differences between 'us' (the workers) and 'them' (the bosses).	Class is not seen as very important – the only real difference between people is that some have more money and possessions than others.

Figure 3.4 The 'traditional' and 'new' working classes

a good career structure, and could eventually expect to take on management positions after long service. They had much better working conditions than factory workers, frequently working in small-scale offices. They had higher status than manual workers, because they had a more middle-class lifestyle and a higher level of education.

Clerical work in the twentieth century

Throughout this century, the position of the clerical worker has changed in a number of important ways.

- The relative pay of clerical workers has declined dramatically, and generally is little better (and often worse) than that of manual workers.
- Promotion opportunities have been reduced. There is little chance of a clerical worker today 'working his or her way up' into management, as managerial jobs are often filled directly by graduates of universities and polytechnics.
- Clerical workers have lost their close association with management and they face increased supervision of their work by managers.
- Office technology such as calculators, computers, and word-processors, has reduced the skills of clerical work – this is called **deskilling** – and much clerical work has become more like routine and repetitious factory work.
- With compulsory education, the skills required for clerical work are far more common today, so the educational differences between clerical and manual workers have been eroded and many more people can do clerical work. This has contributed to the decline in pay.

These changes have brought about a relative decline in status, and in terms of educational level, housing, and living standards there are few differences between clerical and manual workers. A further factor contributing to this decline in status has been the 'feminization' of clerical work – it has become more defined as 'women's work', and in a world dominated by men, women's jobs are often seen as less important simply because they are done by women. In the face of these changes, clerical workers have turned more to trade unions to protect their position, and this brings them more in line with working-class strategies for defending pay and conditions.

Discussion

Do you agree that clerical work has become more defined as 'women's work'? Why are women more likely than men to take up such work?

Technology is changing clerical work.

Source: Ken Pyne, *Labour Party News*, no. 23, 1991.

Are clerical workers now working class?

While there is no doubt that the position of clerical workers has declined dramatically during the twentieth century, clerical workers still have a number of differences from manual workers.

- They have more job security.
- They work shorter hours, have better fringe benefits, such as pension schemes and sickness benefits, and have longer holidays.
- They are still less supervised at work than manual workers: many do not have to clock in, have no pay knocked off for lateness, and have more flexibility in working hours (flexitime).
- They often share canteen and other facilities with management, and they generally cooperate with management, rather than display the mistrust of management shown by manual workers.
- Despite the growth of white-collar trade unions, these unions often maintain a separate identity from manual unions, and they are often concerned with 'staying ahead' of manual workers in terms of pay and conditions and maintaining status differences, rather than recognizing shared or common interests with manual workers.

These differences continue to separate clerical workers from manual workers, and so they cannot be regarded as part of the working class. However, proletarianization is an on-going process and the social position of clerical workers may continue to decline as changes in office technology make office work more and more like factory work.

Social Mobility

Modern industrial societies are said to be open societies because social mobility is possible, and people can move up or down the social class hierarchy. The study of social mobility enables sociologists to find out how open society is – how much people move from the social class into which they were born, and how much they improve their social position during their adult lives.

Measuring Social Mobility

Sociologists use the criterion of occupation to measure mobility, using occupational scales like the Registrar-General's Scale. This means that there are problems with the measuring 'tools' used in social mobility studies. For example, social mobility studies often exclude women, and sociologists differ in the occupational scales they use – some rank occupations according to their status, others by income – so the results of different mobility studies are often hard to compare. Also, the status of occupations changes over time. As we saw earlier, clerical work has changed dramatically over the course of the twentieth century, so someone doing a clerical job in the 1930s may actually have had a much higher status job than someone doing a clerical job today. Social mobility is usually studied in one of two ways:

- **Inter-generational social mobility** compares an adult's present occupation with that of the family she or he was born into (usually measured against the father's occupation). It therefore shows social class mobility between two generations. For example, a refuse collector's daughter who becomes a doctor has experienced upward social mobility compared to the class into which she was born.
- **Intra-generational social mobility** compares a person's present occupation with her or his first occupation, therefore showing how much mobility she or he has achieved in his or her lifetime. An example would be the person who began her or his working life as a small shopkeeper, but who eventually built up a massive supermarket empire.

Activity

Go through the following list, writing down for each one 'upward mobility', 'downward mobility', or 'no change', *and* 'inter-generational mobility' or 'intra-generational mobility'. Refer to the occupational scales in the previous chapter if you find any difficulty.

1. A nurse who decides to become a labourer on a building site.
2. The daughter of a miner who becomes a bank manager.
3. A teacher who decides to retrain as a social worker.
4. A doctor's son who becomes a taxi driver.
5. An immigrant from a poor farming background in Africa who gets a job in Britain as a farm labourer.
6. The daughter of a skilled manual worker who becomes a routine clerical worker.
7. A postal worker who becomes a traffic warden.
8. A pilot whose son becomes a police constable.
9. The owner of a small shop whose daughter becomes an assistant manager in a large supermarket.
10. A sales assistant in a shop who becomes a priest.

How Much Social Mobility is There in Britain?

Social mobility in modern Britain is relatively limited. Most people stay in the broad social class they were born into. Over half of the adults in the working class and the middle class were born to parents of the same class. There are fairly high levels of inter-generational mobility, but most of this is short-range mobility, such as movement from Class V to Class III, and there is relatively little long-range mobility across several occupational classes, such as from Class V to Class I.

There is a high level of self-recruitment at the two extremes of the class hierarchy. This means many children born into Class I themselves enter Class I, and many children born into Class V themselves enter Class V.

Despite more social mobility today, the propertied upper class still remains largely closed, as most wealth is inherited rather than achieved through work or talent. The best way to get rich in modern Britain is to be born to rich parents.

Women and Social Mobility

Studies of social mobility have generally ignored women, because of the mistaken assumption that most women are married, work as housewives, and depend on their husbands for their income. Women have therefore been seen as having their class decided by their husband's occupation. However, this is a wildly outdated view, and ignores the large number of non-married working women and the large increase this century in the numbers of working married women.

What is known is that women have far poorer chances of mobility than men, with women being mainly concentrated in semi-skilled manual occupations, routine clerical work, and the lower professions such as teaching and nursing. Women face major difficulties in entering skilled manual and managerial, technical, and top professional occupations. There are very few women compared to men in the top **elite** positions in society – those small

The 1:2:3 pattern of unequal opportunity

In 1986, whatever the chance a boy from a working-class background had of reaching social Class I or II, a boy from a lower middle-class family had twice the chance, and a boy from an upper middle-class family had three times the chance of entering Class I or II as an adult. This clearly shows an inequality of opportunity in the chances of upward mobility in Britain.

groups of people holding a great deal of power in society, such as judges, leaders of industry, top civil servants, and MPs and government ministers. Women have less chance of promotion than men, and many women experience downward mobility as they abandon careers with bright futures to take care of children, only to return to work at a lower status than when they left. The reasons for this pattern are discussed more fully in chapter 6.

Explanations for Social Mobility

This century has seen a relative decline in the proportion of semi- and unskilled manual occupations and an expansion in non-manual professional, managerial, and routine clerical occupations. This has increased the opportunities for upward mobility for the working class, as there is more room at the top. Middle-class groups generally have fewer children than the increase in the number of top jobs. This means that, even if all middle-class children go into middle-class jobs, there are still higher-level job vacancies to be filled by 'promoting' people from lower down the social scale.

Free and compulsory secondary education since 1944, and the development of comprehensive education in the 1960s, has enabled more working-class children to obtain the educational qualifications required for upward mobility. This is particularly important as intra-generational mobility is generally achieved through promotion at work, and this increasingly depends on educational qualifications, while inter-generational mobility is achieved mainly through educational qualifications.

Some people may achieve upward mobility through marrying a partner from a higher social class. It is mainly women who achieve upward mobility through marriage, but such cross-class marriages are uncommon and most people marry within their own social class.

Exceptional talents, such as in sport or entertainment, or luck, like winning the football pools, provide a route for upward mobility, but only for an extremely small number of people.

Obstacles to Social Mobility

While levels of social mobility have grown a little this century, there remain a number of obstacles to social mobility and the development of a truly 'open' society. The issues summarized below are discussed further in chapters 6, 12 and 15.

- Despite free and compulsory state education, there remains widespread inequality of educational opportunity. Many working-class children face a number of obstacles and disadvantages to success in education, which mean they do not do as well as their ability should allow them to, and this restricts their chances of upward mobility. Middle-class families are generally in a better position to secure for their children a middle-class occupation, as they are more able to afford to support their children in further and higher education.
- There remain biases in recruitment to the upper middle-class elite jobs. For example, judges and top civil servants are recruited almost exclusively from people who have attended very expensive boys' public schools and then gone to Oxford or Cambridge Universities. This is a major obstacle for children from working-class backgrounds, who can't afford these schools and are therefore often denied the chance of getting into these top jobs.
- Women face a range of obstacles in achieving upward mobility, because of a range of factors which hinder their ability to compete in the labour market on equal terms with men (see chapter 6).
- Disadvantages in education, and **racism** (see glossary) in education, training, and employment, often present obstacles to the upward social mobility of some ethnic minority groups. Consequently, a high percentage of people of Afro-Caribbean and Pakistani/Bangladeshi origin are represented in the working class.

Discussion

Do you think everyone who has intelligence, initiative, and skill can make it to the 'top' in modern Britain if they really try? Are those at the top and the bottom of the social class hierarchy there because they deserve to be?

This chapter has shown that social class differences persist as major features of life in contemporary Britain, and most people do not achieve much upward social mobility from the family into which they are born. These class inequalities become even more apparent when the two extremes of the social class hierarchy are studied: the rich and the poor. These themes are explored in the following chapter.

Chapter Summary

After studying this chapter, you should be able to:

- Describe and explain a range of social class differences.
- Describe and explain the main changes in the class structure this century.
- Explain and criticize the suggestion that embourgeoisement has occurred.
- Describe the differences between the 'traditional' and 'new' working classes.
- Describe and explain the changing position of clerical workers this century.
- Describe and explain the patterns of social mobility in Britain this century, and outline the obstacles to social mobility.

Project Suggestions

1. Using secondary sources, do a study of some aspect of social class inequality, such as in health, at work, or in education.
2. Interview a sample of manual and non-manual workers and try to discover what differences exist in their terms and conditions of employment and their experience of work.

Key Terms

affluent worker
deskilling
elite
embourgeoisement
infant mortality
inter-generational social mobility
intra-generational social mobility
perinatal death
proletarianization
racism

4 Wealth, Income, and Poverty

Many believe that large differences in wealth and income and the contrasts between the very rich and the very poor have largely disappeared in modern Britain. Surely the welfare state has got rid of poverty? However, a walk through the streets of any large city will reveal stark contrasts between the mansions, the luxury cars, and the expensive lifestyle of the rich, and the poverty and hardship of many of those who are unemployed, sick, or old, who are single parents, who are homeless or living in decaying housing, and who are faced with a future of hopelessness and despair. This chapter will show the common assumption that the welfare state has resolved the problem of poverty to be misguided, and demonstrate that massive inequalities in wealth and income and widespread poverty remain in modern Britain.

Wealth and Income

- **Wealth** refers to property which can be sold and turned into cash for the benefit of the owner. The main forms of wealth are property such as homes and land, stocks and shares in companies, and personal possessions. **Productive property** is wealth which provides an unearned income for its owner, for example houses which are rented, factories and land, or stocks and shares which provide dividends. **Consumption property** is wealth for use by the owner, such as consumer goods like fridges, cars, and stereo systems, or owning your own home, which do not produce any income.

- **Income** refers to the flow of money which people obtain from work, from their investments, or from the state. This may be earned income, received from paid employment (wages and salaries), or unearned income, which is received from investments, such as rent on property, interest on savings, and dividends on shares.

The Distribution of Wealth and Income

Figure 4.1 shows that in 1988 the poorest 50 per cent of the population owned only 6 per cent of the wealth, while the richest 5 per cent owned 38 per cent. A quarter of the population possessed three-quarters of the nation's wealth. These figures are official figures from *Social Trends*, a major source of official government statistics which is published annually, and they

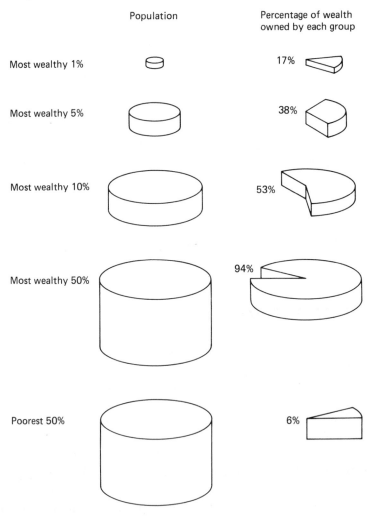

Figure 4.1 Distribution of wealth, United Kingdom, 1988

Source: Data from *Social Trends 21* (HMSO 1991).

therefore under-estimate the inequalities of wealth, as the wealthy have an interest in concealing their wealth to avoid taxation.

As figure 4.2 shows, income is also unequally distributed, with the top fifth of income earners getting about 39 per cent of all income in 1987 – almost twice their 'fair share' if income were equally distributed, and as much as the bottom three-fifths of income earners got between them. The poorest fifth got only about 9 per cent, less than half of their 'fair share'.

Activity

income

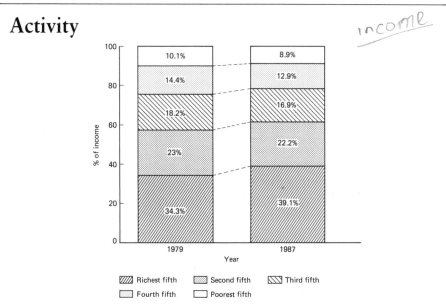

Figure 4.2 Distribution of income: by fifths of the population, Great Britain, 1979–87

Source: Social Trends 21 (HMSO 1991).

Study figure 4.2 and answer the following questions:

1. Which group increased its share of income the most between 1979 and 1987?
2. Which group suffered the least cut in their income share between 1979 and 1987?
3. By how much did the percentage share of the poorest fifth of the population fall between 1979 and 1987?
4. How might the evidence in figure 4.2 be used to show that the rich are getting richer while the poor, in comparison, are getting poorer?
5. Draw a pie chart to illustrate the distribution of income in 1987. Round the numbers up or down to the nearest whole number; for example, make 8.9 per cent = 9 per cent and 39.1 per cent = 39 per cent.

Who Are the Rich?

The rich are:

- The aristocracy. They are major land owners, such as the Duke of Westminster, who owns sizeable chunks of London, Cheshire, the Scottish Highlands, Vancouver, and Hawaii, and whose wealth amounts to an estimated £4.2 billion.
- The owners of industry and commerce – the 'corporate rich' of the business world.
- Stars of entertainment and the media.

The first two of these groups make up Marx's bourgeoisie.

Most wealth is inherited, with those inheriting doing nothing to earn their wealth. Most of the rich live on unearned income from investments rather than from employment.

High-income earners do not necessarily put in more work than those who receive low pay; it is simply that society places different values on people in different positions, and rewards them more or less highly. A senior executive in a large company or a rock star will probably not have to work as hard for his or her high income as a coal miner or an unskilled manual labourer working long hours in a low-paid job. Whenever one hears about 'hard-working Royalty', it is worth bearing in mind that Britain's queen is the world's richest woman, with personal assets estimated at £6.6 billion. What the queen receives in unearned income in one day – an estimated £1.8 million tax free – would take a manual worker on average wages about 142 years to earn.

Attempts to Redistribute Wealth and Income

The massive inequalities in wealth and income which have existed this century, and the inequalities in life chances these have caused, have provoked various measures by governments to redistribute wealth and income more equally. These measures include:

- Inheritance tax, which is a tax payable when people give gifts of wealth either before or after death, and is intended to limit the inheritance of vast quantities of wealth from one generation to the next.
- Capital gains tax, which is intended to reduce profits from dealing in property or shares, and is payable whenever these are sold.

- Income tax, which is payable on unearned and earned income, and rises as earnings increase.
- Social welfare benefits from the state, like income support, which are attempts to divert the resources obtained through taxation to the needy sections of society.

Why Have these Attempts Failed?

Despite these measures, attempts to redistribute wealth and income have been largely unsuccessful. Little real redistribution has occurred, and what redistribution has taken place has mainly been between the very rich and the already well off. This is because their investments often mean the wealthy can make their wealth grow at a faster rate than the rate at which it is taxed.

The state allows tax relief, money normally used to pay income tax, on a wide variety of things such as business expenses, school fees, and mortgages. These are expenses which only the better off are likely to have. This means that they pay a smaller proportion of their income in tax than a person who is poorer but who does not have these expenses.

Tax avoidance schemes, which are perfectly legal, are often thought up by financial advisers and accountants to find loopholes in the tax laws and beat the tax system, thereby saving the rich from paying some tax. Such schemes involve things like living outside of Britain for most of the year, investing in pension schemes to avoid income tax, investing in tax-free or low-tax areas like the Channel Islands, giving wealth away to kin well before death to avoid Inheritance tax, or putting companies in other people's names, such as those of husband/wife, children, or other kin.

Tax evasion is illegal, and involves people not declaring wealth and income to the Inland Revenue. This is suspected to be a common practice among the rich.

A final reason for the failure of attempts at wealth and income redistribution is that many people fail to claim the welfare benefits to which they are entitled. Some reasons for this are discussed later in this chapter.

After the election of the Conservative government in 1979, and throughout the 1980s, the trend which existed throughout the twentieth century towards the redistribution of wealth and income from the rich to the less well off was reversed. Wealth and income became more concentrated in the hands of those who were already rich. The highest rate of income tax paid by top earners was reduced from 83 per cent in 1979 to 40 per cent by 1991, other tax concessions were made to the rich, and the value of welfare benefits to the poor was severely reduced.

Poverty

While there are great inequalities in the distribution of wealth and income in Britain, with a small section of the population possessing large amounts of wealth and income, there is at the other extreme the continued existence of widespread poverty.

Much of the early sociological research into poverty was a reaction against the idea that poverty was the poor's own fault. Charles Booth's study of poverty in London between 1891 and 1903, and Rowntree's studies of poverty in York in 1899, 1936, and 1950, found that the poor were in fact 'deserving' – decent, hard-working families who had fallen into poverty through circumstances beyond their control. Such research helped to overcome the myth of the poor as 'idle scroungers'.

One of the key issues in discussing poverty, and certainly the most controversial, is the problem of defining what poverty is.

Absolute Poverty

Absolute poverty or subsistence poverty refers to a person's biological needs for food, water, clothing, and shelter – the minimum requirements necessary to subsist and maintain life, health, and physical efficiency. A person in absolute poverty lacks the minimum necessary for healthy survival. While

Average daily calorie supply per person (1984-1986)

The average person should consume no less than 2 400 calories every day, according to the United Nations. Below this level chronic malnutrition may eventually occur.

Two 'quarter pounders', two large fries and three milkshakes add up to 2 400 calories.

KEY

■ Less than 2 000 calories

▨ 2 001 to 2 400 calories

▢ 2 401 to 2 800 calories

▨ 2 801 to 3 200 calories

☐ over 3 200 calories

Source: Food and Agriculture Organization, UN

GRAPHIC: JENNY RIDLEY

Figure 4.3 The extent of absolute poverty

- The World Health Organization says that 40 000 children below the age of 5 die from disease, malnutrition, and neglect in developing countries every day. That is 15 million children a year.
- Worldwide, almost 750 million people suffer from hunger and malnutrition. That is more than double the population of Europe.
- In African countries, 27 million people were facing starvation in 1991.

Source: EG, The Guardian, 11 December 1990.

the minimum needed to maintain a healthy life might vary, for example, between hot and cold climates and between people in occupations with different physical demands, absolute or subsistence poverty is roughly the same in every society. People in absolute poverty would be poor anywhere at any time – the standard does not change much over time. The solution to absolute poverty is to raise the living standards of the poor above subsistence level. Absolute poverty is most associated with the countries of the Third World, where it remains a widespread problem. It is unlikely many people live in absolute poverty in Britain today, where poverty is basically relative poverty.

Relative Poverty

Relative poverty involves defining poverty in relation to a generally accepted standard of living in a specific society at a particular time. This takes into account social and cultural needs as well as biological needs. Townsend has provided the classic definition of relative poverty:

> Individuals . . . can be said to be in poverty when they lack the resources to obtain the types of diets, participate in the activities and have the living conditions and amenities which are customary, or at least widely encouraged or approved, in the societies to which they belong. Their resources are so seriously below those commanded by the average individual or family that they are, in effect, excluded from ordinary living patterns, customs or activities.
>
> *Source*: P. Townsend, *Poverty in the United Kingdom* Penguin 1979

This type of poverty is a condition where individuals or families are deprived of the opportunities, comforts, and self-respect which the majority of people in their society enjoy. Minimum needs are then related to the standard of living in any society at any one time, and will therefore vary over time and between societies, as standards of living change. For example, those living in slum housing in Britain would be regarded as poor here, but their housing would appear as relative luxury to poor peasants in the Third World. Similarly, running hot water and an inside bathroom and toilet would have been seen as luxuries one hundred years ago in Britain, but today are seen as basic necessities, and those without them would be regarded as poor by most people.

Activity

1. Either alone or through majority agreement in a group, go through the following list, ticking those items which you think are necessities, which all adults should be able to afford, and no-one should have to go without.

    1. An annual week's holiday away, not with relatives
    2. A bath, not shared with another household
    3. Beds for everyone in the household

4. A 'best outfit' for special occasions
5. A car
6. Carpets in living rooms and bedrooms
7. Celebrations on special occasions such as Christmas
8. Children's friends round for tea/snack fortnightly
9. A damp-free home
10 A decent state of decoration in the home
11 A dishwasher
12 A dressing gown
13 Fares to visit friends in other parts of the country four times a year
14 Fresh fruit and vegetables every day
15 A fridge
16 Friends/family for a meal monthly
17 Heating to warm living areas of the home if it's cold
18 Hobby or leisure activity
19 Holidays abroad annually
20 A home computer
21 An inside toilet (not shared with another household)
22 Insurance of house contents
23 Leisure equipment for children (sports, bicycle etc.)
24 Meat or fish or vegetarian equivalent every other day
25 New, not second-hand, clothes
26 A night out fortnightly
27 Out of school activities, e.g. sports, orchestra, Scouts
28 An outing for children once a week
29 Pack of cigarettes every other day
30 Presents for friends or family once a year
31 Regular savings of £10 a month for 'rainy days' or retirement
32 Restaurant meal monthly
33 A roast joint or vegetarian equivalent once a week
34 Separate bedrooms for every child over 10 of different sexes
35 Special lessons (for children) e.g. music, dance or sport
36 A telephone
37 A television
38 Three meals a day (for children)
39 Toys for children e.g. dolls or models
40 Two meals a day (for adults)
41 Two pairs of all-weather shoes
42 A video
43 A warm waterproof coat
44 A washing machine
(*Breadline Britain 1990s Study Pack*, London Weekend Television)

2. Compare your list with another person or group. How do your decisions compare with others? Were some items clear-cut and others borderline?

3. Now compare your list of necessities with those of the national survey conducted for *Breadline Britain 1990s*, presented in the box below. How far does your list agree or disagree with these national findings? What conclusions might you draw from any differences or similarities between the two?

4. Do you think if you were in a very poor country you would have the same list of necessities? Give reasons for your answer.

5. What does this exercise tell you about the ways of measuring poverty in modern Britain?

The public's perception of necessities in Britain in the 1990s

Research carried out in 1990 tried to establish what the public regarded as necessary for a minimum standard of living in Britain in the 1990s. This research provides a useful guide to public perceptions of relative poverty. At least two out of three members of the public classed the following items as necessities which no-one should have to go without:

- Self-contained damp-free accommodation, with an indoor toilet and bath.
- Carpets and heating.
- Beds for everyone in the household.
- A decent state of decoration in the home.
- A refrigerator.
- A warm, waterproof coat.
- Three meals a day (for children).
- Two meals a day (for adults).
- Insurance.
- Fresh fruit.
- Toys for children.
- Enough bedrooms for every child over 10 of different sex to have his or her own.
- Meat or fish or vegetarian equivalent every other day.

- Enough money for celebrations on special occasions such as Christmas.
- Two pairs of all-weather shoes.
- A washing machine.
- Presents for friends or family once a year.
- Out-of-school activities, such as sports, orchestra, Scouts.
- Regular savings of £10 a month for 'rainy days' or retirement.
- A hobby or leisure activity.

This research estimated that in 1990 in Britain:

- 11 million people – 1 in 5 of the population – lacked three or more of these necessities.
- 10 million people lacked adequate housing.
- 7 million people went without essential clothing.
- 2½ million children lacked at least one of the things they need, such as three meals a day, toys or out-of-school activities.
- 5 million people were not properly fed.
- 31 million people – over half the population – lacked minimal financial security, being unable to insure the contents of their homes or save £10 a month.

Source: Harold Frayman, *Breadline Britain 1990s*, booklet accompanying Domino Films and London Weekend Television's series *Breadline Britain 1990s*, broadcast in April and May 1991. The book *Breadline Britain in the 1990s*, by Stewart Lansley, Joanna Mack, and Harold Frayman, was published by HarperCollins in 1991. The research was funded by the Joseph Rowntree Foundation.

research 1990 by mack + Lansley
Breadline britian

The Controversy over Poverty

The idea of relative poverty and its measurement has been particularly controversial. In 1989, the Conservative Social Security Minister, John Moore, made a speech attacking the idea of relative poverty and the suggestion that many people in Britain were poor. Item A below presents John Moore's view. Item B presents an alternative view put forward by the Child Poverty Action Group (CPAG), with which many sociologists would agree.

Activity

Read item A and item B and then answer the questions which follow.

Item A

In 1989, the Conservative Social Security Minister, John Moore, made a speech attacking the idea of relative poverty and the view that many people in Britain were poor. He argued that poverty 'in the old absolute sense of hunger and want' had been wiped out, and it was simply that some people today were 'less equal'. He claimed the lifestyle of the poorest 20 per cent of families represented 'affluence beyond the wildest dreams' of the Victorians, with half having a telephone, car, and central heating and virtually all having a refrigerator and television set. 'It is hard to believe that poverty stalks the land when even the poorest fifth of families with children spend nearly a tenth of their income on alcohol and tobacco.' He said it was absurd to suggest that a third of the population was living in or on the margins of poverty. Starving children and squalid slums had disappeared. He claimed that the idea of relative poverty amounted to no more than simply inequality, and argued that the use of the concept of relative poverty meant that however rich a society became, the relatively poor would never disappear. 'The poverty lobby would, on their definition, find poverty in Paradise.'

Item B

The Child Poverty Action Group supports the view that poverty should be seen in relation to minimum needs established by the standard of living in a particular society, and all members of the population should have the right to an income which allows them to participate fully in society rather than merely exist. Such participation involves having the means to fulfil responsibilities to others – as parents, sons and daughters, neighbours, friends, workers, and citizens. Poverty filters into every aspect of life. It is about not having access to material goods and services such as decent housing, adequate heating, nutritious food, public transport, credit, and consumer goods.

But living on the breadline is not simply about doing without things; it is also about experiencing poor health, isolation, stress, stigma and exclusion:

> Poverty curtails freedom of choice. The freedom to eat as you wish, to go where and when you like, to seek the leisure pursuits or political activities which others accept; all are denied to those without the resources . . . poverty is most comprehensively under-

stood as a state of partial citizenship. (P. Golding, ed., *Excluding the Poor* (CPAG 1986)).

The gradual raising of the poverty line simply reflects the fact that society generally has become more prosperous and therefore has a more generous definition of a minimum income. The poor should not be excluded as the general level of prosperity rises.

Source: Adapted from Carey Oppenheim, *Poverty: The Facts* (Child Poverty Action Group 1988).

1. With reference to item A, explain briefly in your own words Moore's objections to the idea of relative poverty.
2. Explain in your own words what Moore meant when he said 'The poverty lobby would, on their definition, find poverty in Paradise.'
3. On the basis of what you have studied so far in this chapter, what definition of poverty do you think Moore supports? Give reasons for your answer.
4. With reference to item B, identify four factors apart from material goods and services which the Child Poverty Action Group thinks should be taken into account when defining poverty.
5. What definition of poverty does the Child Poverty Action Group support? Give reasons for your answer.
6. How do you think the Child Poverty Action Group might respond to Moore's comment that 'It is hard to believe that poverty stalks the land when even the poorest fifth of families with children spend nearly a tenth of their income on alcohol and tobacco'?
7. Imagine you are a supporter of the Child Poverty Action Group. Write a response to John Moore's speech.

Discussion

Do you think poverty really exists in modern Britain, given the starving populations in Africa?

The Measurement of Poverty in Britain: The Poverty Line

The **poverty line** is the dividing point between those who are poor and those who are not. There is no official poverty line in Britain today, but there are two separate measures which are widely used as poverty lines:

- The level of income at which income support (supplementary benefit or SB until 1988) becomes payable. The number of poor is calculated as all those claiming, or eligible to claim, income support.
- 50 per cent of average income – the definition of poverty used by the European Community.

Most sociologists also take into account those who are living on the margins of these poverty lines, as those whose incomes are low often slip between being on or below the poverty line and just above it. The margins of poverty include anyone living on between 100 per cent and 140 per cent of supplementary benefit/income support or between 50 per cent and 60 per cent of average income. The statistics on poverty in the rest of this chapter are based on the 50 per cent of average income figure, derived mainly from Carey Oppenheim, *Poverty: The Facts* (Child Poverty Action Group 1990).

The Extent of Poverty in Britain

The figures that follow are from 1987, and it is tempting to dismiss them as out of date. However, social security reforms in 1988 meant that 43 per cent of claimants lost income and 20 per cent experienced no change. Loans to the poor have replaced grants, and these have to be repaid from benefit payments. Unemployment began to increase once again in the early 1990s. Figures from the 1989 Family Expenditure Survey Report showed that the incomes of the poorest fifth of households in the UK – representing seven million people – were about 5 per cent less in 1989 in real terms (after allowing for inflation) than they were in 1979, while the richest fifth were 40 per cent better off. The 'Breadline Britain 1990s' research found that eleven million people lacked three or more items that the public regarded as essential for an adequate standard of living in the 1990s. These factors suggest the figures below are still as relevant in the 1990s as they were in 1987.

How many are poor?

In 1987 in Great Britain:

- 16 150 000 were living in or on the margins of poverty (below 60 per cent of average income) – 30 per cent of the population.
- 10 500 000 were living on or below the poverty line (50 per cent of average income) – 19 per cent of the population.
- Over a third (36 per cent) of all children were living in or on the margins of poverty (below 60 per cent of average income). Over a quarter (26 per cent) of all children were living on or below the poverty line.

Who are the poor?

Poverty is essentially a problem of the working class, because other classes have savings, occupational pensions, and sick pay schemes to protect them when adversity strikes or old age arrives. The major groups in poverty suggest that poverty is not caused by idleness, but by social circumstances beyond the control of the poor themselves. The unemployed, the low-paid, and pensioners account for most of the poor. Of those living in poverty (50 per cent of average income) in 1987:

- 28 per cent were unemployed.
- 26 per cent were in full-time work. Many of the poor work long hours in low-paid jobs.
- 22 per cent were pensioners. Many elderly retired people depend on state pensions for support, and these are inadequate for maintaining other than a very basic standard of living.
- 11 per cent were single parents. Single parents are often prevented from getting a full-time job by the lack of childcare facilities, or only work, at best, part-time, which generally gets lower rates of pay. The costs of childcare often mean they cannot afford to work. The majority of single parents are women, who in any case get less pay than men.
- 5 per cent were sick and disabled. Disability brings with it poorer employment opportunities, lower pay, and dependence on state benefits.
- 9 per cent were 'others' (men aged 60–4, widows, students, carers, and those unemployed but not available for work).

Activity

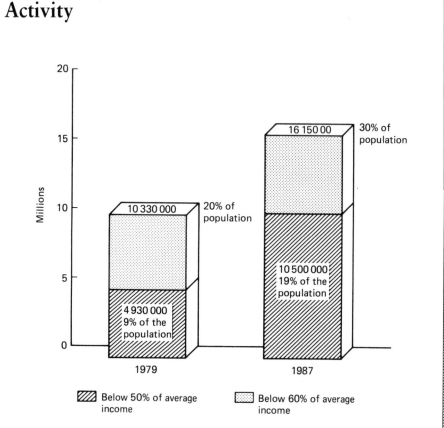

Figure 4.4 Numbers of people living in or on the margins of poverty, Great Britain, 1979 and 1987

Source: Poverty: The Facts (Child Poverty Action Group 1990).

Study figure 4.4 and answer the following questions:

1. By how much did the percentage of the population with below 50 per cent of average income increase between 1979 and 1987?
2. What percentage of the population had between 50 per cent and 60 per cent of average income in 1987?
3. How many more people had below 50 per cent of average income in 1987 compared to 1979?
4. Suggest reasons for the increase in the numbers living in poverty between 1979 and 1987.

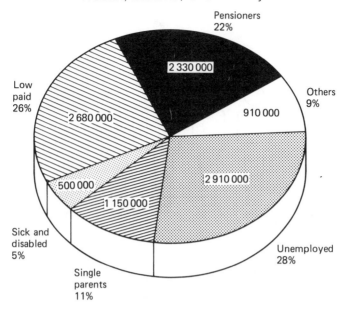

Figure 4.5 Groups in poverty, Great Britain, 1987

Source: Poverty: The Facts (Child Poverty Action Group 1990).

The feminization of poverty

Women are far more likely than men to experience poverty. In 1991, over 60 per cent of adults receiving income support were women. Women face a higher risk of poverty than men because:

- Women are more likely to be in low-paid and part-time work. In 1989, over two-thirds of low-paid workers were women.
- They are far more likely than men to be single parents with sole responsibility for children, leading to reduced possibilities for employment and dependence on state benefits.
- Women live longer than men and retire earlier, and therefore spend a greater proportion of their lives beyond retirement age. However, because of low pay throughout their lives they are less likely than men to have savings, and are less likely than men to be entitled to employers' pensions.
- In many low-income households, it is often mothers rather than fathers who bear the burden of trying to make ends meet, and in the face of poverty sacrifice their own standard of living to provide food, clothing, and extras for the children.

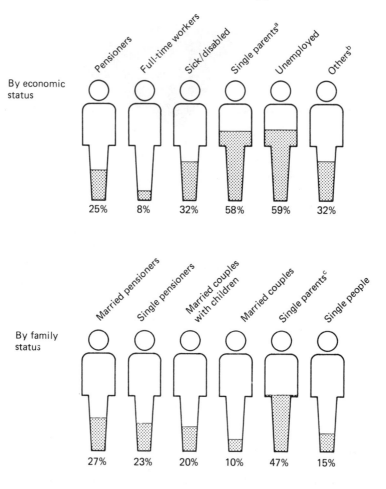

Figure 4.6 The risk of poverty: percentage of total population living in poverty (below 50 per cent of average income after housing costs), Great Britain, 1987

[a] Single parents who are not in full-time work
[b] Men aged 60–4, widows, students, people temporarily away from work, carers, people who are unemployed but not available for work
[c] All single parents

Source: *Poverty: The Facts* (Child Poverty Action Group 1990).

Activity

Study figure 4.6 and answer the following questions:

1. What percentage of sick and disabled people were living in poverty in 1987?
2. What percentage of married couples were living in poverty?
3. What evidence is there in figure 4.6 that might be used to show that low pay is a cause of poverty?
4. What difference is there between the proportion of single and married pensioners living in poverty?
5. Which group overall has the highest risk of poverty?
6. Suggest how the evidence in figure 4.6 might be used to show that the poor are victims of unfortunate circumstances rather than being themselves to blame for their poverty. Could any of the evidence in the figure be used to support the opposite view?

Criticisms of the Poverty Line

Many people are critical of the definition of poverty simply in terms of income, because it takes no account of all the extras most of the population take for granted, such as coping with household emergencies, going on holiday, going out for a drink with friends and taking part in other leisure activities. Poverty is not simply a matter of how much income someone has, but can also involve other aspects of life such as the quality of housing and the quality and availability of public services like transport, hospitals, schools, and play areas for children.

Poverty means going short materially, socially and emotionally. It means spending less on food, on heating, and clothing than someone on an average income. But it is not what is spent that matters, but what isn't. Poverty means staying at home, often being bored, not seeing friends, not going out for a drink and not being able to take the children out for a trip or treat or a holiday. It means coping with the stresses of managing on very little money, often for months or even years. It means having to withstand the onslaught of society's pressure to consume. It impinges on relationships with others and with yourself. Above all, poverty takes away the tools to build the blocks for the future – your 'life chances'. It steals away the opportunity to have a life unmarked by sickness, a decent education, a secure home and a long retirement. It stops people being able to take control of their lives. (Carey Oppenheim, *Poverty: The Facts* (Child Poverty Action Group 1990).)

Let us briefly outline some aspects and consequences of poverty apart from shortage of income. While not all of those in poverty will experience all of these multiple deprivations, the list below shows how poverty can be like a spider's web, trapping the poor in a deprived lifestyle in many aspects of their lives.

- Homelessness. In 1991:
    — 465 700 individuals in Britain were officially without a permanent home.
    — 80 000 were homeless in London, living in bed and breakfast hotels, hostels, and other temporary accommodation.

Britain in the 1990s: homeless young people prepare for another day after spending the night in the doorway of Burton's in the Strand, central London. Some prefer the street to sometimes frightening hostels.

Source: The Guardian, 19 December 1990.

- — An estimated two million single people were homeless.
- — More than 5 000 people were estimated to be sleeping rough in London each night.
- Poverty in health care.
  - — There are few doctors practising in inner-city areas (where many of the poor live), and those who do are often over-worked, because the poor have more health problems.
  - — The poor are less likely to get time off work with pay to visit the doctor.
  - — They face long hospital waiting lists.
  - — Many are not fully aware of what health services are available to them, and the poor tend to be less vocal in demanding proper standards of care from doctors.
- Poverty at school.
  - — Inner-city schools often have older buildings and poorer facilities.
  - — There is often a concentration of social problems in these schools, such as drugs and vandalism, and consequently a higher turnover of teachers.
  - — Parents are less able to help their children with their education, and have less money than non-poor parents to enable the school to buy extra resources.

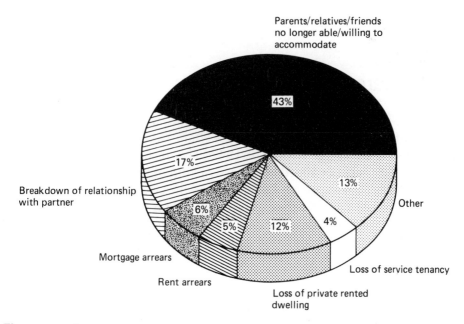

Figure 4.7 Reasons for homelessness, England and Wales, 1989

Source: Hansard, 25 April 1990.

- Poverty at work.
  - Poor working conditions. These include a neglect of health and safety standards and a high accident rate; working at night and long overtime because the pay is so low; lack of trade union organization to protect the workers' interests; lack of entitlement to paid holidays; and no employers' sick pay or pension schemes.
  - Insecure employment, often with very short notice of dismissal.
- Poor health, such as respiratory problems like asthma and infectious diseases, as a result of poor diet and damp, overcrowded housing.
- Going short of food, clothing, and heating, and not being able to replace household goods or carry out household repairs and decoration. A 1991 report by the National Children's Home found that 1 in 10 children under the age of five from low-income families went without enough food to eat at least once a month because their parents couldn't afford it, while 1 in 5 low-income parents denied themselves food on a regular basis. All the families in the study had an unhealthy diet, not because they didn't know or care about a nutritionally healthy diet, but because they couldn't afford it.
- Isolation and boredom. Making friends may be hard because there is no money to get involved in social activities.
- Stress, in the face of mounting bills and debts, perhaps leading to domestic violence, family breakdown, and mental illness.
- Low self-esteem, brought on by dependence on others, the lack of access to the life others have, and difficulties in coping with day-to-day life.

The Welfare State and Poverty

The main measures taken to help the poor have largely developed with the welfare state. The development of the welfare state as we know it today began with the Beveridge Report of 1942. This recommended the development of welfare services aimed at the destruction of the 'five giants' of want, disease, squalor, ignorance, and idleness, and the creation of a society where each individual would have the right to be cared for by the state from womb to tomb. The welfare state came into effect as we know it today on 5 July 1948 – the date of the foundation of the National Health Service.

The welfare state provides a wide range of benefits and services including:

- A range of welfare benefits through the social security system for many groups such as the unemployed, those injured at work, the sick and disabled, widows, the retired, expectant mothers, single parents, and children.

- A comprehensive and largely free National Health Service, including ante- and post-natal care, hospitals, GPs, dentists, and opticians (although some charges are payable – for example to dentists and opticians).
- A free and compulsory state education for all to the age of 16.
- Social services provided by local councils, such as social workers, and special facilities for the mentally and physically handicapped, the elderly, and children. Local councils are also responsible for housing the homeless, and for the adoption and fostering of children.

Voluntary organizations

Voluntary organizations are non-official, non-profit-making organizations which are 'voluntary' in the sense that they are neither created by, nor controlled by, the government. They employ both salaried staff and voluntary helpers, and are funded by donations from the public and grants from central and local government. Voluntary organizations try to fill some of the gaps left by the 'safety net' of the welfare state, by providing help and information in areas where state assistance is too little or non-existent. They also play important roles as **pressure groups**. These seek to put pressure, through public campaigns, on those in positions of power in society to improve welfare benefits for the poor and deprived. Voluntary organizations play a major role in highlighting the weaknesses of the welfare state, and keeping problems such as poverty, homelessness, and the care of the mentally ill in the public eye. They frequently provide expert knowledge and make recommendations to governments for changes to improve social welfare.

Voluntary organizations include groups such as the Salvation Army, which provides hostel accommodation and soup kitchens; Shelter, which campaigns for the homeless and helps with finding accommodation; Help the Aged and Age Concern; the NSPCC (the National Society for the Prevention of Cruelty to Children); NACRO (the National Association for the Care and Resettlement of Offenders). Much of the information on poverty in this chapter has come from one such organization, the Child Poverty Action Group, which promotes action for the relief of poverty among children and families with children.

Table 4.1 Three voluntary organizations in Britain

Organization	Aim	Activities
NSPCC (National Society for the Prevention of Cruelty to Children)	To protect children from abuse in all its forms.	• Taking action to protect children who are deprived, neglected or at risk of abuse, through a network of Child Protection Teams providing a 24-hour service. • Working with parents, children, and social service departments to provide advice, support, counselling, and practical help to overcome family problems and prevent further child abuse. • Providing education and training for professional and voluntary organizations, such as local authority social workers, the police, health visitors, and doctors.
NACRO (National Association for the Care and Resettlement of Offenders)	To work towards a more effective approach to preventing crime and more humane treatment of offenders.	• Running a housing association providing some 700 places for ex-offenders. • Running employment training to help unemployed ex-offenders find work. • Running youth training, education, and advice projects for offenders and people at risk of offending. • Working with others locally and nationally to provide new approaches to criminal justice. • Working with local communities to develop crime prevention and community safety schemes. • Providing research, information, and training services.

Table 4.1 (*cont'd*)

Organization	Aim	Activities
Shelter (National Campaign for the Homeless)	To fight for the right of everyone to a decent home.	• Providing housing aid centres throughout the country which give advice and help. • Working with local authorities to find solutions to the housing problems of young people leaving the care of the local authority. • Campaigning for change and improvements in housing policy by acting as a pressure group on people in positions of power in society – primarily the government. • Providing research and information on the problems of homelessness.

The Persistence of Poverty: Why the Poor Remain Poor

Despite the welfare state, the evidence presented in this chapter suggests that widespread poverty remains in modern Britain. Why is this?

A failure to claim benefits

Welfare benefits have been cut in recent years by inflation and government policies, and they are not high enough to lift people out of poverty. Nevertheless, many people do not claim the welfare benefits to which they are entitled. In 1987 an estimated 800 000 families failed to claim state benefits to which they were entitled. This is often because of the inadequate publicity and the obscure language of leaflets which means people often do not know what their rights are or the procedures for claiming benefits. This is particularly important as the poor are among the least educated sections of the population. The mass media periodically run campaigns about social security 'scroungers'. Headlines such as 'Scroungers by the Sea' (*Daily Mail*, 13 July 1977) and 'How to be a failure and get paid for doing nothing' (*Daily Telegraph*, 29 July 1976) help to attach a stigma to claiming benefits which may deter some people from doing so.

Discussion

Do you agree the media give the impression that people receiving benefits are 'scroungers'? Do you think most people receiving welfare benefits are deserving? Do you think benefits discourage people from taking more responsibility for their own lives? Do you think people should be expected to take a job even if they will be worse off than if they received benefits?

The poor pay more

It is one of the great ironies of poverty that the cost of living is higher for the poor than the non-poor, and this hinders the poor in their attempts to escape poverty. The poor pay more because:

- They often live in poor quality housing, which is expensive to heat and maintain, and they live mainly in inner-city areas where rents are high.
- The price of goods and services is higher in poorer areas, due to factors like shoplifting and vandalism.
- Poverty means buying cheap clothing, which wears out quickly and is therefore more expensive in the long run.
- Their food costs more, as they can only afford to buy it in small quantities, which is more expensive, and from small, often expensive corner shops as they haven't cars to travel to supermarkets. They also lack storage facilities like freezers for buying in bulk.
- House- and car-insurance costs them more, due to higher levels of theft and vandalism in poor areas.
- Credit costs them more, because banks and building societies won't lend them money, as they consider them a 'poor risk'. Loans are therefore often obtained from 'loan sharks' at exorbitant rates of interest.
- They suffer more ill-health and so have to spend more on non-prescription medicines.

The culture of poverty

One explanation for the persistence of poverty is the theory of the **culture of poverty**. This suggests it is the characteristics of the poor themselves, their values and culture, that causes poverty. It is suggested the poor are resigned to their situation, that they seldom take opportunities when they arise, are reluctant to work, and don't plan for the future. They seem to make little effort to change their situation or to help themselves by taking the initiative and trying to break free of their poverty. Children grow up in this culture, and learn these values from their parents, and so poverty continues from one generation to the next.

The weakness of this type of explanation is that it tends to blame the poor for their own poverty, and implies that if only the poor would change their values, then poverty would disappear. However, if the poor do develop a culture of poverty – and this is hotly disputed – it may well be *caused by* poverty and not a *cause of* poverty. For example, the poor cannot afford to save for a 'rainy day', planning for the future is difficult when the future is so uncertain, and it is hard not to give up and become resigned to being unemployed after endless searching for non-existent jobs.

However, the culture-of-poverty explanation is a convenient one for those in power, as it puts the blame for poverty on the poor themselves. If this explanation is adopted, then the problem of poverty will be solved by policies such as cutting welfare benefits to the poor, to make them 'stand on their own two feet', and job training programmes to get them used to working. Such a view of the poor seemed to lie behind many of the Conservative Government's social security reforms in the 1980s, and the cuts in welfare benefits these produced.

The cycle of deprivation

Coates and Silburn in *Poverty: The Forgotten Englishmen*, a study of St Anne's in Nottingham, suggested a further explanation for poverty. They argued that poverty is cumulative, in the sense that one aspect of poverty can lead to further poverty. This builds up into a vicious circle of poverty which the poor find hard to escape from, and it then carries on with their children. Figure 4.8 illustrates examples of possible 'cycles of deprivation'.

The problem with this explanation is that, while it explains why poverty continues, it does not explain how poverty begins in the first place. The final explanation does try to do this.

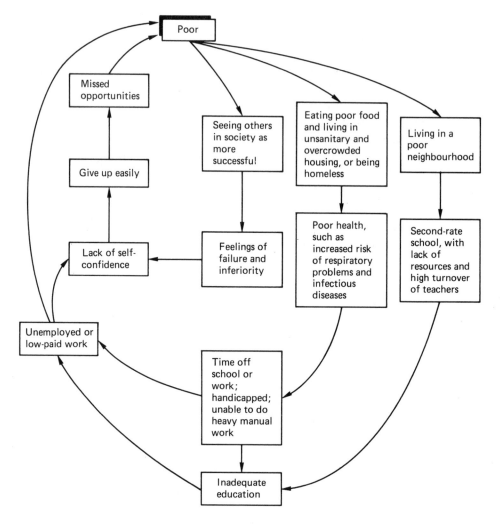

Figure 4.8 Cycles of deprivation

Structural explanations

Structural explanations explain poverty in terms of the structure of society, with its unequal distribution of wealth and income and the inadequate assistance given to the poor. These are mainly Marxist arguments which suggest that the reason the poor remain poor is because they are exploited by the rich. The owners of society's key resources make profits by paying low wages – and their wealthy position depends on poverty. Poverty ensures the dangerous, menial jobs are done, and the poor help to limit the wage demands of those who are non-poor, by providing a threat to their jobs. The poor lack power to change their position, because they do not have the financial resources to change public opinion. Structural explanations suggest that any serious attempt to abolish poverty would involve a widespread redistribution of wealth and income. This would mean the creation of improved social services, higher welfare benefits, and more and better-paid jobs, with the introduction of higher taxes on the rich to pay for these reforms.

Activity

You have become the prime minister, with a huge majority in Parliament enabling you to carry through a successful campaign against poverty. Think carefully about all the explanations for poverty you have read of in this chapter, and the groups in poverty. Devise a series of policies which would help to reduce poverty. Explain in each case why you think your proposed policy would help to reduce poverty.

Chapter Summary

After studying this chapter, you should be able to:

- Explain the difference between wealth and income.
- Describe the attempts made to redistribute wealth and income, and explain why these measures have failed.
- Explain the difference between absolute and relative poverty.
- Describe the poverty line in Britain, and make criticisms of it.
- Describe aspects of poverty apart from lack of income.
- Identify the main groups in poverty in modern Britain, and explain why each of them is poor.
- Explain why women are more likely to be in poverty than men.
- Outline the main features of the welfare state.
- Explain, with examples, the role of voluntary organizations.
- Explain why the cost of living is higher for the poor than for those who are not poor.
- Give a number of explanations why the poor remain poor, despite the welfare state.

Project Suggestions

1. Carry out a survey asking people about poverty in Britain today. Do they think it still exists? What do they mean by 'poor'? Draw up a list of items and ask people whether they think they are essential for a basic standard of living. You could use the list of items earlier in this chapter to help you. Try to draw some conclusions about the idea of relative poverty.
2. Interview a sample of people generally thought to be living in poverty, such as the unemployed or single parents, and try to discover what difficulties they experience compared to those who aren't poor.
3. Do a case study of the activities of a local voluntary organization.

Key Terms

absolute poverty
consumption property
culture of poverty
income
poverty line
pressure groups
productive property
relative poverty
wealth

5 Gender Role Socialization

Stratification by sex is a feature found in most societies, with men generally being in a more dominant position in society than women. Our sex has major influences on how we think about ourselves, how others think about us, and the opportunities and life chances open to us. Men have traditionally been seen in a wide range of active and creative roles – as warriors, hunters, and workers, as political leaders or successful business executives, as scientists, engineers, inventors, or great artists (how many famous women scientists, engineers, inventors, or artists can you name?).

And what roles have women been traditionally seen in? As housewives and mothers confined to the home and caring for their husbands and children. Even when working outside the home, women's jobs often seem to be an extension of their caring role in the home, looking after others as receptionists, secretaries, nurses, teachers, social workers, shop and kitchen assistants, or cleaners. We might almost be forgiven for thinking that men and women exist in two different worlds, united only by belonging to the same species. Are these differences simply an extension of the biological make-up of males and females, or are they a product of the ways that males and females are brought up in society? This chapter will examine this question, and discuss how the social differences between men and women are constructed by socialization in modern Britain. The following chapter examines some of the particular inequalities facing women which are, in part, a product of this socialization.

Sex and Gender

Sex and Gender

The term **sex** (whether someone is male or female) refers to the natural or biological differences between men and women, such as differences in genitals, internal reproductive organs and body hair.

Gender (whether someone is masculine or feminine) refers to the cultural, socially-constructed differences between the two sexes. It refers to the way a society encourages and teaches the two sexes to behave in different ways through socialization.

A **gender role** is the pattern of behaviour and activity which society expects from individuals of either sex – how a boy/man or girl/woman should behave in society. Gender roles may sometimes be referred to as sex roles.

The difference between the terms 'sex' and 'gender' is best illustrated by the case of transsexuals – people who biologically belong to one sex, but are convinced they belong to the opposite sex, for example a woman 'trapped' in a man's body. When these people try to change their biological sex, through surgery and hormone treatment, they also have to learn to act in a different way and adopt new masculine or feminine gender roles. *The Independent on Sunday* (16 December 1990) reported the case of a man who changed sex twice: from male to female and back again. On taking on the female role, he had to adopt a new feminine gender identity, like changing his name from Colin to Cathy, wearing a dress and high-heel shoes, putting on a black wig as his hair was too masculine in texture, and shaving off his beard. However, the importance of gender identity meant that, while losing his male friends, barriers remained in forming close relations with female friends. He felt he was simply changing from acting as a man to acting as a woman, and that the only group with which he could find full acceptance was with other transsexuals. After three years of living as a woman, the pressures of being accepted as neither male nor female meant he stopped hormone treatment, reverted to his former male identity, and started dressing as a man again. It is experiences such as these that show the fundamental importance of gender identities, and how influential they are, not only in how we see ourselves, but in how others see us too.

Gender and Biology

It is sometimes suggested that the different gender roles played by women and men are 'obvious' extensions of the biological differences between the sexes. Therefore women are thought to be 'natural' mothers, with a maternal and caring 'instinct' and a biological inclination towards child rearing and domestic tasks. Men, on the other hand, it is suggested are 'naturally' assertive and dominant members of society, inclined towards the 'breadwinner' role of supporting the family.

If this argument were correct, then one would expect the typical roles played by men and women in Britain to be the same in every society: after all, the biological differences between men and women are the same everywhere. However, the comparative study of other societies suggests this is not the case.

Three Tribes in New Guinea

Margaret Mead described three tribes in New Guinea (*Sex and Temperament* 1935) where the roles of men and women were quite different from those found in modern Britain.

- Among the *Mundugumar*, both sexes showed what we in Britain would regard as masculine characteristics – both sexes were aggressive, both hated childbirth and child rearing, and both treated children in an offhand way.
- Among the *Arapesh*, there were few 'natural' differences between the behaviour of the sexes. Both sexes were gentle and passive; women did the heavy carrying; the men tried to share the pains of childbirth with their wives by lying with them during childbirth. Both sexes shared equally the tasks of bringing up children (women's traditional role in Britain).
- In the *Tchambuli* tribe, the traditional gender roles found in modern Britain were reversed – it was the men who displayed what we would regard as 'feminine' characteristics', such as doing the shopping and putting on make-up and jewellery to make themselves attractive. Women were the more aggressive practical ones, who made the sexual advances to men and did all the trading.

These three examples suggest that gender roles are not natural, since they differ between societies even though biological differences remain the same. There is also evidence of children who, although biologically male, have been brought up as females and developed feminine forms of behaviour. It is evidence like this which has led sociologists to conclude that masculine and feminine gender identities are primarily constructed through socialization, rather than a product of the biological differences between men and women.

Gender Stereotyping in Britain

A **stereotype** is a generalized, over-simplified view of the features of a social group, allowing for few individual differences among members of the group. The assumption is made that all members of the group share the same features. Examples of stereotypes include views such as 'all women are lousy drivers', 'all young people are vandals and layabouts', or 'the unemployed are all on the fiddle.'

A gender stereotype is a generalized view of the 'typical' or 'ideal' characteristics of men and women. In modern Britain, for example, girls and women are expected to show the 'feminine' characteristics of being pretty, slim, gentle, caring, sensitive, submissive, non-competitive, and dependent. The masculine stereotype, on the other hand, emphasizes characteristics like physical strength, aggression and assertiveness, independence, competitiveness, and ambition. Girls and women who fail to conform to the feminine stereotype are liable to be seen as 'tomboys', while men and boys who fail to conform to the masculine stereotype are likely to be seen as 'cissies' or 'wimps'.

Some jobs and activities are also stereotyped as more suitable for men or women; housework and childcare, for example, are still seen as predominantly 'women's work', while 'men's work' is predominantly seen as something that takes place outside the home in paid employment.

Activity

1. What other groups of people tend to get stereotyped in the world today apart from men and women?
2. What are the main features of these stereotypes?
3. Do you consider these stereotypes to be flattering or insulting to the groups concerned? Give reasons for your answer.

4. Look at the following list of words, and divide them into three groups: those you might use to describe women, those you might use to describe men, and those you might use to describe both men and women.

clever	aggressive	tender	thoughtful
powerful	gentle	caring	attractive
emotional	beautiful	pretty	soft
cold	assertive	kind	clinging
sweet	logical	quiet	ruthless
sly	delicate	brave	active
muscular	weak	handsome	competitive
slim	submissive	bitchy	bastard
bachelor	spinster	tart	blonde
domineering	hysterical	frigid	elegant
raving	plain	cute	slag
hideous	passive	tender	gracious

5. Now compare the two lists of words used to describe men and women. Do they present gender stereotypes? You will probably have found there are some words in both lists that have a similar meaning. Discuss why these words are not used to describe both sexes, and how they show stereotyped assumptions about women and men.

There is a wide range of social institutions which influence the socialization of males and females into their gender roles in modern Britain, but here the family, the education system, the peer group, and the mass media will be focused on.

The Role of the Family

Children begin to learn their gender roles at a very early age, and by the time children start school they have already learnt much about masculine and feminine roles. For example, a survey conducted in 1991 for the NAS/UWT and the Engineering Council among five-year-olds found that car-repairing, woodwork, fire-fighting, mountain-climbing, and seeing war films were seen by most children to be mainly for men, and 73 per cent of the boys and 66

Gender stereotyping of the worst kind. This was how Mr Justice Harman responded in 1991 when someone explained to him the difference between Miss, Mrs, and Ms.

per cent of the girls thought that only men could be scientists. The family plays a very important part in this primary socialization.

Parents' stereotypes

Parents and relatives tend to hold stereotyped views of the 'typical' or 'ideal' characteristics of boys and girls, and they often try to bring up their children in accordance with their stereotyped view of 'normal' masculine or feminine behaviour. Comer argues in *Wedlocked Women* (Feminist Books 1974) that girls are expected and encouraged to show dependence, obedience, conformity, and domesticity, while boys are encouraged to be dominant, self-reliant, active, and outward looking. Young children soon learn that approval from parents and relatives often depends on conforming to these stereotypes, and as Michelle Stanworth in *Gender and Schooling* (Hutchinson 1983) notes,

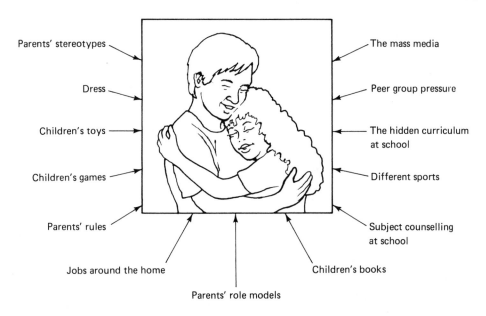

Parents' stereotypes

Dress

Children's toys

Children's games

Parents' rules

Jobs around the home

Parents' role models

The mass media

Peer group pressure

The hidden curriculum
at school

Different sports

Subject counselling
at school

Children's books

Figure 5.1 The social construction of gender differences through socialization

'parents may scarcely be aware that they praise their daughters for being pretty and loving, their sons for being courageous and resourceful.'

From birth, girls and boys are frequently dressed in different clothes and colours – 'blue for a boy and pink for a girl' – and parents generally buy girls clothes which are more colourful and 'pretty', and boys more practical clothing. Such different forms of dress continue, of course, right throughout life.

Children's toys

Children are generally given different sorts of toys to play with according to their sex, which increases the pressure on them to follow at an early age the different roles to which they will be expected to conform in adult life. Table 5.1 illustrates the way toys tend to be stereotyped according to their suitability for either boys or girls.

Boys tend to be given, for example, meccano sets, cricket bats, footballs, chemistry sets, electronic toys, guns, cars, aeroplanes, and computers: more active and technical toys, which take them outside the home, both physically and in their imagination. On the other hand, girls are generally given toys like sewing machines, dolls, prams, toy hoovers, cookers, and tea sets – toys which are often played with inside the home, and serve to restrict girls to the domestic situation.

Activity

Table 5.1 Sex-stereotyping of toys

Masculine toys		Either sex		Feminine toys	
Toy	Rating	Toy	Rating	Toy	Rating
Football	1.5	Banjo	4.5	Skipping rope	7.0
Plane	1.7	Rocking horse	4.6	Sewing machine	8.2
Toolset	2.0	Alphabet ball	4.9	Dish cabinet	8.3
Racing car	2.2	Paddling pool	5.0	Cleaning set	8.4
Dumper truck	2.5	Blackboard	5.3	Dolls pram	8.5
Construction set	2.7	Rollerskates	5.3	Dolls wardrobe	8.7
Tractor	3.0	Telephone	5.6	Cosmetics	8.8
Wheelbarrow	3.2	Teddy bear	5.8		
Sports car	3.6				

The ratings were made by 20-year-old psychology students, and were found to correspond strongly with the choices made by children of either sex. 1 = strongly masculine, 5 = appropriate for both sexes, 9 = strongly feminine.

Source: Data adapted from A. Oakley *Sex, Gender and Society* (Gower Publishing 1985).

1. Look at the two lists of strongly masculine and strongly feminine toys in table 5.1, and add any other toys to the lists you can think of.
2. Explain all the main differences you can between the masculine and feminine toys, and suggest how these differences might encourage boys and girls to learn different skills and behave differently as adults. Make sure you refer to examples of particular toys and particular adult roles in your answer.

Children's games

Children's games frequently involve practising adult gender roles, such as girls playing the role of nurse to their brothers' doctor, or girls playing at being mothers or housewives by playing with dolls, trying on make-up, cooking, or serving tea to brothers with toy tea sets. Boys play more aggressive and dominant games, such as war games or cowboys and Indians.

Little girls' dreams?
Barbie's worldwide sales total more than £300 million a year. If each Barbie doll that has been sold were placed head to toe, they would circle the world more than three-and-a-half times.

Source: Sean Smith, *The Guardian*.

Parents' rules

Research has suggested that girls face different rules to boys of the same age, and are more strictly supervised by parents. Girls are more likely to be collected by parents from school than boys, and are less likely to be allowed to play outside or in the street. Girls are also more likely to be told to be in at a certain time, and to have to tell their parents where they are going.

Jobs around the home

As table 5.2 shows, participation by children in household duties shows a marked difference between the sexes, with girls more likely to do indoor housework, generally helping their mothers with domestic jobs, while boys are more likely to do outdoor jobs with their fathers, like cleaning the car, sweeping the yard and being shown how to do repairs and make things.

Activity

Table 5.2 Eleven-year-olds' participation in household duties

Duty	Boys %	Girls %	Both %
Washing up	40	63	51
Indoor housework (tidying, vacuum cleaning, dusting, bedmaking, etc.)	19	44	32
Miscellaneous dirty/outside jobs (gardening, sweeping yard, cleaning car or windows, making or mending fires, peeling potatoes, shoecleaning, emptying bin, etc.)	36	8	22
Going on errands	39	21	30

Source: Adapted from J. Newson, E. Newson, D. Richardson and J. Scaife, 'Perspectives in sex role stereotyping' in J. Chetwynd, and O. Hartnett, (eds), *The Sex Role System: Psychological and Sociological Perspectives* (Routledge & Kegan Paul 1978).

Study table 5.2 and answer the following questions:

1. What household duty is most likely to be performed by both sexes?
2. What household duty is least likely to be performed by (a) boys and (b) girls?
3. How do you think the divisions in household duties among eleven-year-olds could be seen as preparation for adult gender roles? Give examples of particular adult roles.

Watching and imitating parents

Small children mainly learn by watching and imitating the **role models** provided by others. A role model is simply a pattern of behaviour which others model their behaviour on. Children often observe their parents carrying out their respective gender roles every day. If children see their mothers spending more time in the home while their fathers go out to work, their mothers spending more time doing cooking, cleaning, and other housework than their fathers, and if they see it is their mothers, rather than their fathers, who always take time off work to look after them when they are sick or take them to the doctor, then children may well begin to view these roles as the 'normal' ways for men and women to behave.

The Role of the School

The process of gender socialization begun in the home often carries on through schooling, and this has been excellently documented in Michelle Stanworth's study *Gender and Schooling* (Hutchinson 1983). Much of this socialization goes on through the school's **hidden curriculum**. This consists of the hidden teaching of attitudes and behaviour, which are taught at school through the school's organization and teachers' attitudes but which are not part of the formal timetable. This is discussed in more detail in chapter 11. The hidden curriculum emphasizes the differences between males and females, and encourages different forms of behaviour. Three examples help to illustrate this.

Teachers' attitudes

Teachers have also been socialized into gender roles, and there is evidence suggesting that teachers have higher expectations of boys than girls, encourage them more (especially in sciences and computing), and place more emphasis on their progress than that of girls, because they expect boys to be the future 'breadwinners'. Teachers also give different career advice to boys and girls, such as steering girls towards nursing and clerical work, and boys towards a much wider range of occupations.

Boys demand more of the teacher's time, and disruptive, unruly behaviour from boys is more likely to be tolerated than the same behaviour from girls. Girls fighting in the playground, for example, are likely to be punished far more severely than boys fighting, since girls are not expected to show such 'unfeminine' behaviour.

Schoolbooks

Reading books in infant schools often show women and little girls in the housewife/mother role, such as helping mother in the home, or watching their brothers climbing trees, mending the car, and 'getting into mischief'.

Boys are more likely to be portrayed as playing with cars or trains, playing football, exploring, building things, climbing trees, and so on.

In secondary school, gender differences are reinforced by the illustrations in textbooks for different subjects – science books rarely show girls doing science, and boys rarely appear in home economics books, suggesting that some subjects are more suited to one sex rather than the other.

Subject choice

Girls and boys have traditionally been counselled by parents and teachers into taking different subjects. Girls have been more likely to take arts subjects (like English Literature, History, and foreign languages) and study Home Economics, Commerce, and Typing, while boys have been more likely to take sciences, Technical Drawing, and CDT – subjects which are more likely to lead to more skilled and technical occupations after school. This gender division is also found in sport, with football and cricket for the boys and hockey and netball for the girls. The National Curriculum introduced in 1988 (see chapter 11) has meant that *all* 11–14-year-olds have to take Technology, which includes Home Economics, Business Studies, and CDT. This may mean that these gender divisions between subjects break down during the 1990s, but this remains to be seen.

Discussion

On the basis of your own experiences at both primary and secondary school, discuss any difficulties or pressures you might have experienced at school because of your sex in choosing subjects and options that you wanted to do. Take into account factors such as the views of your parents, friends, and teachers, and the advice of careers and subject teachers.

The Importance of the Peer Group

A **peer group** is a group of people of similar age and status with whom a person mixes socially. Generally, people try to gain acceptance among their peers by conforming to the norms of their peer group. These norms frequently involve stereotyped masculine and feminine roles. For example, among male peer groups, interests and norms often centre on activities like football, music, cars, motor-bikes, stereo equipment, and computers. Female interests often centre on things such as fashion, make-up, and dancing. The peer group can exert strong pressure to conform to these interests: a boy, for example, who collected soft toys would be quite likely to find himself ridiculed by his peer group; a girl who played football might be seen as a bit of a 'tomboy'. Such pressures can help to discourage participation in activities which don't conform to gender stereotypes.

Double standards

Among teenage boys (and often adult men too) sexual promiscuity and sexual 'conquest' is often encouraged and admired as approved masculine behaviour, and is seen as a means of achieving status in the male peer group. However, males will condemn this same promiscuity among women – promiscuous girls/women are likely to be seen as 'slags' or some other insulting term. This attitude is often reinforced even by the female peer group, where sexual relations by girls are only approved in the context of a steady, close relationship. Girls/women who have sex outside some 'steady relationship' are therefore likely to find themselves condemned by men and women alike. This double standard helps to encourage conformity to separate gender identities for men and women, with the stereotyped man as 'sexual athlete' and woman as the passive and faithful lover, wife, or 'girlfriend'.

Discussion

Do you believe that there is a 'double standard' applied to the behaviour of females when it comes to sexual activity?

The Role of the Mass Media

The mass media include films, television, newspapers, records, radio, advertising, books, comics, and magazines. The mass media create and reinforce gender stereotypes in a number of ways.

Comics, for example, present different images of men and women: girls are usually presented as pretty, romantic, helpless, easily upset, and dependent on boys for support and guidance, and boys and girls are often presented in traditional stereotyped gender roles such as soldiers (boys) or nurses (girls). A similar pattern is shown on children's television. Belotti argues that many traditional fairy tales, indeed much children's fiction, often portray females as either evil or fairly stupid and dependent on men for their ultimate safety, as the following suggests:

> 'Little Red Riding Hood' is the story of a girl, bordering on mental deficiency, who is sent out by an irresponsible mother through dark wolf-infested woods to take a little basket full to the brim with cakes to her sick grandmother. Given these circumstances her end is hardly surprising. But such foolishness, which would never have been attributed to a male, depends on the assurance that one will always find at the right moment and in the right place a brave huntsman ready to save grandmother and granddaughter from the wolf. (E. G. Belotti, *Little Girls* (Writers and Readers Publishing Co-operative 1975), quoted in A. Oakley, *Subject Women* (Fontana 1982), p. 109)

Activity

1. Do you agree with the view that female figures in children's fairy stories are mainly portrayed as either good but fairly stupid or evil and wicked? Try to think of evidence drawn from stories, other than the one given above, which either confirms or denies your view.
2. Examine some children's reading books, comics, or male or female adult magazines and see if you can identify any pattern in the different roles and interests allocated to boys and girls or men and women. Provide evidence for your conclusions.

You may have found from the previous activity that there are often very different types of story and magazine aimed at males and females. Romantic fiction is almost exclusively aimed at a female readership. A glance at the magazine shelves of any large newsagents will reveal a 'Women's interests' section, consisting almost exclusively of magazines on cooking, homecare and housekeeping, health and slimming, lifestyle, fashion and haircare, knitting, mother and baby, and weddings. This shows very clearly the way the media both encourage and cater for a particular view of a woman's role. There is no similar 'Men's interests' section. However, men (and not women) can often be seen queuing up to read magazines (classified as of 'general interest') concerned with photography, stereos, computers, DIY, and all manner of transport: cars, motor-bikes, aircraft, trains, and boats. The 'top shelf' soft-porn magazines are aimed exclusively at men.

Images of men and women

When women appear in the mass media, it is usually in one of two main roles (and rarely any other):
- *As a 'sex object'* – the image of the slim, sexually seductive, scantily clad figure typically found on page 3 of the *Sun* newspaper is used by the advertising industry to sell everything from peanuts to motor-bikes and newspapers.

or:

- *In the housewife/mother role* – as the content, capable, and caring housewife and mother, whose constant concern is with the whiteness of clothes, the cleanliness of floors, and the evening meal.

When men appear in the media, it is in a very wide range of roles, but the masculine stereotype of the tall, strong, handsome, brave, non-domestic male often appears. These differing roles of men and women are most evident in advertising, even when young children are used. For example, television advertisements for washing-up liquid or washing powder nearly always show mothers and small daughters working together, and boys are usually the ones who come in covered in dirt. While men/small boys hardly ever appear in such advertisements, when they do appear in a domestic role it is nearly always made clear it is an exception, or that they are not very good at domestic tasks.

Activity

1. What do the two 'Men – a user's guide' cartoons on the next page suggest are the main forces which contribute to the gender socialization process?
2. Study the result of the socialization of men shown in the cartoons, and describe the stereotype of a 'typical male'.
3. Do you think the cartoons give an accurate impression of masculine behaviour? Back up your view with evidence of both child and adult male behaviour.

Men — a user's guide

Mark Haddon and Clara Vulliamy

Men — a user's guide

Mark Haddon and Clara Vulliamy

Some consequences of media stereotyping

The images of men and women presented in the mass media in most cases do not conform to the reality of people's everyday lives. However, they may succeed in inducing feelings of guilt, inadequacy, and lack of self-confidence among the majority of women who don't 'measure up' to the 'sex object' or the 'happy housewife' images. This may partly explain why so many women are concerned with slimming and dieting, why anorexia is an illness affecting mainly teenage girls, and why many housewives in this country are on tranquillizers.

With men, the consequences may take a more sinister turn, and it is possible that the rising number of violent crimes against women might in part be traced back to these media stereotypes, as the following writer argues:

> The only image the media will accept of a male is muscle-bound and dominant to the extent that when Prince Edward left the marines not even the pacifists applauded his rejection of a military lifestyle and he became Prince Wimp – a wimp in media terms being anyone incapable of fighting off alligators while delivering a box of chocolates. So if this is true, then men are reacting to their perceived ideal image in the same way as women react to theirs and violence can be the only result. An inadequate male will try to emulate screen heroes and then feel even more rejected when his life is not filled immediately with women who look like centre-folds.
>
> The fact that, as his refusal to cross the Atlantic after the Libyan bombing raid shows, not even Sylvester Stallone can live up to the Rambo image would be ignored and these men would react in the only way the media has taught them – aggressively. Possibly towards other men but more likely towards women who are an easier target.
>
> The rising number of violent crimes against women might not be because they are portrayed as sex objects but because men are shown to be all-powerful, irresistible and capable of solving problems with a karate kick or a Kalashnikov*. The proof might turn out to be the number of rapists who, when caught, are found to be bodybuilders trying to conform physically, if not emotionally, to the male image as it is portrayed. (R. R. C. Penfold, 'Image fakers' *The Guardian* 15 June 1988)

---

* A Russian assault rifle

Activity/Discussion

1. In the passage above, list all the features which make up the mass media stereotype of men.
2. Suggest ways that each of these features might affect adult male behaviour.
3. Do you agree with the writer's view in the passage above that there is a link between male stereotyping in the media and violence against women?

The Sexual Division of Labour

The processes of gender role socialization outlined in this chapter often mean that men and women have different expectations of life. Socialization has the general effect of restricting girls' experience to the domestic sphere, limiting their self-confidence, and pushing them towards marriage and the roles of housewife and mother as their primary roles in life. Boys, on the other hand, are more likely to grow up conforming to the stereotype of the non-domestic, practical, independent, and assertive male, whose role in life is that of worker and 'breadwinner' for wife and family.

The different socialization of males and females shows itself in the **sexual division of labour** in the job market, with jobs being divided into 'men's jobs' and 'women's jobs', and with young men and women choosing different types of work. These divisions in the labour market, and the inequalities which women face in a number of areas of social life as a result of the socialization process, are examined in the following chapter.

Chapter Summary

After studying this chapter, you should be able to:
- Explain the difference between sex and gender.
- Argue against the view that gender roles are biologically based.
- Describe the main features of gender stereotypes in modern Britain.

- Explain how gender socialization is carried out through the family, the school, the peer group, and the mass media.
- Explain some of the effects of the gender socialization process on both men and women.

Project Suggestions

1. Observe children in a playgroup and see if boys and girls play different types of game or play with different toys. Interview their mothers or fathers about the types of toy they had for birthday or Christmas presents. Try to reach some conclusions about gender role socialization.
2. Study children's comics for a week (or reading books in an infant school, daily newspapers, children's books, television programmes and films, etc.), and see if boys/men and girls/women are presented in stereotyped ways. Give some detail on what the various stereotypes are and explain how they might contribute to gender role stereotyping.
3. Examine subject or option choices, or exam entries, at your school or college and see if there are differences between males and females. Interview male and female students about why they chose their options, and interview teachers about your findings.

Key Terms

gender
gender role
hidden curriculum
peer group
role model
sex
sexual division of labour
stereotype

6 Women

The theme of the previous chapter was the way our ideas about masculinity and femininity, and the different roles expected of men and women in Britain, are constructed through the influence of a wide range of agencies of socialization. A popular assumption today is that throughout the twentieth century our ideas about women and the traditional housewife/mother role allocated to them have been changing. Women, it is often assumed, have achieved both full participation in society beyond the confines of the home, and equal status with men in most areas of social life.

The primary concern of this chapter is to examine this assumption. To what extent has the position of women in society improved, and what explanations are there for any changes? To what extent do women still face barriers to their full participation in society on an equal footing with men? The major focus here will be on identifying and explaining the continuing inequalities which women face in the world of work, both inside and outside the home, but other aspects of the inequalities confronting women are discussed in chapters 4, 5, 10 and 12.

The Changing Status of Women in Britain

Women in the Nineteenth Century

In nineteenth-century Britain, most women lacked many of the legal and political rights which men had. Women were in most cases dependent on men for money and support, and faced major discrimination at work and in education, with a wide range of jobs and opportunities barred to them. Women's main role in life was expected to be that of a housewife and mother, and a typical working-class woman could expect to be pregnant about ten times, and spend many years of her life bearing and nursing children.

Women in the Twentieth Century

During the twentieth century, there has been a gradual improvement in the status of women in Britain, the outlines of which it is useful to list here. However, as will be seen later, women still face major inequalities compared to men, particularly the conflicting demands of family life and career success.

- Women have achieved more political equality with men, beginning with the powerful and often violent campaign waged by the Suffragette Movement at the beginning of this century. This won the right for women to vote in parliamentary elections. By 1918, all women over age 30 could vote, and this was lowered to age 21 in 1928. This put women in the same position as men for the first time in relation to voting rights.
- Women today have equal rights with men in education. It is now illegal to discriminate against women or men by denying them access to certain subjects and courses at school or in further and higher education because of their sex.
- More types of job are seen as suitable for women today, and many more women are going out to work in paid employment. Women now make up about 43 per cent of the workforce in Britain, which gives them more financial independence.
- Equal opportunity laws have helped women to get a better deal and overcome prejudice and discrimination. For example, the Equal Pay Act of 1970 made it illegal for employers to offer different rates of pay to men and women doing the same or similar work. The Sex Discrimination Act of 1975 made it illegal to distinguish between men and women in work, leisure, and educational opportunities, and the Equal Opportunities Commission has been formed to help enforce the Sex Discrimination Act and the Equal Pay Act, and to promote equality of opportunity between men and women.
- Women have won equal rights with men in property ownership. The Married Women's Property Acts of 1880 and 1882 gave married women the right to own their own property, and the 1970 Matrimonial Proceedings Act established that all property was to be equally divided between husband and wife in the event of a divorce.
- Women have had equal rights with men in divorce since the 1923 Matrimonial Causes Act.

Equal Opportunities

the law is on your side – and so are we

The Equal Opportunities Commission was established by Parliament in 1975 to ensure effective enforcement of the Sex Discrimination Act and the Equal Pay Act.

It is the responsibility of the Commission to work towards the elimination of sex discrimination in employment, in education and training opportunities and in the provision to the public of goods, facilities services and accommodation.

As well as investigating areas of inequality between the sexes, the Commission has a duty to make recommendations to the Government about the operation of existing law.

One important function of the Commission is to advise you of your rights under the Sex Discrimination Act and the Equal Pay Act – rights which could have an effect on your career prospects as well as your pay packet.

Send second class stamp for free catalogue of publications, dealing with all aspects of sex discrimination.

Publicity Section

Equal Opportunities Commission

Overseas House, Quay Street, Manchester M3 3HN.

- The welfare state has provided more support for single-parent families, the majority of whom are women, and for women caring for dependent husbands and the elderly in the home.

Why has the status of women changed in twentieth-century Britain?

The changing status of women in twentieth-century Britain outlined above can be explained by a number of factors.

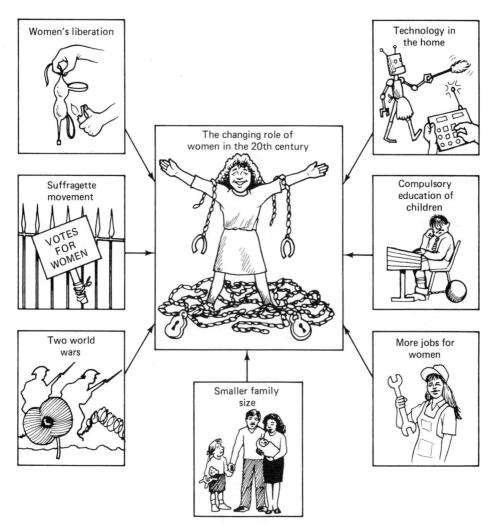

Figure 6.1 Why has the status of women changed in twentieth-century Britain?

The Suffragette Movement

The Suffragette Movement, which started at the turn of the twentieth century and lasted until 1918, aimed to achieve equal voting rights for women with men in parliamentary elections. This involved a long and often violent struggle against men's ideas about a woman's role. It was the first major struggle by women for equality with men, and began to change the ideas held by both men and women about a woman's role. The success of this campaign gave women political power for the first time in elections, and MPs had to begin to take women's interests into account if they were to be elected.

Activity

Go to a library and find out what you can about the kinds of actions carried out by the suffragettes in their campaign to achieve 'Votes for Women'. (You may find this information in a good encyclopedia, or in the history or sociology sections.) How do you think these activities might have changed both men's and women's views on women's traditional roles?

The two world wars

During the First (1914–18) and Second (1939–45) World Wars, women took over many jobs in factories and farms which were formerly done by men, as the men went off to be soldiers. Women showed during these war years that they were quite capable of doing what had previously been seen as 'men's jobs', and this began to change people's ideas about a woman's role.

Smaller family size

The declining size of families is both a cause and a consequence of the improving status of women. This has reduced the time spent in child rearing and given women greater opportunities to enter paid employment. A typical mother today spends about four years bearing and nursing children, and she can expect to live a much longer life than her nineteenth-century counterpart. This means once a woman has had children today, she still has a long life stretching ahead to pursue a career.

More jobs for women

There are more types of job seen as suitable for women today, and legal obstacles to the employment of women have been removed in most cases. Although there still remains a lot of prejudice and discrimination by employers about the suitability of some jobs for women, the way women took over men's jobs during the world wars, the pressures of the Suffragette Movement, and more recently the Women's Liberation Movement have helped to erode hostility to female workers among male bosses and workers.

This increase in employment opportunities for women has come about with the expansion of light industry, manufacturing, and the tertiary sector of the economy. The tertiary sector is concerned with services, finance, administration, distribution, transport, and government agencies, such as the NHS, the social services, and education. The expansion of this sector has increased the number of routine clerical and secretarial jobs which are overwhelmingly done by women. There has also been an increase in the number of jobs in the lower professions, such as teaching, social work, and nursing, which employ many women.

Maternity benefits and maternity leave now provide additional encouragement and opportunity for women to return to work after childbirth, as their jobs are kept open for them while they are absent having children. The fact that more women are working gives them greater financial independence and therefore more authority in both the family and society.

The compulsory education of children

Compulsory schooling since 1880, and particularly since 1944, has reduced the time necessary for the care and supervision of children in the family. This has given women with children a greater opportunity to go out to work than earlier this century.

Technology in the home

Advances in technology have brought many improvements to the home environment, including better housing standards like central heating, labour-saving devices like freezers, washing machines, microwave cookers, food processors, and vacuum cleaners, manufactured foodstuffs such as canned and frozen foods, and 'instant meals'. It has been suggested that these improvements have reduced the time spent on housework. However, others argue that these developments have simply meant higher standards are expected, and therefore more housework has to be performed. For example, automatic washing machines mean that washing is done several times a week instead of just once on 'washing day', and people change their clothes more often. This also creates, of course, more ironing. Similarly, vacuum cleaners mean that houses are expected to be kept cleaner than they used to be.

The Women's Liberation Movement

The Women's Liberation Movement is a broad movement of women concerned with the fight to achieve equality with men. This movement is not a single group, but consists of a large number of different women's groups with various aims, both in Britain and abroad. These groups are united by the need to improve the status and rights of women, and are concerned with ending **patriarchy**, which is the dominance of men in society. Since the 1960s, the Women's Liberation Movement has challenged many ideas about the traditional role of women, particularly the stereotype that 'a woman's place is in the home'. It has campaigned for:

- Better nursery facilities.
- Free contraception and free abortion on demand, and 'a woman's right to choose' whether to have an abortion or not.
- Equal pay and job opportunities.
- The removal of tax and financial discrimination against women.
- Freedom from violence against women.
- The right of women to define their own sexuality.

The Women's Liberation Movement has challenged many people's ideas about women, and has created a 'climate of expectation' where women expect to be treated equally and not as simply lovers, housewives, and mothers. It is mainly because of pressures from the women's movement that equal opportunity laws have been passed, and that **sexism**, or prejudice and discrimination against people because of their sex, is increasingly seen as unacceptable behaviour.

Discussion

Do you think that women are treated more equally today? What obstacles and problems do women still face that men don't?

Women at Work

Unpaid Work: Domestic Labour

When talking about women at work, many people assume this refers to paid employment. However, it is important to remember there is one job which is performed full-time almost exclusively by women – unpaid housework or **domestic labour**. This domestic labour of women is hardly recognized as 'real work' at all, and carries little status compared to paid employment. Many women who are housewives themselves often devalue the status of their job, as is summed up in the phrase 'I'm only a housewife.' Oakley found that an average 77 hours a week are spent on housework and related tasks – far more than most people spend in paid employment. However, domestic labour has none of the advantages of paid employment, like regular working hours, chances of promotion, holiday pay, or sick pay. As table 6.1 shows, housewives experience far more monotony, fragmentation, and speed in their work than workers on even the most gruelling assembly line, but without the compensation of being paid for it.

Activity

Table 6.1 The experience of monotony, fragmentation and speed in work: housewives and factory workers compared

| | | Percentage experiencing: | |
Workers	Monotony[a]	Fragmentation[b]	Speed[c]
Housewives	75	90	50
Factory workers	41	70	31
Assembly line workers	67	86	36

[a]Monotony refers to the feeling that the work is boring and repetitive.
[b]Fragmentation refers to the feeling that the work is divided into a series of unconnected tasks not requiring the worker's full attention.
[c]Speed refers to the feeling that the worker has too much to do, with too little time to complete the task, and so has to work at too fast a pace.
Source: A. Oakley, *The Sociology of Housework* (Martin Robertson 1974).

Table 6.1 compares housewives' experience of their work with that of factory and assembly line workers.
1. Which group experiences the most monotony in their work?
2. Which group experiences the least speed in their work?
3. In which group did 31 per cent complain of too much speed in their work?
4. Suggest ways the evidence shown in table 6.1 might explain the finding that women who are exclusively housewives suffer more mental health problems than many of the population.
5. What differences are there between working exclusively as a housewife in the home and working in a factory which might make factory workers better able to cope with the monotony, fragmentation, and speed of their work?
6. Suggest reasons why housework is often not seen by many people as 'real work'.

Housework and childcare are still seen as primarily the responsibility of women. As shown in table 6.2, even when both partners are working full-time outside the home in paid employment, it is still women who are in most cases expected to take the major responsibility for housework and childcare. In 1987, 70 per cent of women in marriages or cohabiting couples where both partners were working full-time had responsibility for general domestic duties. What this means, of course, is that many full-time working women have two jobs to their male partner's one!

Activity

Table 6.2 Who performs jobs in the home?: married or cohabiting couples with both partners working full-time, 1987

Domestic job	Mainly man (%)	Mainly woman (%)	Shared equally %
Household shopping	8	43	49
Making evening meal	7	63	28
Washing evening dishes	22	33	41
Household cleaning	4	60	33
Washing and ironing	1	81	18
Repairing household equipment	86	3	10
Organizing household bills/money	36	31	33
Looking after sick children	1	56	40
Teaching children discipline	10	6	81
Summary: is responsible for general domestic duties	8	70	22

Source: Adapted from British Social Attitudes: 5th Report (Gower Publishing 1989), table 10.2.

Table 6.2 looks at the way work is divided in the home where both husbands and wives, or cohabiting couples, have full-time jobs.
1. Which household task is most likely to be performed mainly by women?
2. Which household task is least likely to be shared equally?
3. Which household task is shared equally by 81 per cent of couples?
4. In the light of table 6.2, list each of the following statements as true or false:

Mostly men alone wash up the evening dishes.
Looking after sick children is most likely to be shared by men and women today.

When their partners work full-time as well, men are most likely to make the evening meal.

Even when they work full-time, women are still mainly responsible for general domestic duties.

The only thing that men still seem to take the main responsibility for is repairing household equipment.

5. How does the evidence in table 6.2 support the view that women do two jobs compared to men's one job? Refer to particular examples to back up your case.
6. How might sociologists explain the division of household tasks shown in table 6.2?

Women in Paid Employment

Many of the factors discussed above explaining the changing status of women have brought about a large increase in the employment of women this century. In 1991, women made up about 43 per cent of the workforce, compared to less than 30 per cent at the beginning of the twentieth century. Over 75 per cent of women of working age were in employment in 1991. Much of this increase has been among married women: less than 10 per cent of married women were working in the early twentieth century, but this had increased to about 60 per cent in 1990, with 1 in 10 of these wives being the sole breadwinners in their families.

The inequality of women in paid employment

Although during the twentieth century the role and status of women have gradually improved, and women have obtained job opportunities and rights previously denied to them, women still have an unequal position with men at work. Much of this inequality arises because, as Oakley argues, the central role of women is still seen by a male-dominated society as that of housewife and mother. The following section summarizes the key features of women's employment situation, and describes and explains the main inequalities women face in the labour market.

The sexual division of labour

The sexual division of labour simply means that jobs are divided into 'men's jobs' and 'women's jobs', with women's jobs often having lower pay, poorer promotion prospects, and lower status than men's.

As shown in figure 6.2, fewer women than men are employed in the top managerial and professional group, and table 6.3 shows that few women in this group are in the top professional jobs. Figure 6.2 also shows that women are mainly employed in jobs which are concentrated at the lower end of the occupational scale: in unskilled and semi-skilled manual jobs and in routine, low-level clerical jobs like filing and typing, which require little or no training.

Women are also spread over a far narrower range of jobs than men. Figure 6.3 shows that nearly 75 per cent of women are concentrated in four main occupational groups: professional and related in education, welfare, and health; clerical; selling; and catering, cleaning, hairdressing, and other personal services.

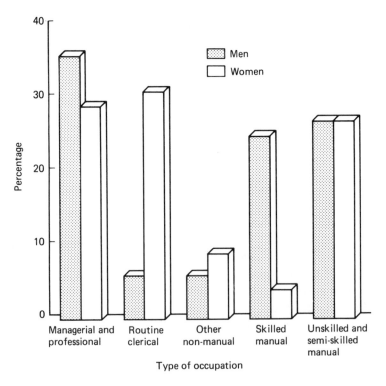

Figure 6.2 The occupations of women and men, Great Britain, 1990

Source: Department of Employment Labour Force Survey, 1990.

Table 6.3 Women and men in top professional jobs in the 1980s

Job	Men (%)	Women (%)
General practitioner	79	21
Hospital consultant or senior medical officer	86	14
Senior civil servant or MP	92	8
Cabinet minister (1991)	100	0
Senior local government officer	83	17
Local authority chief executive	99	1
Engineer or technologist	99	1
Accountant	96	4
Dentist	82	18
High court judge (1991)	97	3
Barrister	86	14
Solicitor	81	19
University professor	97	3
Full-time university lecturer	88	12
Bank manager	99	1
Company director	99	1
Chartered surveyor	99	1
Architect	95	5

Source: Equal Opportunities Commission and *The Report of the Hansard Society Commission on Women at the Top* (Hansard Society 1990).

Occupational grouping

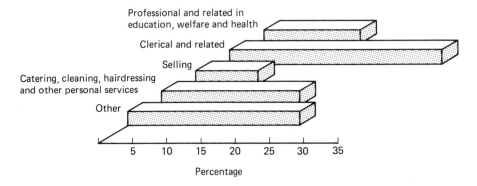

Figure 6.3 Occupational distribution of working women, Great Britain, 1990

Source: Department of Employment Labour Force Survey, 1990.

Activity

Table 6.3 shows that there are very few women in top professional jobs.
1. Why do you think this might be the case? What obstacles prevent women from getting into these jobs?
2. What steps might be taken to overcome these obstacles?

Female occupations Women are mainly employed in low-grade and low-paid jobs which are seen as 'female occupations'. These are often extensions of the traditional domestic roles of housewives and mothers into which many women continue to be socialized. These involve serving and waiting on people, caring for them, cleaning and clearing up after others – all jobs that women have traditionally done in the home. Such jobs include nursing, primary school teaching, secretarial and routine clerical work, low-grade catering work, such as that of waitresses and canteen assistants, and working as shop assistants, supermarket 'shelf-fillers' and check-out operators. For example, typists and secretaries serve their (usually male) bosses, organizing the office to make things easier for them, making them coffee, and providing papers for and clearing up after their meetings; primary school teaching involves childcare; nursing is caring for the sick; catering involves cooking, serving, and clearing up meals.

Part-time work

In 1990, more than four out of five part-time workers were women, and about 43 per cent of women in paid employment worked only part-time. Surveys suggest this is closely related to women's responsibilities for children and other domestic tasks. Many working women are limited in the jobs they can do and the hours they can work because they are still expected to take responsibility for housework and childcare, and to be at home for the children leaving for and returning from school. There are still few workplaces today with childcare facilities which would allow working mothers to take full-time jobs. The presence of dependent children (under the age of 16), and the age of the youngest child, are the most important factors related to whether or not women are in paid employment, and whether they work full or part-time. Figure 6.4 illustrates the importance of this link between dependent children and part-time status.

Much part-time work is particularly vulnerable to economic recession, and therefore involves higher risks of unemployment. Many employment-protection laws do not apply to part-time workers, and often part-time workers do not belong to trade unions and so lack trade union protection.

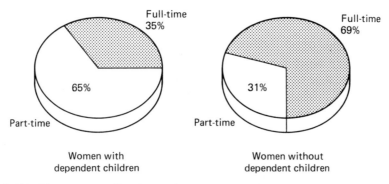

Figure 6.4 Working women: by dependent children and full- or part-time employment status, Great Britain, 1990

Source: OPCS General Household Survey, 1990

Activity

Source: Labour Research Department, *Part-time Workers*.

1. What does the cartoon suggest might be some of the reasons why women are less likely to attend trade union meetings than men?
2. How might more women be encouraged to attend union meetings?
3. Women are less likely to belong to trade unions than men. Suggest possible reasons for this.

These factors mean many women often face high risks of redundancy and unemployment.

Limited career opportunities

Women have more limited career opportunities than men for a number of reasons. Because of gender stereotyping at school and the wider gender-role socialization process, women often lack the necessary educational qualifications for the 'top jobs' and, equally important, the self-confidence and assertiveness required to apply for such jobs.

There is widespread male prejudice about women in career jobs and senior positions. There is evidence that some men are reluctant to be supervised by female managers, and there is a common male belief that men make better bosses. It is often assumed single women will eventually leave paid employment to marry and have children, and married women, particularly, are often seen as 'unreliable' because of the assumption they will be absent to look after sick children – although research has shown there is little difference in absence from work between men and women who share the same circumstances. As a result of these factors, women are often overlooked for training and promotion to senior positions by male employers.

In addition, women with promising careers may have temporarily to leave jobs to have children, and therefore miss out on promotion opportunities. Top jobs require a continuous career pattern in the 20–30 age period – yet these are the usual childbearing years for women, so while men continue to work and get promoted, women miss their opportunities.

Finally, married women are still more likely to move house and area for their husband's job promotion rather than their own. This means women interrupt their careers and have to start again, often at a lower level, in a new job, which means the men are getting promotion at the expense of lost opportunities for their wives.

Discussion

Do you agree with the suggestion in the cartoon that the questions being asked at the interview discriminate against women, or do you think employers have a right to ask such questions? Do you think discrimination against women is still a problem in education, work, and leisure activities?

Limited access to training

Women are less likely than men to enter training for better paid and more secure skilled work. Often women are denied training, and therefore promotion opportunities, because employers, parents, teachers, and sometimes the women themselves see training as 'wasted' on women. Employers,

Many employers still ask
women discriminatory
questions

The ten worst-paid jobs in Britain...

Kitchen hand
Women's-wear worker
Sewing machinist
Shop assistant
Men's-wear worker
Hat or glove maker
Barmaid
Hotel worker
Retail check-out operator
Hairdresser

...and they're nearly all done by women!

as a product of gender socialization, may assume women will leave work to produce and raise children. They may therefore be unwilling to invest in expensive training programmes for women. Rather, they prefer to employ women in low-skilled jobs where they can be easily and quickly trained and replaced. Of the small number of women who do obtain training, the vast majority are employed in 'feminine occupations' such as hairdressing, beauty, and clerical work, which are generally low-paid with limited career prospects.

Lower pay

While the Equal Pay Act gives equal pay to women if they do the same work as men, it has been shown above that women often do not do the same work as men, and consequently have no-one to claim equal pay with. The average pay of women is only about 70 per cent of the average male wage, and in 1990 women made up two-thirds of all low-paid workers. The ten worst-paid jobs in Britain are all performed mainly by women. In a nutshell, this is because many women are concentrated in low-skilled and part-time work, which lacks promotion prospects, trade union protection, and often sick pay, holiday pay, and redundancy payments – a situation which does not apply to the majority of men.

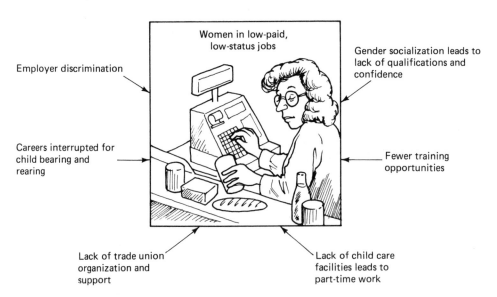

Figure 6.5 Why are women concentrated in lower-paid and lower-status jobs than men?

Conclusion

There have been great improvements in the position of women in the twentieth century, particularly in the 1970s and 1980s under the impact of the Women's Movement. Attitudes have changed, and sexism has become less acceptable. Women have become more self-confident and assertive, and they are beginning to achieve more success and influence in society.

However, it is still women who are most likely to face poverty, and women alone head 18 per cent of families with dependent children. Women still earn less than men, have poorer career opportunities and less job security, and there are few women in any of the top positions in society. Housework and childcare remain the primary responsibility of women, undermining their ability to compete with men in paid employment, reducing their financial independence, and restricting their power and influence in society. While women have gained much this century, there still remains some considerable distance to travel before women achieve equality with men in society.

Discussion/Activity

1. This chapter has mainly focused on the inequalities facing women at work. What other inequalities do women face in their daily lives compared to men? Think about things like going into pubs alone, fear of attack and sexual assault, politics, and so on.
2. In the light of the issues raised in this and the previous chapter and your responses to the activity above, consider what steps might be taken to break down these inequalities. To help you do this, draw three columns. In the first column, list all the inequalities you can think of that women still face today compared to men; in the second column, list the causes of these inequalities; in the third column, list the changes that would need to be made in society to remove these inequalities.

Chapter Summary

After studying this chapter, you should be able to:

- Describe and explain how and why the position of women has changed in Britain this century.
- Describe the main features of domestic labour.
- Explain why more married women are entering paid employment.
- Describe and explain a range of inequalities facing women in paid employment.
- Explain why women get only two-thirds of the average male wage and are poorly represented in top jobs.

Project Suggestions

1. Interview a sample of married or cohabiting women in paid employment who have small children, and try to discover any problems or role conflict they experience at work and in the home.
2. Interview a sample of full-time housewives and try to discover what they enjoy most and dislike most about being full-time housewives, how much time they spend each week on housework, and how much help, if any, they get from their male partners.
3. Do a survey among men and women of different age-groups asking about their attitudes to the growing equality of women.

Key Terms

domestic labour
patriarchy
sexism

7 Power and Politics

When most people in Britain think about politics, they usually think about voting and elections, councillors and MPs, and often boring party political broadcasts on television. This is quite a narrow view of politics, and of course in many parts of the world people are unable to vote in elections, and don't even have the right to be bored by the television broadcasts of competing political parties. Politics is not simply about councils and governments, but is more widely about the exercise of power.

Power is the ability of people or groups to exert their will over others and get their own way, even if sometimes others resist this. Politics is concerned with the struggle to gain power and control, by getting in a position to make decisions and implement policies. This means that when partners in a personal relationship argue about decisions affecting them, we can talk about the 'politics of the personal'. In family life, disputes between husbands and wives, and parents and children, can be considered as part of the 'politics of family life'. The power differences between men and women can be considered as 'sexual politics'.

In this chapter, the focus will be on the political system in society as a whole – the extent to which individuals can influence the decisions of governments, the policies of the political parties, and the factors which affect the way people vote. A key question will be to what extent Britain can be regarded as a democratic society.

Authority and coercion

A distinction is often made between two types of power:

- **Authority** is power which is accepted as legitimate (fair and right) by those without power. We obey those with authority because we accept they have the right to tell us what to do.

- **Coercion** is that type of power which is not accepted as legitimate by those without power, as the power holders rule without the consent of those they govern. People only obey because they are forced to by violence or the threat of violence.

Activity

1. Look at the following situations where people are using their power in modern Britain. In each case, briefly explain whether they are using authority or coercion and give reasons for your answer. Be warned – some may involve bits of both authority and coercion, and so it may be worth discussing your answers with someone else.

   - A police officer who stops and searches people simply because they're black, and then arrests them for objecting. C
   - A traffic warden who gives someone a parking ticket for illegal parking. A
   - A school pupil who beats other pupils up if they won't give him or her money. C
   - A teacher in a school who puts a student in detention for not doing his or her homework. A
   - A couple who beat their children because they won't do as they're told. C/A
   - A prime minister who orders his or her detectives to clear a restaurant of other customers so he or she can eat in peace. C
   - A manager who tells workers to stop chatting and get on with their work. A
   - A man who beats his wife because she displays too much independence. C/A
   - A prison officer who puts a prisoner in solitary confinement for refusing to follow orders. A

2. Depending on your answers to the activity above, explain in relation to each example how the use of coercion might be changed into authority, or how authority might become coercion. You may not find this is possible in every case.

3. What are the circumstances which influence whether the use of power is seen as fair or not?

Types of Political System

There are differences between societies in the amounts of power ordinary people have to influence government decisions, and these differences are shown in two opposing political systems: **democracy** and **totalitarianism**. While these two are presented as opposing systems, most political systems will fall somewhere between the two. It will be seen later, for example, that even in Britain, often seen as the 'home' of democracy, aspects of totalitarianism remain.

Democracy

Democracy is a system of government which basically involves 'government of the people, by the people, for the people', where ordinary people have some control over government decision-making. It is impractical for everyone in society to be permanently and directly involved in political decision-making, so often representatives are elected to represent people's opinions – such as MPs (members of parliament) and local councillors in Britain. This is known as representative or parliamentary democracy, and is found in Britain, France, Germany, the other countries of the European Community, and the USA. Electing representatives is an important part of a democracy. However, a democratic society usually includes many other features to ensure that representatives can be replaced if they follow unpopular policies and that people can freely express their opinions. Figure 7.1 illustrates the main features of a democracy.

Discussion

In the light of figure 7.1, do you think Britain is a democratic society? Do you think all individuals and groups have the same amount of power in society?

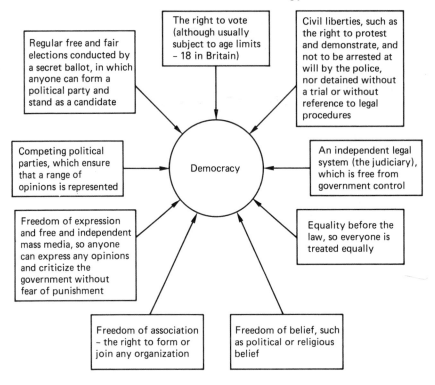

Figure 7.1 The features of a democracy

Totalitarianism

Totalitarianism is a system of government where society is controlled by a small powerful group – an elite – and ordinary people lack any control over government decision-making. There are no free elections and no civil liberties, and most of the features found in a democracy do not exist. The government rules by coercion rather than consent. People are forced to obey the government because of its control of the police, the courts, and the army. All the major social institutions like the economy, the education system, religion, the legal system, the police, and the mass media are strictly controlled by the government. Ideas opposed to those of the government are censored, and any opposition organizations crushed by force. Examples of totalitarian societies include Hitler's Germany and the People's Republic of China ('Communist' China).

A **dictatorship** is a form of totalitarianism where power tends to be concentrated in the hands of one person, such as Hitler.

Political Parties in Britain

A **political party** is a group of people organized with the aim of forming the government in a society. In a democracy, the existence of a range of political parties is essential if voters are to have a choice of candidates and policies to choose from. The discussion below covers the major parties in Britain which put up candidates for election to local councils, the British Parliament at Westminster, or the European Parliament in Strasbourg.

The Labour Party

The Labour Party was founded in 1906. It relies mainly on working-class support and receives most of its income from the trade union movement. It is one of the two main political parties in Britain. Traditionally the Labour Party placed great emphasis on state ownership and workers' control of key sectors of the economy, such as the banks, insurance companies, and all the major industrial companies. Labour Party membership cards still stress this aspect of Labour policy.

In 1988–90, many of the Labour Party's traditional policies were reviewed and changed extensively in a 'policy review', with the Party adopting policies which it was thought would have more appeal to voters.

To secure for the workers by hand or by brain the full fruits of their industry and the most equitable distribution thereof that may be possible upon the basis of the common ownership of the means of production, distribution and exchange, and the best obtainable system of popular administration and control of each industry or service. *Labour Party Constitution Clause IV (4)*

Labour
membership/card

The Labour Party 150 Walworth Road London SE17 1JT 071-701 1234

Some policies of the Labour Party

- State ownership of the public services such as gas, water, electricity, the post office, and the railways.
- A more equal distribution of wealth and income.
- Support for trade unions and workers' rights.
- Defence of the welfare state, including state education and the National Health Service.
- Support for the disadvantaged, such as the poor, the unemployed, women, and ethnic minorities.
- International nuclear and conventional disarmament.

The 'Centre' Parties

The 'centre' parties have policies which fall between those of Labour and the Conservatives. They generally share a belief in freedom of the individual, some state assistance to the poor, and some state ownership of the economy, but largely support private industry.

- The *Social Democratic Party* (SDP) was founded in 1981 by former members of the Labour Party who left because they thought its policies were too left-wing. It stood in elections in 1983 and 1987 in alliance with the Liberal Party (the SDP/Liberal Alliance), but it was dissolved in 1990 due to lack of support.
- The *Liberal Democrats* were founded in 1988 by a merger of the Liberal Party and people who left the SDP, and they are today the main 'third party' in British politics.
- The *Green Party* is a fairly new party, mainly campaigning around environmental issues, and drawing support from a wide range of people who are more concerned about this than any other political issue. There is also some evidence it attracts support from those who wish to register a 'protest vote' against the other parties.

The Conservative (Tory) Party

The Conservative Party is opposed to any form of state ownership of the economy. It gets the majority of its funds from big business, and draws much of its traditional support from the upper and middle classes and private business.

Some policies of the Conservative Party

- Private ownership of the economy, opposition to nationalization (state ownership), and putting already nationalized industries back into private ownership. Between 1979 and 1990, British Gas, British Steel, British Airways, British Telecom, and the water and electricity industries were all sold off to private ownership.
- Free enterprise: limiting the interference of the state in the affairs of private business and the economy generally.
- Self-help, by making the individual rely less on support from the state.
- Cutting the burden of taxes on the better off.
- Law and order, through a strong police force.
- Limiting the power of trade unions.
- A strong defence policy, based on nuclear weapons.

Activity

1. In addition to the policies outlined above, try to find out what other policies the political parties have.
2. On the basis of the policies of the parties, why do you think many working-class people have traditionally voted Labour, while many middle-class people have voted Conservative?

Influencing Decision-making in a Democracy

There are a number of ways individuals can influence the decision-making process in a democracy. Joining a political party is an obvious way, which enables them to take part in formulating the policies of that party, which may eventually become government policy if the party wins a general election.

The existence of competing political parties, combined with free elections and freedom of speech, means that parties must represent a range of interests if they are to be elected or to stay in power: the need to attract voters means parties have to respond to the wishes of the electorate. Voting is the most obvious way ordinary people can influence political decisions.

A further method is by writing to their local MP or councillor to try to have their concerns taken up, or by writing to the press and using public opinion to pressurize elected politicians. However, individuals on their own have limited power, and the most effective way of influencing decision-making is to join together with others concerned about the same issue, by forming or joining a pressure group.

Pressure Groups

Pressure groups are organizations which try to put pressure on governments, councillors, and others with power to implement policies which they favour. Pressure groups, which are sometimes called interest groups, are important in a democracy as channels for the representation of interests and opinions which might otherwise be forgotten or ignored by those with power. They therefore help to keep political parties and governments in touch with public opinion.

Pressure groups and political parties

Pressure groups differ from political parties in three main ways:

- They do not try to take power themselves by having their members elected to Parliament and forming a government.
- They do not claim to represent the interests of everyone, but only the particular concerns of some sections of the population.
- They are generally concerned with only one issue or a group of related issues rather than the wide range of issues on which political parties have to form policies.

There are two main types of pressure group.

Protective or Defensive Groups

These are concerned with defending the shared interests of their membership. Examples of these groups include the AA (the Automobile Association), Help the Aged, the NSPCC, trade unions and professional associations, and employers' organizations like the CBI (the Confederation of British Industry).

Promotional Groups

These are concerned with promoting a particular cause rather than protecting the interests of a particular group. Examples include ASH (Action on Smoking and Health), the Child Poverty Action Group (concerned with raising welfare benefits), the Anti-Apartheid Movement, Greenpeace, CND, and animal rights groups like the Animal Liberation Front. Table 7.1 gives examples of some pressure groups in Britain and indicates what the aims of each group are.

Table 7.1 Examples of pressure groups in Britain

Organization	Aim
Protective or defensive groups:	
Automobile Association	To protect the interest of motorists
Age Concern	To campaign on matters of concern to the elderly and to promote dignity and quality of life for the retired.
Lord's Day Observance Society	To preserve Sunday as the Christian Sabbath
National Society for the Prevention of Cruelty to Children (NSPCC)	To protect children who are deprived, neglected or at risk of abuse
Confederation of British Industry (CBI)	To protect and promote the interests of British business and the private enterprise system
British Medical Association	To protect and promote the interests of doctors
Law Society	To protect and promote the interests of lawyers

Table 7.1 Examples of pressure groups in Britain

Organization	Aim
Trades Union Congress (TUC)	To protect and promote the interests of affiliated trade unions and the economic and social conditions and rights of workers
National Union of Teachers	To protect and promote the interest of teachers

Promotional groups:

Action on Smoking and Health (ASH)	To promote opposition to tobacco smoking
Child Poverty Action Group	To promote action for the relief of poverty among children and families with children and to campaign for higher welfare benefits
Electoral Reform Society	To secure the use of the single transferrable voting system in all elections and to establish proportional representation
Anti-Apartheid Movement	To isolate and eliminate the apartheid regime in South Africa
Greenpeace	To protect the environment and the ecological balance of the earth
Shelter	To provide assistance to the homeless and promote changes in housing policy to eliminate homelessness and poor housing
Campaign for Nuclear Disarmament (CND)	To eliminate nuclear weapons
Campaign Against Pornography	To build a mass campaign against pornography and the violence against women it produces

Methods Used by Pressure Groups

There is a range of methods used by pressure groups to influence public opinion, political parties and governments.

- Contributions to the funds of political parties; for example, trade union support to the Labour Party or contributions to the Conservative Party by industry. The large contribution of the big brewers to Conservative Party funds encouraged the Conservative government in 1989 to abandon proposals aimed at eliminating the monopoly of the large breweries on pubs. This is a clear example of a powerful pressure group in action.
- Lobbying MPs and government ministers. This means going to the entrance hall or lobby of the House of Commons or local MPs' 'surgeries' to put the group's case.
- Sponsorship of MPs: paying their election and other expenses in exchange for their support in the House of Commons. Trade unions and the Police Federation both do this.
- Advertising in the mass media.
- Leafleting.
- Organizing petitions or opinion polls to show how much support they have.
- Holding public meetings.
- Letter-writing campaigns to the newspapers, local councillors, and MPs.
- Demonstrations.
- Organizing mass campaigns, such as CND's campaigns against nuclear weapons, or the campaign against the poll tax in 1989–91, which helped to bring about the abolition of this massively unpopular tax.
- Civil disobedience – breaking the law to bring attention to their cause. This kind of tactic is used by the Animal Liberation Front when it breaks into laboratories and releases animals used for experiments in scientific research.
- Strikes, to bring economic pressure on the government to change its policies.
- The provision of expertise. Pressure groups often have specialized knowledge gathered through research which they can lay at the disposal of the government, giving them a direct influence on government policy. For example, the Child Poverty Action Group, Shelter, and the CBI are all providers of expert knowledge to governments.

Activity

Imagine *either* that the council is planning to close a local school *or* that there are plans to open a dump for nuclear waste in your area. Plan out how you might organize a campaign to keep the school open or to stop the nuclear waste dump being opened. Think carefully of how you might get people together and all the activities you might engage in to influence those with power. What obstacles, including money, might you find in carrying out a successful campaign?

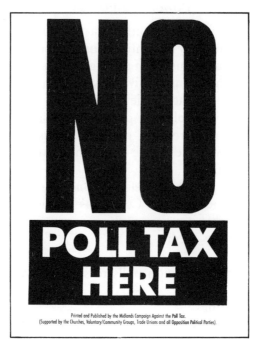

Pressure groups in action: a 1990 poster for display, by the Midlands Campaign Against the Poll Tax

Pressure groups in action: a 1991 demonstration against the poll tax

Source: Denis Thorpe, *The Guardian*.

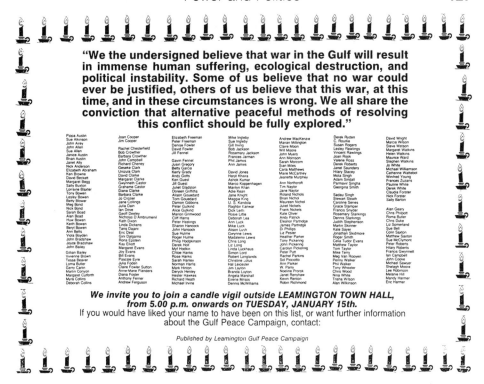

"We the undersigned believe that war in the Gulf will result in immense human suffering, ecological destruction, and political instability. Some of us believe that no war could ever be justified, others of us believe that this war, at this time, and in these circumstances is wrong. We all share the conviction that alternative peaceful methods of resolving this conflict should be fully explored."

We invite you to join a candle vigil outside LEAMINGTON TOWN HALL, from 5.00 p.m. onwards on TUESDAY, JANUARY 15th.
If you would have liked your name to have been on this list, or want further information about the Gulf Peace Campaign, contact:

Published by Leamington Gulf Peace Campaign

Pressure groups in action: a 1991 newspaper advertisement against the Gulf War

Source: Leamington Spa Courier.

Are All Pressure Groups Equally Effective?

Pressure groups are important in a democracy as a means of representing a wide range of interests and influencing those with power. However, there are a number of criticisms of pressure groups and their effectiveness in influencing power-holders.

- Not all interests are represented through pressure groups. Not all groups in the population are equally capable of forming pressure groups. Disadvantaged groups like the poor, the unemployed, ethnic minorities, the handicapped, the mentally ill, and the old often lack the resources or education to make their voices heard. Substantial wealth and education mean some groups can run more effective campaigns to make their demands heard, such as employers' organizations like the CBI.
- Not everyone has the same chance of meeting top decision-makers. Getting to see decision-makers is far easier if you are from the same social

class background. 'Friends in high places' and the 'old boys' network', which is considered in the discussion of public schools in chapter 12, mean that the interests of the upper and middle classes are generally more effectively represented than those of the working class.

- Some groups holding key positions in the economy are able to bring pressure to bear on the government through strike action. For example, railway or power workers can cause widespread disruption by strike action, and so are more likely to get action on their grievances than, say, old age pensioners or students. *strategic position*

These factors are of some concern in a democracy, as not all pressure groups have the same amount of influence. Some interests get represented more effectively than others and some interests may not be represented at all.

Influences on Voting Behaviour

Research suggests that the decision on which political party people vote for is influenced by a range of factors.

The Family

As in other areas of life, the family plays an important role in political socialization or the formation of an individual's political beliefs. Many people tend to share the general political beliefs and attitudes of their parents, and continue to support the political party their parents did.

Geographical Area

Voting patterns seem to be associated with the geographical area in which people live. Those in the north of England, Scotland, Wales, and inner-city areas are more likely to support the Labour Party. Those in the southern parts of England and rural areas are more likely to support the Conservative Party. This could be because of social class differences between these areas, with higher numbers of traditional working-class people, more unemployment, and social deprivation in areas supporting Labour.

Ethnic Origin

The ethnic group to which people belong appears to have an influence on their voting habits (see chapter 15 on ethnic groups). As table 7.2 shows, black and Asian people have traditionally been more inclined to support the Labour Party than other parties. This is because Labour has sympathetic policies on immigration and race relations, and is more concerned with reducing the racial discrimination, social deprivation, and unemployment which ethnic minorities are more likely to encounter.

Activity

Table 7.2 The voting intentions of ethnic minorities in Britain, 1983–7

Party	Asians (%)		Afro-Caribbeans(%)	
	1983	1987	1983	1987
Conservatives	9	23	7	6
Labour	81	67	88	86
Lib./SDP	10	10	5	7

Source: Adapted from *The Guardian*, 19th June 1987.

Study table 7.2 and answer the following questions:

1. In which ethnic group and in which year did 88 per cent of people intend to vote Labour?
2. By how much did Asian support for the Conservatives increase between 1983 and 1987?
3. Which ethnic group showed the greatest support for the Labour Party in both 1983 and 1987?
4. For which party did Asian support show no change between 1983 and 1987?
5. Draw a pie chart to show the voting intentions of Asians and Afro-Caribbeans in 1987.

Religion

Religion is not a particularly important influence on voting in most of the United Kingdom, although members of the Church of England are more likely to support the Conservative Party. However, in Northern Ireland voting coincides almost exactly with the divisions between Protestants and Catholics, with Protestants supporting parties which support Union with Britain, and Catholics supporting parties sympathetic to a United Ireland.

Party Images

image of the leader

Most people have general impressions or images of what the political parties stand for, rather than real knowledge of their policies. Evidence suggests the way most people vote is influenced by this 'party image', rather than by knowledge of what the actual policies of the political parties are. For example, working-class people might vote Labour because it presents a more 'caring' image, supporting the Health Service and workers' rights, and appears more sympathetic to the needs of the poor and disadvantaged than the 'uncaring' Conservatives who seem to support business and law and order.

This is perhaps why political parties, during election campaigns, often concentrate more in their advertising and television broadcasts on presenting particular images or impressions of parties and party leaders (such as 'caring', 'efficient', and 'friendly') rather than on explaining what their actual policies are.

The Mass Media

The mass media are major agencies of socialization, and have important influences on people's general beliefs and opinions. Chapter 8 shows how many of the mass media tend to present a very conservative view of society – generally supporting the 'Establishment' and the way things are currently organized in society. This may help to establish a long-term climate of opinion which benefits the Conservative Party at the expense of Labour and other parties. As table 7.3 shows for the 1987 general election, nearly all the major national daily newspapers support the Conservative Party, with the exception of the Labour-supporting *Daily Mirror* and *The Guardian*. This illustrates in a very clear way the conservative bias which tends to mark many of the mass media, and would appear to justify complaints that the

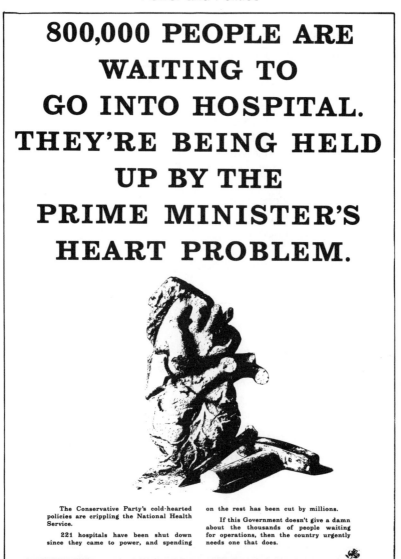

800,000 PEOPLE ARE WAITING TO GO INTO HOSPITAL. THEY'RE BEING HELD UP BY THE PRIME MINISTER'S HEART PROBLEM.

The Conservative Party's cold-hearted policies are crippling the National Health Service.

221 hospitals have been shut down since they came to power, and spending on the rest has been cut by millions.

If this Government doesn't give a damn about the thousands of people waiting for operations, then the country urgently needs one that does.

THE COUNTRY'S CRYING OUT FOR LABOUR.

Party images in the 1987 general election: a Labour Party poster

mass media represent mainly the interests of the privileged upper- and upper-middle class, at the expense of working-class and minority-group interests.

Because newspapers tend to put forward a particular political opinion, many people see them as unreliable sources of evidence, and turn to the television instead. There is not much evidence to suggest that party political broadcasts on television have much influence in changing people's voting habits, except in cases when people find it difficult to make up their minds which way to vote. '**Floating voters**' are those with no fixed political

Table 7.3 Political parties supported by national daily newspapers in the 1987 General Election[a]

Newspaper	Party support	Circulation (1986)	% of market
Sun	Conservatives	4 151 478	28.1
Daily Mail	Conservatives	1 790 228	12.1
Daily Express	Conservatives	1 806 247	12.2
Daily Star	Conservatives	1 347 759	9.1
Daily Telegraph	Conservatives	1 131 004	7.7
The Times	Conservatives	488 681	3.3
Financial Times	Conservatives	258 312	1.7
Daily Mirror	Labour	3 260 516	22.1
The Guardian	Labour	527 194	3.6
Today	Alliance	N/A[b]	N/A
The Independent	No party support	N/A	N/A
Total		14 761 419	100.0

[a]The party support of each newspaper is derived from its voting recommendation for the 1987 general election.
[b]N/A means figures were not available at the time.

Source: Adapted from Stephen Wagg, 'Mass communications: the debate about ownership and control', *Social Studies Review,* vol. 2, no. 4 (March 1987) and John Beynon, 'General election 1987', *Social Studies Review*, vol. 3, no. 2 (November 1987).

opinions and who therefore regularly switch votes between parties from one election to the next. It is these voters who are most likely to be influenced by the media, and it is at these floating voters that many TV party election broadcasts are aimed.

The mass media and voting: key findings

- Where people already have established political views, the mass media are more likely to reinforce those views than to change them.
- People tend to be selective in their choice of programmes and newspapers, and they only see and hear what they want to. They will either choose those that present information which confirms their existing opinions and avoid those that conflict with them, or reject those aspects which do not conform with their existing ideas. For example, there are committed Labour voters and *Sun* readers who ridicule Conservative election broadcasts and ignore the Tory politics of the *Sun*.

- While the media are unlikely to change people's voting behaviour in the short term (such as in the run-up to a general election), they might be effective in changing attitudes over a longer period of time. For example, they might gradually change people's perception of a particular party or political leader.
- The mass media are most likely to be influential on issues and parties which are new to people and about which people have little knowledge or experience.
- Floating voters are those most likely to be influenced by the media, particularly by party political broadcasts on television.
- Most of the media support the Conservative Party, and this can create a long-term climate of opinion where more people are favourable to the Conservatives.

Britain's Tory press
All these newspapers supported the Conservatives in the 1987 general election. Their combined circulation accounted for 74.2 per cent of all national daily newspapers sold in Britain

Social Class

Social class has traditionally been the single most important factor influencing the way people vote, though in the 1970s and 1980s this has been of declining importance. In Britain, the Labour Party has been seen as the party with policies representing the interests of the working class, and traditionally most working-class people have voted Labour. In contrast, the Conservatives have been associated with the interests of the middle and upper classes.

However, if all working-class people did vote Labour, there could never be a Conservative government, because the working class makes up the majority of the electorate. In fact, traditionally about one-third of manual workers have voted Conservative, and about one-fifth of the middle class have voted Labour. In the 1979, 1983, and 1987 general elections, even more manual workers voted Conservative. Working-class people who vote Conservative, and middle-class Labour voters, are known as **deviant voters**, because they seem to be voting against the party representing the interests of their class. Why do they do this?

Working-class Conservative voters

Deference voters
Working-class deference voters are those who see members of the upper and middle class as superior in 'breeding', coming from 'better families' who make better 'natural leaders' than those from their own class. The Conservative Party contains these sort of people, and therefore it is supported. Such voters tend to be older, be female, and have lower incomes. They are found in manual occupations where individuals are isolated from other workers, work close to their bosses, and 'know their place'. Such groups might include farmworkers and domestic servants.

Pragmatic voters
Pragmatic voters are those working-class people who have an instrumental attitude to voting, and will support whichever party offers them the greatest personal gain, such as more money, lower mortgage rates, and a higher standard of living. They are therefore motivated by pragmatic or practical reasons. Such voters will support the Conservative Party only so long as they feel it has more practical benefits to offer them than other parties.

This pragmatic, instrumental attitude means such voters have no particular party loyalty. They are more volatile, which means they are more likely to switch votes if another party offers them better personal benefits. Such workers tend to be those found in the 'new' working class, which was discussed in chapter 3.

In the 1970s and 1980s, the numbers of the traditional working class which provided the secure base of Labour support declined, and the new, 'pragmatic', instrumental working class expanded to become the largest section of the working class. This has meant that while the bulk of support for the Labour Party still comes from the working class, fewer working-class people are supporting Labour. In 1987 only 42 per cent of manual workers voted Labour, and as table 7.4 shows, only 50 per cent of semi-skilled and unskilled manual workers voted for the Labour Party.

Activity

Table 7.4 How the social classes voted for the three main parties, 1979–87

	1979			1983			1987		
Class	Con. (%)	Lab. (%)	Lib./SDP (%)	Con. (%)	Lab. (%)	Lib./SDP (%)	Con. (%)	Lab. (%)	Lib./SDP (%)
I and II	67	18	15	62	12	27	59	14	27
III n-manual	58	21	20	55	21	24	52	22	26
III manual	45	45	10	39	35	27	43	34	24
IV and V	32	55	14	29	44	27	31	50	19

Source: Adapted from Ivor Crewe 'Why Mrs Thatcher was returned with a landslide', *Social Studies Review*, vol. 3, no. 1, September 1987.

Study table 7.4 and answer the following questions:

1. Which social classes were least likely to support the Labour Party in 1979, 1983, and 1987?
2. Which classes in the table make up the working class?
3. In which social class did support for Labour decline the most between 1979 and 1987?
4. Which party increased its support in all social classes between 1979 and 1983?
5. The table shows that working-class support for Labour declined between 1979 and 1987. Which party gained most from this? Give evidence from the table to back up your answer.

No longer can the Labour Party automatically rely on support from the majority of the working class, because most of them are now part of the volatile and pragmatic 'new' working class. Throughout the 1980s, the Conservatives proved more successful in persuading this expanding group that they had more benefits to offer than the Labour Party, and the new working class provided much of the working-class support for the Conservative Party in the 1979, 1983, and 1987 general elections.

The new 'pragmatism' among working-class voters suggests that perhaps social class is becoming of less importance in affecting the way people vote than it has traditionally been, particularly where the Labour Party is concerned.

Middle-class Labour voters

About one-fifth of the middle class have traditionally voted Labour against what would appear to be their middle-class interests. These voters are most likely to be found in three main occupational groups:

- Those in the 'caring' welfare professions, like teachers and social workers. These people tend to vote Labour because their daily work brings them into contact with the disadvantaged and their problems, and they feel the Labour Party is more likely to tackle such issues. A Labour Party membership survey in 1990 found that school teachers were the single largest occupational group of Labour Party members (*Labour Party News*, no. 21 (Sept./Oct. 1990)).
- Those who have experienced upward social mobility from working-class backgrounds may vote Labour out of a sense of loyalty to their working-class origins.
- Routine clerical workers who are facing proletarianization may support Labour because they see their living and working conditions getting worse, and their social status declining.

Volatility and dealignment

The pattern of voting in Britain since the 1970s suggests two major related changes have occurred:

- The electorate has become more volatile – voters are more willing to change the party they vote for if another party offers them better personal benefits. People are voting more on the basis of a party's

policies and how well they perform, or might perform, in government. Voters have less loyalty to any one party, and the support of voters swings to and fro between different political parties.
- There is no longer a clear alignment (a matching up) of particular social classes with one of the two main parties – in particular, the working class is no longer clearly aligned with the Labour Party, but neither is the the middle class with the Conservatives. Most voters no longer show loyalty to a party according to their social class – dealignment (a mismatch) between class and voting has occurred.

Activity

1. If there were a general election tomorrow, which political party would you vote for? Give reasons for your answer, explaining carefully what influenced you in making your decision.
2. Figure 7.2 summarizes the key influences that sociologists have identified on voting behaviour. In the light of the exercise above, how far do you think the findings of sociologists confirm or deny your view? Which influences do you think are the most important?

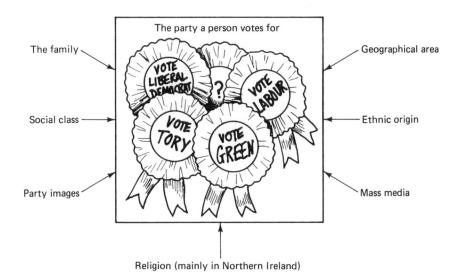

Figure 7.2 Factors influencing the way people vote

Why do People Abstain in Elections?

About 25 per cent of the electorate in general elections, and as many as 60 per cent or more in local elections, abstain – they fail to vote. Disadvantaged groups, such as the least educated and the poor, and younger people and old people are the most likely groups to abstain from voting. In marginal seats, where the difference between the votes of the parties is very small – sometimes as little as one or two votes – abstention can actually swing the election result.

Aside from factors such as apathy, forgetfulness, bad weather, being away on holiday, or being kept in by illness, people may make a positive decision to abstain for several reasons. In safe seats, where there has traditionally been a large majority for one party, voters may not feel it is worth voting since the outcome of the election is so predictable. It may be there is no candidate standing from the party people would normally vote for, or they may not support or understand the policies of any of the different parties. Some voters might think elections are a waste of time, since the policies of all the parties are too similar and 'elections don't change anything anyway'. In such circumstances they may not bother to vote at all.

Opinion Polls and Elections

Opinion polls are social surveys which try to find out people's attitudes on many issues, and they are widely used to discover how people intend to vote in elections. They most commonly involve face-to-face interviews in the street, but telephone polls are becoming more popular in Britain.

The results of opinion polls provide the basis for reports about the 'state of the parties' which are regularly published in the newspapers. In election periods, polls are conducted daily. For example, during the four weeks of the 1987 general election campaign, 54 opinion polls were carried out.

Why Opinion Polls are Sometimes Inaccurate

Opinion polls use sophisticated sampling techniques to obtain representative samples of the voting population. Often they can predict the outcome of elections very accurately from asking no more than about two thousand people. This is because the group they have questioned are a good representative cross-section of the entire population in terms of factors such as age, sex, social class, and geographical spread around the country. However, sometimes the opinion polls fail to predict accurately the results of elections. The reasons for this are quite varied, and many possible explanations are discussed in the final chapter of this book on the general problems of sampling and survey methods. Some possible problems of opinion polls are outlined below.

- They may not contain a representative sample of voters, which may lead to inaccurate results.
- Interviewer bias may mean people give inaccurate answers.
- The format and wording of questions may affect the results of the poll. For example, respondents prefer to agree rather than disagree with statements which are put to them.
- People may change their minds during the course of the election campaign, after the poll was conducted, when they have heard more arguments and have had more time to make up their minds. Because of this, opinion polls are likely to become more accurate the closer they are to the day of the election.
- Some of those interviewed may decide not to vote when it comes to the actual election, and this will distort the opinion poll's predictions.
- Opinion polls might themselves change the way people decide to vote and therefore the results of the election.

How Opinion Polls Might Influence the Results of Elections

There is some evidence that opinion polls might not simply reflect voters' opinions, but actually help to form and change them, and therefore affect the eventual election results. For example, if the polls predict a large win for one party, its supporters may not bother to vote, thinking that it is a safe seat and the result a foregone conclusion. This could possibly result in that party actually losing the election if too many of its supporters did this. In the 1970 general election campaign, for example, four out of five polls predicted that Labour would win by a small majority. In fact, the Conservatives won with a majority of 30 parliamentary seats. The Labour Party thought that its lead in the opinion polls might have made the party workers and supporters assume they would win the election regardless of how they conducted their campaign. It was thought this complacency, created by the opinion polls, may have cost Labour the election.

If the polls predict that a certain party is going to win by a large margin, then supporters of another party which has no chance of winning might decide to vote for a third party in the hope of defeating the predicted winning party. This is known as *tactical voting*. An example might be committed Labour voters in a safe Tory seat, where Labour stands no chance of winning. If the opinion polls show that a Liberal Democrat is in second place, then Labour voters may decide to vote for the Liberal Democrat in the hope of defeating the Tory.

A final influence of opinion polls might be the *bandwagon effect*, where, if the polls show one party to be in the lead, people may want to jump on the bandwagon and be on the side of what they think will be the winning party.

Because opinion polls can affect the results of elections, some people have actually suggested that they are banned immediately before elections, as happens in France, Germany, and Spain.

Is Britain a Democracy?

Earlier in this chapter you may have discussed whether Britain is a democracy or not. Much of this chapter has emphasized the democratic features of modern Britain, and if you look back to figure 7.1, then you may agree that many of the features listed there are indeed to be found in modern Britain. However, there are a number of weaknesses in British democracy.

Non-elected Rulers

Democracy is meant to involve governments reflecting the interests of the people through elected representatives. However, the House of Lords and the monarchy are not elected, but both have considerable power in controlling which laws are passed.

The Voting System

Voting in the UK is by the first-past-the-post system, under which the party that gets most votes in any constituency (voting area) wins that constituency. In general elections, the representative of the winning party becomes the constituency's MP, and the party getting the most MPs forms the government. This means governments are often elected which represent only a minority of voters in the country as a whole. In fact, every government in Britain since 1945 has been elected with the support of less than half of the voting population. Figure 7.3 shows that in the 1987 general election, the number of MPs elected for each party in no way represented their share of

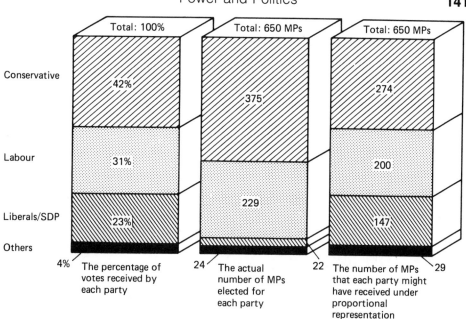

Figure 7.3 General election results, United Kingdom, 1987

the votes in the country as a whole. Such circumstances mean that, while minority parties might collect a lot of votes in the country as a whole, they get few MPs, or none at all, in Parliament and therefore no representation. **Proportional representation** – which means the number of MPs elected for each party reflects the share of the vote received – would ensure that minority parties and interests were more adequately represented. Figure 7.3 shows the number of MPs that might have been elected for each party in 1987 if proportional representation had been adopted.

Elite Rule

As seen in chapter 4, wealth remains highly concentrated in the hands of a small upper class, which gives it major influence in economic decision-making. For example, this class can decide where factories should be located and whether they should be opened or closed down, and it can control the workforce through hiring and firing. Democratically-elected governments cannot afford to ignore this power, otherwise they might face rising unemployment and other social problems if this class decided not to invest its money.

Most of those in the top elite jobs which wield power and influence in this country come from public school and upper- and upper-middle-class backgrounds (see chapter 12 on this). Even among Labour MPs, only about 25 per cent come from working-class backgrounds. This raises questions about the extent to which working-class interests are adequately represented.

Unequal Pressure Groups

As seen earlier in this chapter, not all interests are represented through pressure groups, and some pressure groups have a lot more wealth and power than others. It is the voices of the disadvantaged and the poor which are least likely to be heard.

Deciding the Issues

The political parties – not the population as a whole – often decide what the important issues are and which ones they are going to fight elections around. The mass media are mainly privately owned and controlled by a rich and powerful minority and have a conservative bias. They have an important role in forming 'public opinion' and, like political leaders, can decide the issues around which elections are fought.

The points raised above suggest that perhaps Britain is not quite as democratic as many people might believe, and that not everyone gets an equal chance to express their opinions and influence decision-making. This is likely to be true particularly of those holding radical opinions who want to change the way society is presently organized. While democracy in Britain has many strengths and freedoms which must be defended, it also has its limitations. The interests of democracy are perhaps best served by removing the limitations and reinforcing the strengths.

Chapter Summary

After studying this chapter, you should be able to:

- Explain briefly what is meant by the terms 'power', 'authority', 'coercion', and 'politics'.

- Describe and explain the main features of a democracy, and how democracy differs from totalitarianism and dictatorship.
- Identify the main political parties in Britain which put up candidates in elections, and briefly describe some of their main policies.
- Explain what pressure groups are and how they differ from political parties.
- Describe, with examples, two types of pressure group.
- Describe the methods pressure groups use to influence those with power.
- Explain why some interests are better represented by pressure groups than others.
- Discuss the range of factors influencing voting behaviour.
- Discuss how the mass media might influence political attitudes.
- Explain what is meant by 'deviant voting' and explain both working-class and middle-class deviant voting.
- Suggest reasons why people abstain in elections.
- Explain why opinion polls might sometimes fail to predict accurately the outcome of elections.
- Explain how opinion polls might themselves affect election results.
- Discuss the extent to which Britain might be regarded as a democracy.

Project Suggestions

1. Study the aims and activities of a local or national pressure group, interviewing members of the group and studying its literature and reports in newspapers. What methods does the group use to influence public opinion and how effective/successful is the group?
2. Carry out an opinion poll on the attitudes of students, workmates, or members of the public to the different political parties, their policies, and their leaders.
3. Carry out a survey among a sample of people of different ages and/or sexes and/or social classes asking about their attitudes to some current political issue of major importance. Are there any differences between different groups?
4. Ask a sample of people what factors they think have the most influence on the way they vote, or the way they would vote if they are under voting age.
5. Carry out an opinion poll in your school, college or workplace, including the question, 'If there were a general election tomorrow, for which party would you vote?' Compare your findings with those of a current national opinion poll.

Key Terms

authority
coercion
democracy
deviant voter
dictatorship
floating voter
political party
politics
power
proportional representation
totalitarianism

8 The Mass Media

The Power of the Media: Key Questions

The term 'mass media' refers to forms of communication which are directed at large mass audiences without any personal contact. The main media of mass communication include television, radio, newspapers and magazines, books, cinema, advertising, and records.

In Britain, 97 per cent of the population watch television, and fifteen million newspapers are sold every day. The media have become important

---

Activity

1. Work out approximately how many hours in a typical week you spend watching television or videos, listening to the radio or music, reading newspapers and magazines, or at the cinema.
2. Work out approximately how many hours a week you spend sleeping.
3. There are 168 hours in a week. Take away the number of hours you spend sleeping from this total. Now work out what percentage of your waking life you spend under the direct influence of the mass media (you can do this by dividing the number of hours spent watching TV etc. by the number of waking hours and multiplying by 100).
4. List all the ways you think the mass media influences you in your life, such as your knowledge about current affairs, opinions, tastes in music and fashion, roles of men and women, etc.

sources of information, entertainment, and leisure activity for large numbers of people, and they have become key agencies of secondary socialization and informal education. Most people will base their opinions and attitudes, not on personal experience, but on evidence and knowledge provided by newspapers and television.

You may have found from the previous activity that you spend a great deal of time under the direct influence of the mass media. You may also have found that the mass media provide the source of many of your ideas and opinions about the world.

If most of our opinions are based on knowledge obtained 'second hand' through the mass media, then this raises the important issue of the power of the mass media to influence our lives. Most people think and act in particular ways because of the opinions they hold and the knowledge they have, and many would agree that an 'informed' opinion – based on evidence – is the best opinion. However, do the mass media inform us about everything, and do they stress certain things in more favourable ways than others? Do they give false impressions of what is happening in society? The main mass media are privately owned and controlled, and run to make a profit. What effects does this pattern of ownership and control have on the content of the media? Does it create bias in the media? What are the implications of this in a democracy? These are the sorts of question which have interested sociologists and which will be explored in this chapter.

Formal Controls on the Media

Although the mass media in Britain are formally free to report whatever they like, and the government has no power in normal times to stop the spreading of any opinions through censorship, there are some formal limits to this freedom.

The Law

The law restricts the media's freedom to report anything they choose in any way they like. The principal legal limits to the media's freedom are shown in the next box below.

Legal limits to the media's freedom

- *The laws of libel* forbid the publication of an untrue statement about a person which might bring him or her into contempt, ridicule, dislike, or hostility in society.
- *The Official Secrets Acts* make it a criminal offence to report without authorization any official government activity which the government defines as an official secret. These are extremely wide-ranging Acts, which are meant to protect the 'public interest'. However, many people argue they are often used to protect the political interests of governments.
- *Defence or 'D' Notices* are issued by the government as requests to journalists not to report certain news items which the government believes to be 'against the national interest'. These usually concern military secrets and other information which might be useful to an 'enemy'.
- *The Race Relations Act* forbids the expression of opinions which will encourage hatred or discrimination against people because of their race.
- *The Obscene Publications Act* forbids the printing of anything that the high court considers to be obscene and indecent, and likely to 'deprave and corrupt' the public.
- *The Prevention Of Terrorism Act* makes it illegal to broadcast interviews with members of the IRA, Sinn Fein, and some other organizations in Northern Ireland.
- *Contempt of Court* provision forbids the reporting and expression of opinions about cases which are in the process of being dealt with in a court of law. This is to prevent the jury forming opinions about a case from what they see or hear in the mass media, before they have heard the evidence for themselves.

The Government and the State

The government and the state have a number of direct and indirect controls over the mass media, particularly television and radio.

The BBC

The BBC is a state-owned body, which is controlled by a board of governors whose members are appointed by the Home Secretary. The BBC is financed by the state through the television licence fee, topped up by government subsidies raised from taxation. The state can therefore have some control over the BBC by refusing to raise the licence fee or increase subsidies. Although the BBC is not a private business run solely to make a profit like the independent commercial broadcasting services (independent TV and radio), and is not dependent on advertising for its income, it still has to compete with commercial broadcasting by attracting audiences large enough to justify the licence fee and government subsidies.

Independent broadcasting

Independent broadcasting includes all the non-BBC television and radio stations. These are controlled by a series of regulatory bodies whose members are appointed by the Home Secretary. These bodies include the Independent Television Commission, the Radio Authority, the Broadcasting Standards Council, and the Broadcasting Complaints Commission. These organizations are concerned with licensing the companies which can operate in the private sector, and between them they are responsible for the amount, quality, and standard of advertising and programmes on independent television and radio, and deal with any complaints.

The Press Complaints Commission

The Press Complaints Commission is a voluntary body appointed by the newspaper industry itself to maintain certain standards of newspaper journalism. It will deal with public complaints against newspapers, but it has no real power to enforce effective sanctions as a result of these complaints.

Ownership of the Mass Media

The mass media are very big business. The ownership of the main mass media in modern Britain is concentrated in the hands of a few large companies, who are interested in making profits. This concentration of ownership is shown in figure 8.1. Of the total circulation of daily and

Figure 8.1 Who owns what: national newspaper group interests in publishing, television, and radio, 1991

Source: Adapted from *The Guardian*, 12 June 1989.

Sunday newspapers, 86 per cent is controlled by just four companies, and over 60 per cent by two companies (News International and the Maxwell Foundation). One individual, Rupert Murdoch of News International, owns the *Sun, Today* and *The Times*, newspapers which make up about 34 per cent of all national daily newspaper sales in Britain. Robert Maxwell, before his death in November 1991, and Rupert Murdoch between them accounted for about 56 per cent of the total daily newspaper sales in 1991. As figure 8.1 shows, this concentration extends also to TV, radio, and book and magazine publishing. The details of who owns what are continually changing, but in 1991 Rupert Murdoch, for example, also owned 50 per cent of British Sky Broadcasting and HarperCollins, the book publishers, and Maxwell had interests in Central and Border TV. The same few people therefore control a wide range of different media. This means that a large proportion of what we see and hear in the media is controlled by a few large companies.

Activity

Explain why the concentration of ownership of the mass media might be of some concern in a democracy (refer to the previous chapter if you're not really sure what a democracy is).

Newspaper readership and the social class

There are noticeable social-class differences in newspaper readership, as shown in table 8.1.

Newspapers can be separated into three main groups: the 'quality' newspapers, the 'middle-brow' newspapers, and the mass-circulation 'popular' newspapers, also called the tabloid press. The middle class are far more likely to read the 'quality' newspapers and the manual working class make up the main readership of the 'popular' newspapers, particularly the *Sun, Daily Mirror*, and *Daily Star*. The *Daily Express* and *Daily Mail*, and increasingly *Today*, are aimed primarily at the 'middle-brow' lower middle class, but have readers drawn from the whole social spectrum.

'Quality' newspapers
The 'quality' newspapers are large in size and serious in tone and content. They are concerned with news and features about politics, economic and financial problems, sport, literature and the arts, and give

The **Guardian**

THE INDEPENDENT

FINANCIAL TIMES

The Daily Telegraph

THE TIMES

in-depth, analytical coverage in longer articles and news stories. The main 'quality' national daily newspapers in Britain are *The Times*, *The Guardian*, the *Daily Telegraph*, *The Independent* and the *Financial Times*.

'Middle-brow' newspapers

These fall between the 'quality' and the 'popular' newspapers, and include features of each. While they tend to have a more serious tone

Daily Express

Daily Mail

and content than the 'popular' press, they also cover a range of the more colourful issues found in the 'popular' papers and are also of the tabloid type (small in page size). The *Daily Mail* and the *Daily Express* are the main 'middle-brow' papers, but *Today* seems to be moving into this market.

'Popular' newspapers

In contrast to the 'quality' newspapers, 'popular' newspapers are of the tabloid type, and are generally referred to as the tabloid press. Although they carry 'news', they are much more likely to concentrate on the sensational aspects of the news, 'human interest' stories, such as scandals and celebrities, entertainment, sport, and other 'light' topics, written in very simple language combined with large headlines and many colour photographs. The 'popular' national daily newspapers in Britain are the *Daily Mirror*, the *Sun*, and the *Daily Star*.

Activity

Study table 8.1 and answer the following questions:

1. What percentage of social class IIIM read the 'Sun' in 1987?
2. Which newspaper was most widely read by those in class I?
3. Which two newspapers were most widely read by the working class?
4. What was the difference in the percentage of those in social class I who read 'The Guardian' compared to those in social class V?
5. Compare one 'quality' and one 'popular' newspaper for the same day. Study the kinds of stories, advertisements, photographs and cartoons, and the language they use. List all the differences between them. In the light of your findings, suggest explanations for the different social classes of their readerships.

Table 8.1 Reading of national daily newspapers by social class, 1987

Newspaper	Percentage of adults in each social class reading each paper in 1987					
	I	II	IIIN-m	IIIM	IV	V
Sun	5	10	20	32	37	27
Daily Mirror	4	8	16	27	29	19
Daily Mail	14	14	14	9	6	5
Daily Express	9	12	13	10	6	6
Daily Star	2	2	6	12	15	9
Daily Telegraph	28	16	8	3	1	2
The Guardian	9	10	4	1	1	1
The Times	16	8	3	1	1	1
Today	1	2	3	3	3	1
The Independent	6	6	3	1	1	0
Financial Times	8	5	2	1	0	0

Source: Adapted from Social Trends 19 (HMSO 1989).

The Mass Media, Public Opinion, and Social Control

The mass media play a key role in providing the ideas and images which people use to interpret and understand much of their everyday experience, and they actively shape people's ideas, attitudes, and actions. The mass media therefore have an important role in forming public opinion. The pressure of public opinion can be a significant source of social control, in so far as most people prefer to have their behaviour approved of by others rather than feeling isolated and condemned by them.

The survey results in table 8.2 (next page) show that most people do use and believe the mass media, particularly television, as their main source of news. However, their reliance on such sources may be misguided. This is because the mass media don't simply show 'the facts' on which people can then form opinions. They select facts and put an interpretation on them, frequently stressing the more conservative values of society. The mass media can then be said to act as an agency of social control. They carry this out in two main ways: agenda-setting and gate-keeping, and norm-setting.

Table 8.2 People's sources of news, and which source they see as the most believable

	All respondents (%)	No regular newspaper (%)	Regular readers of:			
			Any newspaper (%)	Daily Telegraph, The Guardian, The Times or Financial Times (%)	Daily Express or Daily Mail (%)	Daily Mirror, Sun or Daily Star (%)
Main source of news						
Television	61	76	59	32	62	65
Newspapers	20	3	30	57	28	24
Radio	15	23	15	25	14	14
Most believable source of news						
Television	–	–	57	30	59	66
Newspaper	–	–	15	35	13	11
Radio	–	–	15	20	16	13
Don't know/not answered	–	–	12	16	12	11

Source: Adapted from *British Social Attitudes: The 1985 Report* (Gower Publishing 1985).

Activity

Study table 8.2 and answer the following questions:

1. Which of the mass media did all respondents use as their main source of news?
2. What percentage of regular readers of any newspaper used newspapers as their main source of news?
3. What percentage of *Daily Mirror*, *Sun*, or *Daily Star* readers used newspapers as their main source of news?
4. What percentage of regular newspaper readers saw television as the most believable source of news?
5. What group of regular newspaper readers saw newspapers as a more believable source of news than television?
6. What percentage of regular readers of any newspaper saw newspapers as the most believable source of news?
7. Suggest reasons why most newspaper readers don't use newspapers as their main source of news and see them as less believable than television.

Agenda-setting and Gate-keeping

Agenda-setting is the idea that the media have an important influence over the issues that people think about because the agenda, or list of subjects, for public discussion is laid down by the mass media.

Obviously, people can only discuss and form opinions about things they have been informed about, and it is the mass media which provides this information in most cases. This gives those who own, control, and work in the mass media a great deal of power in society, for what they choose to include in or leave out of their newspapers and television programmes will influence the main topics of public discussion and public concern. This may mean that some subjects are never discussed by the public because they are not informed about them.

The media's refusal to cover some issues is called **gate-keeping**. Such issues are frequently those potentially most damaging to the values and interests of the upper class. For example, strikes are widely reported (nearly always unfavourably), while industrial injuries and diseases, which lead to a much greater loss of working hours (and life), hardly ever get reported. This means that there is more public concern with tightening up trade union laws to stop strikes than there is with improving health and safety laws. Similarly, black crime gets widely covered in the media, but little attention is paid to attacks on black people by white racists. This tends to reinforce people's racial prejudices. A final example is the way welfare benefit 'fiddles' are widely reported, but not tax evasion, with the result that there are calls for tightening up benefit claim procedures, rather than strengthening agencies concerned with chasing tax evaders.

Activity

1. Study the main newspaper headlines or major television or radio news stories for a week. Draw up a list of the key stories, perhaps under the headings of 'popular newspapers', 'quality newspapers', 'BBC TV news' 'ITN news', and 'radio news' (this is easiest to do if a group of people divide up the work).
2. Compare your lists, and see if there is any evidence of agreement on the 'agenda' of news items for that week. If there are differences between the lists (check particularly the newspapers), suggest explanations for them.

Norm-setting

Norm-setting means the mass media emphasize and reinforce conformity to social norms, and seek to isolate those who do not conform by making them the victims of unfavourable public opinion. This is achieved in two main ways.

- Encouraging conformist behaviour, such as not going on strike, obeying the law, being brave, helping people, and so on. Advertising, for example, reinforces the gender role stereotypes of men and women.

- Discouraging non-conformist behaviour. The mass media often give extensive and sensational treatment to stories about murder and other crimes of violence, riots, social security 'fiddles', football 'hooliganism', homosexuality, and so on. Such stories, by emphasizing the serious consequences which follow for those who break social norms, are giving 'lessons' in how people are expected *not* to behave. For example, the early treatment of AIDS in the mass media nearly always suggested it was a disease that only homosexuals could catch. This was presented as a

warning to those who strayed from the paths of monogamy and hetero-
sexuality – both core values of British society.

Stan Cohen illustrates this idea of norm-setting very well in the following
passage:

> A large amount of space in newspapers, magazines and television and a
> large amount of time in daily conversation are devoted to reporting and
> discussing behaviour which sociologists call deviant: behaviour which
> somehow departs from what a group expects to be done or what it
> considers the desirable way of doing things. We read of murders and
> drug-taking, vicars eloping with members of their congregation and film
> stars announcing the birth of their illegitimate children, football trains
> being wrecked and children being stolen from their prams, drunken
> drivers being breathalysed and accountants fiddling the books. Sometimes
> the stories are tragic and arouse anger, disgust or horror; sometimes they
> are merely absurd. Whatever the emotions, the stories are always to be
> found, and, indeed, so much space in the mass media is given to deviance
> that some sociologists have argued that this interest functions to reassure
> society that the boundary lines between conformist and deviant, good and
> bad, healthy and sick, are still valid ones. The value of the boundary line
> must continually be reasserted: we can only know what it is to be saintly
> by being told just what the shape of the devil is. The rogues, feckless fools
> and villains are presented to us as if they were playing parts in some
> gigantic morality play. (Source: Stanley Cohen, ed., *Images of Deviance*
> (Penguin 1982), introduction)

Activity

1. How is deviance defined in the passage above?
2. What does the passage suggest is one of the functions of the mass
   media's interest in deviance?
3. Give examples from the passage of:
   (a) Two types of deviant behaviour which are not regarded as
       criminal in modern Britain.
   (b) Two types of deviant behaviour which are regarded as criminal
       in modern Britain.
4. Think of one example of deviance which is currently receiving a lot
   of attention in the mass media and is of major public concern.
   Explain how this might be reasserting the 'boundary line' between
   conformist and deviant behaviour.

5. Look at a range of newspapers and try to find examples of norm-setting headlines and stories. Explain in each case what types of behaviour are being encouraged or discouraged.

What Affects the Content of the Media?

The mass media obviously cannot report all events and issues happening in the world. Of all the happenings that occur in the world every day, how is 'news' selected? Who decides which of these events is 'newsworthy'? The 'news', like any other product for sale, is a manufactured product. What factors affect the production and 'packaging' of this product? What decides the content of the mass media?

The Owners

Sometimes the private owners of the mass media will impose their own views on their editors. Two of the largest newspaper owners in Britain in 1991 – Robert Maxwell and Rupert Murdoch – have both been known to do this.

Even when the owners don't directly impose their own views, it is unlikely that those who work for them will produce stories which actively oppose their owners' prejudices and interests, if they want to keep their jobs! The political leanings of the owners and editors are overwhelmingly conservative.

When he bought the *Daily Mirror*, Robert Maxwell announced: 'I have invested £90 million. There can be only one boss, and that is me.'

Making a Profit

The mass media are predominantly run by large business corporations with the aim of making money, and the source of much of this profit is advertising, particularly in newspapers and commercial television. It is this dependence on advertising which explains why so much concern is expressed about 'ratings' for television programmes, the circulation figures of newspapers, and the social class of their readers. Advertisers will usually advertise only if they know that there is a large audience for their advertisements, or, if the audience is small, that it is very well off and likely to buy their products or services.

That newspapers are very concerned about selling advertising is shown by their commissioning of readership surveys, such as the one carried out among business readers of the 'quality' newspapers in 1990 which is summarized in figure 8.2. Such statistics are important to newspapers because they help them to sell highly profitable advertising aimed at business people.

Advertising and media content

The importance of advertising affects the content of the media in the following ways:

- Audiences or readers must be attracted. If they are not, then circulation figures or TV ratings will fall, advertisers will not advertise, and the particular channel or newspaper may go out of business. The *Sunday Correspondent*, *News on Sunday* and the *London Daily News* are all newspapers which have collapsed in recent years for this reason. This means that what becomes 'news' is partly a result of commercial pressures to attract audiences by selecting and presenting the more colourful, and 'interesting' events in society.

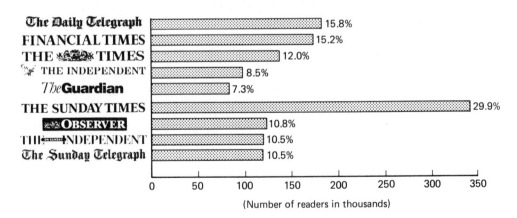

Figure 8.2 Quality newspapers read by business people. Numbers of readers are in thousands.
Figures at ends of bars are percentages of total market, estimated at 1 148 000.

Source: Adapted from *The Independent on Sunday*, 28 October 1990.

- In order to attract the widest possible audience or readership, it becomes important to appeal to everyone and offend no-one. This leads to a conservatism in the media, which tries to avoid too much criticism of the way society is organized in case it offends the readers or advertisers. This may mean that minority or unpopular points of view go unrepresented in the mass media.
- It may lead to a distortion of the 'news' by concentrating on sensational stories, conflict, gossip, and scandal which are more likely to attract a mass audience than more serious issues. Alternatively, for those media which aim at a 'select' readership from the upper- and upper-middle classes, it is important that the news stories chosen should generally be treated in a conservative way, so as not to offend an audience which has little to gain (and everything to lose!) by changes in the existing arrangements in society.

News Values and 'Newsworthiness'

Journalists obviously play an important role in deciding the content of the mass media, as it is journalists who basically select what 'the news' is and decide on its style of presentation. News doesn't just happen, but is made by journalists. Research has shown that journalists operate with values and assumptions about which events are 'newsworthy' – these assumptions are called **news values**. These guide journalists in deciding what to report and what to leave out, and how what they choose to report should be presented.

Issues or events that are newsworthy include:

- Issues that are easily understood.
- Events that occur quickly or unexpectedly, such as disasters.
- Events that involve drama, conflict, excitement, and action
- Events that are in some way out of the ordinary.
- Events that have some human drama or interest to them, such as the activities of famous personalities, scandal, or the release of hostages, like those freed in Beirut in 1991.
- Events that are considered important – events in Britain are generally considered more important than those happening in the rest of the world, and national events are generally considered more important than local ones.
- Stories which it is assumed will be of interest to the newspaper's readership or TV audience – giving the readers what they want! This is of great importance if the audience or readership is to continue to be attracted and viewing figures kept up or papers sold.

The idea of news values means that journalists tend to play up those elements of a story which make it more newsworthy, and the stories that are most likely to be reported are those which include many newsworthy aspects.

These features affecting the content of the media suggest that the mass media present, at best, only a partial view of the world.

Activity

1. Why do you think the story in the cartoon on the next page might be 'newsworthy'?
2. Take any current major news story which is receiving wide coverage in the mass media. List the features of this story which make it 'newsworthy'.
3. Study one 'quality' and one 'popular' newspaper of the same day and compare their coverage of this story. For example, do they sensationalize it and present new 'angles'? What evidence is there, if any, that the news values of the 'popular' press differ from those of the 'quality' press? Give examples to back up your answer.
4. Imagine you wanted to run a campaign to prevent a nuclear waste dump being built in your neighbourhood (or choose any issue that interests you). In the light of your expert knowledge about news values, suggest activities you might undertake to achieve media coverage of your campaign, and explain why they might be considered newsworthy.

Stereotyping, Scapegoating, and the Media

Stereotyping of different social groups is a common feature of media coverage of events. Chapter 5 on gender role socialization considered the way that gender stereotypes are formed and reinforced throughout the whole range of the mass media. Two other groups which are frequently victims of media stereotyping are young people and black people. These two groups are also frequently used as **scapegoats** for many of society's problems. Scapegoats are simply groups or individuals blamed for something which is not their fault.

News Values

Stereotyping and Scapegoating of the Young

The mass media often create a stereotype of all young people as trouble-makers, layabouts, and vandals, by exaggerating the occasional deviant behaviour of a few young people, such as 'lager louts', out of proportion to its real significance in society. The mass media provide for many people the only source of information about events, and therefore distort people's attitudes and give a misleading impression of young people as a whole. Old people, who tend to be more home-based, are particularly vulnerable to such stereotypes, as their impressions are formed very strongly by the media.

Folk devils and moral panics

In his book on the mods and rockers of the 1960s, *Folk Devils and Moral Panics*, Stan Cohen suggests that mass media stereotypes of young people, particularly where unusual or exceptional behaviour is involved, provide exciting stories and sensational headlines, and help to sell newspapers. He argues that young people have been used as a scapegoat to create a sense of unity in society, by uniting the public against a common 'enemy'. Young people are relatively powerless, and an easily identifiable group to blame for all of society's ills. Some young people who get involved in relatively trivial deviant or delinquent actions or groups, such as hooliganism, vandalism, 'lager louts', glue-sniffing, minor drug abuse, dressing as punks, the mods and rockers and hippies, are labelled in the media as **folk devils** or groups posing a threat to society. (**Labelling** is defining a person or group in a certain way – as a particular 'type' of person.) This causes a **moral panic** in society – an over-reaction suggesting that society itself is under threat. Editors, politicians, churchpeople, police, magistrates, and social workers then 'pull together' to overcome this imagined threat to society. The folk devils become visible reminders of what we should not be. In this view, young people play much the same role as witches in the past – an easy scapegoat to blame for all of society's problems. As a result of these moral panics, all young people may then get labelled and stereotyped as potentially troublesome or as a 'problem group'.

Stereotyping and Scapegoating of Black People

Black people are another social group which the mass media tends both to stereotype and to use as scapegoats. Black and Asian people make up less than 5 per cent of the population of Britain, yet frequently this small minority are presented in quite negative ways in the media, as if they were major causes of conflict and 'social problems' that otherwise wouldn't exist. These ethnic minorities often only appear in the media in the context of crime, drugs, and inner-city riots, as scapegoats on which to blame these problems. This creates, confirms, and reinforces public prejudices about black people among whites.

Degrading stereotypes of black people are still frequently found in books, films, and comics. Little is heard about their successes and achievements, their history and culture, or about the discrimination and deprivation they often face in housing, employment, and education. Attacks on black people by white racists rarely receive media coverage. Although these things are beginning to change, with more positive media coverage and television programmes aimed at black people, the media can still be said to produce negative stereotypes of black people and thereby reinforce the racism which is deeply entrenched in British society.

Discussion

Do you agree that the media stereotype the activities of black people and young people? What evidence, if any, can you point to that this happens?

Crime and the Media

The mass media provide knowledge about crime and deviance for most people in society, including politicians, the police, social workers, and the public at large. The mass media tend to be very selective in their coverage of crime, exploiting the possibilities for a 'good story' by dramatizing, exaggerating, and sensationalizing some crimes out of all proportion to their actual extent in society. For example, attacks on old people and other crimes of violence – which are quite rare – are massively over-reported, giving a false and misleading impression of the real pattern and extent of such crimes. This process can create many unnecessary fears among people by suggesting that violence is a normal and common feature of everyday life. This is particularly likely in the case of the housebound elderly. A Home Office report in 1989 confirmed this view, arguing that TV programmes which stage reconstructions of unsolved crimes, such as the BBC's *Crimewatch UK* and the *Crimestoppers* campaign, exaggerate the level of dangerous crime and unnecessarily frighten viewers.

The Media, Labelling, and Deviancy Amplification

As seen earlier in this chapter, the media's pursuit of 'good stories' means they often distort, exaggerate, and sensationalize the activities of some groups. The media have the power to label and stereotype certain groups and activities as deviant, and present them as folk devils causing some imagined threat to society. Even if much of what is reported is untrue, this may be enough to whip up a moral panic – growing public anxiety and concern about the alleged deviance.

This can raise demands for action by the agencies of social control to stop it. Often these agencies, such as schools, social services, the police, and

'A pit bull terrier? No, they've cornered a social worker!'

Folk devils of 1991
Reproduced by permission of *Punch*.

magistrates, will respond to the exaggerated threat presented in the media by taking harsher measures against the apparent 'troublemakers'. Such action, particularly by the police, can often make what was a minor issue much worse, for example by causing more arrests, and amplify (or make worse) the original deviance. This is known as **deviancy amplification**. Groups which have fitted this pattern include mods and rockers in the 1960s and other youth sub-cultures, glue-sniffers, football 'hooligans', 'hippy convoys' on their way to Glastonbury or Stonehenge, and organizers of Acid House parties. Figure 8.3 illustrates the way the media can amplify deviance and generate a moral panic. Figure 8.4 shows a range of moral panics which have arisen in Britain since the 1950s.

Activity

Study figure 8.3 and try to fill in each of the stages of any current moral panic which is going on in society.

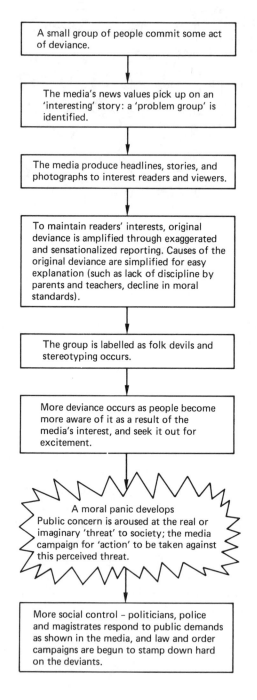

Figure 8.3 Deviancy amplification, moral panics, and the media

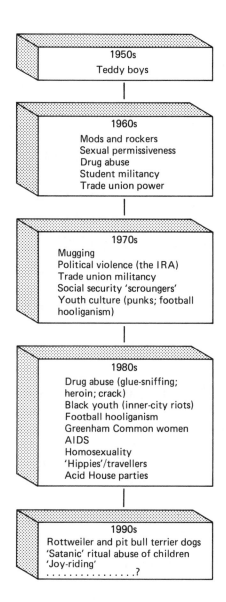

Figure 8.4 Folk devils and moral panics, Great Britain, 1950s–90s

Bias in the Media

Bias in the media is concerned with whether the media favour one point of view at the expense of others. Figure 8.5 summarizes a range of influences which can cause bias in the media. Many of these have been discussed elsewhere in this chapter.

Source: Socialist Worker.

Selection

The processes of agenda-setting, gate-keeping, and norm-setting mean some events are simply not reported and brought to public attention. Some of those that are reported may be singled out for particularly unfavourable treatment. In these ways, the mass media can decide what the important issues are, what 'news' is, what the public should and should not be concerned about, and what should or should not be regarded as 'normal' behaviour in society.

The Presentation of News

The way news items are presented may be important in influencing the way people are encouraged to view stories. For example, the physical position of a news story in a newspaper (front page or small inside column), the order of importance given to stories in TV news bulletins, the choice of headlines, and whether there is accompanying film or photographs will all influence the attention given to particular items. A story may be treated sensationally, and it may even be considered of such importance as to justify a TV 'newsflash'.

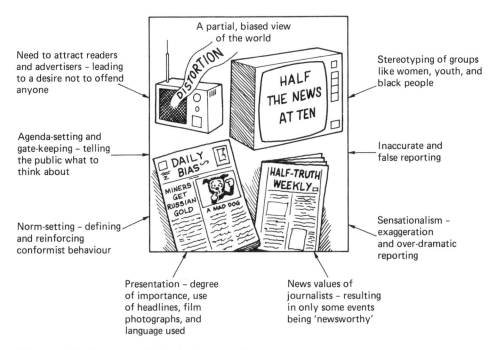

Need to attract readers and advertisers – leading to a desire not to offend anyone

A partial, biased view of the world

DISTORTION

HALF THE NEWS AT TEN

Stereotyping of groups like women, youth, and black people

Agenda-setting and gate-keeping – telling the public what to think about

DAILY BIAS

MINERS GET RUSSIAN GOLD

A MAD DOG

HALF-TRUTH WEEKLY

Inaccurate and false reporting

Norm-setting – defining and reinforcing conformist behaviour

Sensationalism – exaggeration and over-dramatic reporting

Presentation – degree of importance, use of headlines, film photographs, and language used

News values of journalists – resulting in only some events being 'newsworthy'

Figure 8.5 Sources of bias in the media

Where film is used, the pictures shown are always selected from the total footage shot, and may not accurately reflect the event. The actual images used in news films may themselves have a hidden bias. For example, in the reporting of industrial disputes, employers are often filmed in the peace and quiet of their offices, while workers are seen shouting on the picket lines or trying to be interviewed against a background of traffic noise. This gives the impression that employers are more calm and reasonable people and have a better case than the workers.

The language used in news reporting can also create bias, by giving particular impressions to their audiences. Figure 8.6 illustrates this bias in the use of language in newspaper reporting during the first week of the Gulf War in 1991.

Inaccurate and False Reporting

Other sources of bias lie in inaccurate reporting, because important details of a story may be incorrect. Politicians are always complaining that they have been inaccurately quoted in the press. False reporting, through either completely making up stories or inventing a few details, and the media's tendency to dramatize events out of all proportion to their actual significance

Mad dogs and Englishmen

We have	They have
Army, Navy and Air Force	A war machine
Reporting guidelines	Censorship
Press briefings	Propaganda

We	They
Take out	Destroy
Suppress	Destroy
Eliminate	Kill
Neutralize	Kill
Decapitate	Kill
Dig in	Cower in their foxholes

We launch	They launch
First strikes	Sneak missile attacks
Pre-emptively	Without provocation

Our men are . . .	Their men are . . .
Boys	Troops
Lads	Hordes

Our boys are . . .	Theirs are . . .
Professional	Brainwashed
Lion-hearts	Paper tigers
Cautious	Cowardly
Confident	Desperate
Heroes	Cornered
Dare-devils	Cannon fodder
Young knights of the skies	Bastards of Baghdad
Loyal	Blindly obedient
Desert rats	Mad dogs
Resolute	Ruthless
Brave	Fanatical

Our boys are motivated by	Their boys are motivated by
An old-fashioned sense of duty	Fear of Saddam

Our boys	Their boys
Fly into the jaws of hell	Cower in concrete bunkers

Our ships are . . .	Iraqi ships are . . .
An armada	A navy

Israeli non-retaliation is	Iraqi non-retaliation is
An act of great statesmanship	Blundering/Cowardly

The Belgians are . . .	The Belgians are also . . .
Yellow	Two-faced

Our missiles are . . .	Their missiles are . . .
Like Luke Skywalker zapping Darth Vader	Ageing duds (*rhymes with Scuds*)

Our missiles cause . . .	Their missiles cause . . .
Collateral damage	Civilian casualties

We . . .	They . . .
Precision bomb	Fire wildly at anything in the skies

Our PoWs are . . .	Their PoWs are . . .
Gallant boys	Overgrown schoolchildren

George Bush is . . .	Saddam Hussein is . . .
At peace with himself	Demented
Resolute	Defiant
Statesmanlike	An evil tyrant
Assured	A crackpot monster

Our planes . . .	Their planes . . .
Suffer a high rate of attrition	Are shot out of the sky
Fail to return from missions	Are zapped

Figure 8.6 Mad dogs and Englishmen

Source: The Guardian, 23 January 1991.

in society, typical of much reporting of the Royal Family, are devices used to make a story 'more interesting' and sell newspapers – this is particularly common in the mass circulation tabloid press. Such methods mean the media can be accused of manipulating their audiences. The media can also create false impressions by the sort of language used in reporting. For example, Figure 8.6 shows a number of expressions that were used by the British press in the first week of the Gulf War against Iraq, January 1991.

Activity

In figure 8.6, 'we' refers to the American, British, and other allied forces; 'they' refers to the Iraqis with whom 'we' were at war.

1. Explain with particular examples how the language used to describe Iraq differs from the language used to describe the allied forces. What general impression is given of the Iraqis?
2. Try to think of examples of other sorts of language used in newspaper stories and headlines which might give a distorted or biased impression – for example, football fans described as 'animals'.

The Mass Media and Democracy

Much of this chapter has suggested that the mass media act as a conservative influence in society, and give only a biased view of the world. However, some argue that the wealth of information provided by the mass media encourages and promotes a variety of opinions, and this enables the population to be informed on a wide range of issues, which is essential in a democratic society. It is perhaps useful to finish this chapter by examining briefly some of the competing views on this aspect of the role of the mass media in modern Britain.

The media promote democracy.

- Because the media in Britain are not controlled by the state, the risk of censorship by governments is reduced, and free speech is protected. Journalists are free to report and comment – within legal limits.

- The wide variety of privately owned media means a range of opinions are considered and public debates take place. By criticizing the actions of governments, the mass media can play an important 'watch dog' role, and keep governments in touch with public opinion.

- The media give an unbiased account of news. TV news has, by law, to be impartial.

- The media accurately reflect public opinions that already exist in society rather than creating new ones. People wouldn't read newspapers or watch TV unless they were providing what their audiences wanted.

The media restrict democracy

- The media (particularly newspapers) reflect the conservative views of their wealthy owners. While journalists are often critical and expose wrongdoing, they will frequently avoid issues which might cost them their jobs by upsetting newspaper owners.

- The variety of opinion presented is limited. Working-class political views, such as their views of strikes, are rarely reported. The ideas and actions of the least powerful groups are the most likely to be excluded. Those who in some way present a challenge or threat to the status quo – the existing way society is organized – are presented as irresponsible or unreasonable extremists.

- News values, agenda-setting, and norm-setting, and other sources of bias mean only some issues are covered, and these are not presented in neutral ways. The media choose what to report and how to report it, and therefore provide a biased view of the world.

- The media does not simply reflect public opinion, but actively forms it. People can only form opinions on the basis of the knowledge they have, and the media is primarily responsible for providing this knowledge.

  The owners of the mass media hold overwhelmingly conservative views, and their ownership gives them the power to defend their position by forming favourable public opinion.

- Anyone can put his or her views across, by setting up a newspaper, distributing leaflets and other means of communicating ideas.

- Only the rich have the resources necessary to publish and distribute a newspaper on a large scale, or to set up a television or radio station. The concentration of ownership of the mass media is a threat to democracy, as a small powerful group of media owners can control access to ideas, information, and knowledge. Those who wish to put forward alternative views to that presented in the mass media may not be allowed access to the media by their owners. They will therefore be denied any real opportunity to persuade public opinion of their ideas.

Discussion

That the mass media in Britain are owned by a small group of individuals who control the spread of ideas and information, and who are not elected nor answerable to the public, means people's opinions are manipulated by a small minority. Far from promoting democracy, the mass media in Britain are a major threat to it.

Chapter Summary

After studying this chapter, you should be able to:

- Explain what is meant by the term 'mass media'.
- Describe briefly the ways the law and the government might exercise control over the mass media.
- Describe the concentration of ownership of the mass media and explain why this might be of some concern in a democracy.

- Describe the differences between the 'quality' and the 'popular' newspapers, and their relationship to different social classes.
- Explain a variety of ways in which the mass media might form public opinion and exercise social control.
- Explain the terms 'agenda-setting', 'gate-keeping', and 'norm-setting'.
- Explain a range of factors influencing the content of the mass media.
- Explain, with examples, what are meant by 'news values'.
- Discuss, with examples, the role of the mass media in stereotyping and scapegoating.
- Explain how the mass media might give false impressions of crime.
- Explain how the mass media might amplify deviance.
- Explain a variety of ways in which bias may occur in the media.
- Explain the competing views of the role of the mass media in a democracy.

Project Suggestions

1. Video BBC and ITV news bulletins for a week, or study 'popular' and 'quality' newspapers for a week, and compare their coverage of different events. What evidence is there of agenda-setting?
2. Study some of the 'popular' and 'quality' newspapers for a week and discuss the differences between them, for example, by measuring up the column inches given to different categories of news, advertising, TV, and photographs.
3. Carry out a study of newspapers, advertisements, or children's comics, looking at the presentation of ethnic minorities or women.
4. Carry out a survey to find out which of the mass media people see as most reliable in presenting the news. The questionnaire in chapter 16 could be used as a starting point. You could compare your results with those given in Table 8.2 earlier in this chapter.
5. Compare two 'quality' and two 'popular' national Sunday or daily newspapers for the same days. Carefully analyse the headlines, types of story, photographs, and cartoons they contain. On the basis of this evidence, draw up a list of the news values you think each newspaper uses to decide which stories to include and which to exclude.
6. Interview the editor and other journalists on a local newspaper to find out how they decide what to print and what not to, what makes a story 'newsworthy', how far they think they exaggerate stories, and so on.

Key Terms

agenda-setting
deviancy amplification
folk devils
gate-keeping
labelling
moral panic
news values
norm-setting
scapegoats

9 Social Control, Deviance and Crime

In order for people to know how to behave in society, to be able to predict how others will behave, and therefore to live together in some orderly way, some shared values and norms are necessary. Without some measure of agreement on the basic ground rules, social life would soon fall into confusion and disorder. For example, imagine the chaos on the British roads if drivers stopped following the rules about driving on the left-hand side of the road, or stopping at red traffic lights.

Norms and values are learnt through socialization, but knowing what the norms are does not necessarily mean people will follow them. Social control is concerned with the various methods used to make sure people continue to obey those social values and norms which have been learnt through socialization. This is achieved by various positive and negative sanctions – rewards and punishments.

Together, socialization and social control help to maintain social conformity – conforming to social values and norms. Deviance is the term given to behaviour which is in some way socially unacceptable or not approved of – non-conformist behaviour.

Agencies of Social Control

Social control is carried out through a series of agencies of social control, many of which are discussed in fuller detail in other parts of this book, but it is useful to summarize them here.

Formal Social Control

Formal social control is that which is carried out by an agency specifically set up to ensure that people conform to a particular set of norms, particularly the law. The police, courts, prisons, and sometimes the army, as in Northern Ireland, force people to obey the law through formal sanctions such as arresting, fining, or imprisoning those who break society's laws.

Informal Social Control

The following agencies carry out social control in an informal way. This means their primary purpose is not social control, but they play an important role in it none the less.

The family

This is where primary socialization takes place and children first learn about the basic values and norms of society. For example, children learn the difference between right and wrong, 'good' and 'bad' behaviour, norms governing gender roles, and acceptance of parental authority. Children may become embarrassed or develop a guilty conscience if they break these rules. The approval or disapproval of parents can themselves be important elements in encouraging children to conform, along with other sanctions such as praise and rewards, threats, teasing, and physical violence.

The school

This socializes pupils and sets standards of 'correct' behaviour, the forms of dress and so on which are expected by society. This is achieved by sanctions such as detentions, suspensions, expulsions, merit points, and other aspects of the hidden curriculum (see chapter 11 for a discussion of this). Through the actions of teachers and the way the school is organized, for example through streaming and examinations, pupils are encouraged to accept norms like the competitiveness, the gender roles, the ranking of people with unequal pay and status, and the inequalities in power and authority to which they are expected to conform in the wider society. In this way, the school helps to maintain the way society as a whole is presently organized, such as the inequalities between men and women and between managers and workers.

The peer group

The peer group is a very important group in providing an individual's view of her or himself, and the desire for approval and acceptance by peers is itself an important source of social control. The fear of rejection and ridicule by peers may exert an enormous influence on an individual's behaviour. Such pressure may promote conformity to the wider norms of society, such as acceptance of traditional gender roles. However, conformity to the peer group may also promote deviance. This is particularly likely among young people, where peer pressure may encourage them to adopt forms of deviant behaviour, such as playing truant from school or under-age drinking.

The workplace

At work, there are frequently strong pressures from fellow workers to conform to work-related norms, and an individual who is labelled as a troublemaker or uncooperative may find her- or himself denied promotion opportunities, allocated unpleasant jobs, or even dismissed. Fellow workers may use such negative sanctions as refusing to talk to or mix with workmates, ridiculing them, or playing practical jokes on those who fail to conform to their norms.

Activity

1. Give examples of six norms in each case to which you are generally expected to conform in *two* of the following:
    (a) At your school or college.
    (b) In your peer group.
    (c) At work.
2. Explain in each case how these norms are enforced, and outline the sanctions applied if you fail to conform to them.

The mass media

These are a major source of information and ideas, and can have powerful influences on people's attitudes, opinions, and behaviour. As discussed in chapter 8, the mass media carry out social control through the processes of norm-setting and agenda-setting. These generally encourage conformist

Social control: people make
rules and then enforce them
on the carrot and stick principle

Activity

Look at the cartoon above.

1. Explain in your own words the point the cartoon is illustrating.
2. List six possible consequences that might face a person who followed a deviant path as an adult.
3. Suggest four reasons why a person might fail to conform to social norms.
4. Identify and explain two ways in which not conforming to social norms might lead to success in society.
5. Much deviance is disapproved of to some extent, but can you think of forms of deviance in any society which might be welcomed by the majority of the public as opening the way for society to change and improve?

behaviour, such as conformity to gender roles, promoted through advertising, or monogamy, through the AIDS campaign. This is achieved through such devices as the selection and presentation of news items, advertising, sensationalism, stereotyping and scapegoating. By reporting the serious consequences which follow for those who break society's norms, and telling people what they should be thinking about, norm-setting and agenda-setting are effectively carrying out social control.

Religion

Religion is a belief system which may influence people's ideas about 'right' and 'wrong' behaviour, and this in turn may affect their behaviour. For example, the Christian religion promises rewards (heaven) to those who conform to its teachings, and punishments (an eternity in hell) to those who do not. Religious beliefs and teachings often support and reinforce the values and norms of society by giving them a 'sacred' quality. The Ten Commandments in Christianity – 'thou shalt not kill...steal...commit adultery' – reinforce values such as respect for human life, private property, and monogamous marriage. Feelings of guilt (a guilty conscience) may result if religious rules are broken by believers – a sort of inner police officer controlling behaviour.

Crime and Deviance

The difference between crime and deviance

Deviance is any non-conformist behaviour which is disapproved of by society or a social group, whether it is illegal or not. It is norm-breaking behaviour, and can range from being eccentric to criminal activity.

Crime is the term used to describe behaviour which is against the law – law-breaking.

Delinquency is crime committed by those between the ages of 10 and 17.

The Difficulty of Defining Deviance

Crime is easy to define, as the law states what a criminal act is. However, while deviance appears to be easy to define as any non-conformist behaviour, it is, in fact, quite difficult to pin down what members of any society or group actually regard as deviant behaviour. Deviance covers a very wide range of behaviour, and what is regarded as deviant will depend on the norms of a group or society, and these differ between societies and between groups within the same society, and they change over time. Whether or not an act is defined as deviant will therefore depend on the time, the place, the society, and the attitudes of those who view the act. The following examples illustrate how definitions of deviance can vary according to a range of circumstances.

Non-deviant crime?

Most people commit deviant and even illegal acts at some stage in their lives, and there are many illegal acts which most people don't regard as particularly deviant. For example, parking and speeding offences, under-age drinking, pinching office stationery, or making unauthorized personal calls on the office phone are all illegal but extremely common, so it is difficult to see them as deviant. Some offences, like under-age drinking, are often seen as expected behaviour, and those who don't commit the offence may even be seen as deviant by those around them.

The time

Deviance can only be defined in relation to particular norms, and norms change over time. For example, cigarette smoking used to be a very popular and socially acceptable activity, but is increasingly becoming branded as deviant, and smokers are now unwelcome in many places. Attitudes to abortion and homosexuality have also changed dramatically, and homosexuality is no longer seen as being as deviant as it once was. However, in Britain changes in the law in the late 1980s and early 1990s suggested that the government was trying to make homosexuality more unacceptable once again, by taking steps to make it a criminal offence. Fashion, of course, is an obvious example of changing norms – people today would generally be regarded as deviant were they to wear the fashions of seventeenth-century England.

Attitudes to smoking
have changed

The society

Norms, and therefore definitions of deviance, differ between societies. For example, consumption of alcohol is often seen as deviant and illegal in many Islamic countries, but is seen as normal in Britain. Topless bathing on a Mediterranean beach is quite acceptable, but not so in a local park in England. Smoking marijuana is generally regarded as deviant by most people in modern Britain (but see the next paragraph), but is normal behaviour in many countries of the Middle East.

The social group

Norms can vary between social groups in the same society, and so what may be acceptable in a particular group may be regarded as deviant in the wider society. For example, smoking ganja (marijuana) is perfectly acceptable behaviour among Rastafarians in Britain, even though it is generally regarded as deviant and is illegal.

The place

The place an act takes place may influence whether it is regarded as deviant or not. For example, it is seen as deviant if people have sex in the street, but not if it takes place between couples in a bedroom; fighting in the street is seen as deviant, but not if it takes place in a boxing ring. Similarly, killing may be seen as 'heroic' on a battlefield in wartime, but as murder in peacetime.

Activity

Apart from the examples given above:

1. Identify and explain two examples of acts which are against the law but are not usually regarded as deviant by most people.
2. Give three examples of deviant acts which are not against the law.
3. Identify and explain two examples of acts which are generally accepted by the majority of people in Britain, but which might be regarded as deviant in some social groups in Britain, for example ethnic minority or religious groups.
4. Explain the circumstances in which the following acts might not be regarded as deviant or illegal:

   Two men having sex together.
   Killing 10 people.
   Driving through red traffic lights.
   Deliberately breaking someone's arm.
   Punching someone in the face.
   Breaking into someone's house and removing her or his possessions.
   Taking children away from their parents by force.

Why are Some Deviant Acts Defined as Criminal While Others are Not?

Marijuana use in some countries of the Middle East is an extremely common practice, with few laws controlling its use, and yet alcohol consumption is strictly banned by laws which are vigorously enforced. In Britain, the opposite is more or less the case, despite the massive social cost caused by alcoholism in terms of family breakdown, days off work, acts of violence, and costs to the NHS, and little evidence that marijuana has any addictive properties. Why are there such differences in the way some acts are defined as criminal while other, similar acts are not? There are two broad competing views on this.

The consensus view

This view suggests that social rules are made and enforced for the benefit of everyone. The law and the definition of crime represent a consensus – a widespread agreement among most people – that some deviant acts are so serious that they require legal punishments to prevent them occurring. This may seem fairly clear in cases such as murder, rape, and armed robbery, but it is not so clear on other issues, like those of alcohol and marijuana. From the consensus view, this would be explained by the varying norms found in different societies, which mean alcohol and drugs are viewed differently.

Inequalities in power

This view suggests that the law reflects the interests of the richest and most powerful groups in society who have managed to impose their ideas and way of thinking on the rest of the population through the agencies of social control. Those in positions of influence in society, such as newspaper editors, politicians, owners of industry, powerful pressure groups, judges, and the police, are much better placed to make their definition of a crime stick than the ordinary person in the street. They also have the power to define some acts as criminal through newspaper campaigns, by passing laws in Parliament, or by treating some offences more seriously than others.

In this way the powerful are able to maintain their own position of power and influence by defining those activities which are against their interests as deviant or criminal. The issue of alcohol raised above could well be explained by the power of the wealthy large brewers and distillers. A further example is the way laws against picketing by trade unionists are much stronger and more rigidly enforced than those imposing health and safety standards on employers. Middle-class crimes such as tax evasion are often neither prosecuted nor pursued as vigorously nor punished as severely as a working-class offence such as social security fraud, which is much more likely to result in prosecution and a prison sentence.

Discussion

Which view explaining why some deviant acts are defined as criminal while others are not do you find most convincing? Do you think the law is biased in deciding both which acts are defined as criminal, and which ones get pursued by the police and the courts?

The Pattern of Crime

Information on the pattern of crime is obtained from the official crime statistics. These are published each year by the Home Office from the records of local police forces.

Figure 9.1 shows a breakdown of the types of offence recorded by the police in 1990–1. It is notable that, despite wide media coverage of dramatic incidents such as attacks on the elderly, crimes against the person made up only about 5 per cent of all offences in 1990–1. Most recorded assaults and crimes of violence do not result in any serious physical injury – in 1987, only 15 per cent of such cases needed professional medical attention, and in only 1 per cent of such cases was the victim admitted to hospital. In fact, as figure 9.1 shows, most crime is fairly small-scale property crime.

Criminal statistics are notoriously unreliable, so the pattern of crime shown in them must be treated with considerable caution. The problem of the crime statistics will be discussed shortly, but for the moment our concern will be with explaining the pattern shown in the official statistics.

The official crime statistics show that most crime is committed:

- In urban areas.
- Against property.
- By young, working-class males.

Why is the crime rate higher in urban areas?

The official crime rate is significantly higher in urban areas than in rural areas. There are four main reasons for this.

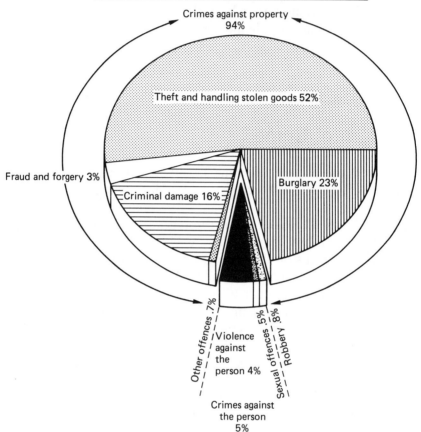

Figure 9.1 Notifiable offences[a] recorded by the police, England and Wales, July 1990–June 1991.

[a]Notifiable offences are the more serious types of offence, either indictable offences, for which any suspect would have to be tried by jury at a crown court, or triable-either-way offences, which may be tried at either a magistrates' court or a crown court.

Source: Adapted from Home Office Statistical Bulletin 18/91. 13 September 1991.

More opportunity for crime
Large urban areas provide greater opportunities for crime: more and larger shops, warehouses and business premises, cars, houses, and other typical targets of crime.

Policing
There is a greater police presence in urban areas, so more crime is likely to be detected. Different policing methods also mean the police are more likely to take formal action (arrest and prosecution) in urban areas. In rural areas they are less likely to arrest offenders, preferring merely to issue more informal warnings, or in the case of young people perhaps visiting the offender's parents or her or his school.

Less chance of being caught
In the large cities, life is more impersonal and people do not know each other so well. Strangers are more likely to go unrecognized, and are therefore more able to get away with offences. Potential criminals are less likely to steal within a small rural community where everyone knows almost everybody else and suspicious 'strangers' in the community are likely to be noticed. Any local offenders are quite likely to be known in the community.

Social deprivation
Social deprivation and social problems, such as poor housing, unemployment, and poverty, are at their worst in the inner cities. These have been linked to crime, as people try to resolve their desperate situations through illegal means.

Why are most convicted criminals young?

Official statistics show that roughly half of all those convicted are aged 21 or under. Young people are caught in the transition between child and adult status: they are no longer expected to behave as children, but are denied the full rights and responsibilities of adults. They therefore often feel deprived of status in society. The peer group provides some support for an identity and status independent of school or family, and therefore takes on a greater importance among young people than at any other age. Many young people lack the responsibilities involved in having children, paying rent or mortgage repayments, and often in keeping down a job.

This lack of responsibilities and status, and the search for excitement and peer group status, mean many young people drift into minor acts of delinquency and clashes with the law. Peer group pressure may also give young people the confidence and encouragement to involve themselves in minor acts of delinquency which they would not engage in on their own.

While most young people will break the law at some time, the kinds of offence they commit are usually fairly trivial and peer-group related. For example, research conducted at the Centre of Criminology at Edinburgh University in 1990 found that about half the offences committed by 11–15-year-olds involved rowdiness and fighting in the street, with the rest consisting mainly of shoplifting (usually sweets) and vandalism (usually graffiti).

The police are likely to see young people as the source of problems, and this stereotype means the police spend more time observing and checking youth. As a result, more get caught, get defined as offenders, and appear in the statistics. In fact, the Edinburgh research found that young people are far more likely to be the victims of crime than to commit them, and these crimes are often committed by adults. The young complained of being followed by 'weirdos', bothered by 'flashers', alcoholics, and junkies, and in fear of rape and other sexual assaults. However, the research found that the police often didn't take the complaints of the young seriously, seeing them primarily as troublemakers. More than half had been moved on, told off, stopped and questioned, or stopped and searched during the previous nine months. This situation discourages young people from reporting offences against them,

Source: The Guardian, 2 November 1990, reproduced by permission of David Haldane.

and reinforces the impression of young people as delinquents rather than the victims of crime.

Discussion

Do you think the police stereotype young people, and unfairly make them out to be troublemakers? What evidence do you have to back up your opinions?

Why are most convicted criminals male?

Males outnumber females by about 7:1 in the official statistics, and only about 3 per cent of the prison population are women. Why is this?

Evidence suggests more paternalism/sexism on the part of the police means they regard female offenders as a less serious 'threat' than men. They therefore adopt more informal approaches to their offences, such as unrecorded cautions or simply letting them off. The police are more likely to press charges in the case of men.

Due to gender role socialization, men are more likely than women to carry out crimes of violence and other serious offences. While women are far less likely to commit violent crimes than men, those who do are likely to face more serious punishment than men, as it violates socially acceptable patterns of feminine behaviour. A typical example of this was the case of Sara Thornton, who in 1991 was given a life prison sentence for killing her violent husband, while a man tried for killing his 'nagging' wife in the same year walked free after receiving a suspended sentence.

Women who commit crimes may benefit from the police stereotype that they are less likely than men to be criminals, and so are less likely to have their behaviour watched and get caught. Teenage girls are also likely to be more closely supervised by their parents, reducing the chances of their getting into trouble in the first place. Adult females may be less likely to get involved in crime due to the constraints placed upon them by the demands of the housewife/mother role – caring for husbands, children, and dependent elderly relatives.

Women's offences are more likely to be less detectable offences, such as sexual offences, like prostitution, or petty theft, like shoplifting. The tough and dominant behaviour expected of men is more likely to lead to more serious and detectable criminal behaviour, and the police expect men to be the more likely criminals.

Activity

1. Read carefully the previous section on why most convicted criminals are male. Make a list in order of importance of the reasons why women are less likely to be criminals than men.
2. How do you think police attitudes to women and crime could affect the number of female offenders recorded in the official crime statistics? Explain your answer carefully, with examples of particular crimes.
3. Women are more likely to be victims of some crimes than men. Suggest, with reasons, examples of some of these crimes.

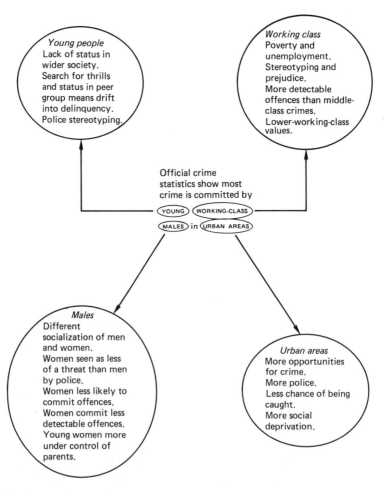

Figure 9.2 A summary of explanations for the pattern of crime shown in the official crime statistics

Why are most convicted criminals working class?

According to the official statistics, working-class people are more likely to be arrested and charged with crimes than those of other social classes. There are a number of possible explanations for this.

Poverty and unemployment

A Home Office research paper in August 1990 found a link between the level of crime and the state of the economy. Property crime in particular seems to rise when people are hard up, when poverty is on the increase and people need to provide for their families. Such hardship provides an obvious explanation for the most common offences of property crime, and would account for the high proportion of working-class criminals. In a society where there are wide inequalities in wealth and income, some level of crime is to be expected from those who live a more deprived life than others in society.

Stereotyping and prejudice

Working-class youth fit more the police stereotype of the 'typical criminal', and there is therefore a greater police presence in working-class areas than in middle-class areas. This means there is a greater likelihood of offenders being seen and arrested by the police when committing an offence than in middle-class areas. Crime rates will therefore be higher in working-class areas simply because there are more police to notice or respond quickly to criminal acts.

The activities of working-class youth are more likely to be defined by the police as criminal than the same behaviour in the middle class. For example, a case of university students getting drunk and wrecking a restaurant might result in their having to pay for the damage and be dismissed by the police as 'high jinks', but the same behaviour by working-class football supporters would be more likely to be seen as 'hooliganism', with resulting prosecutions for criminal damage.

Working-class youth are also more likely to be prosecuted if they are caught than the middle class. This is perhaps because they are less likely to benefit from informal processes of social control. For petty offences, middle-class youth are more likely to be dealt with by parents and teachers than the law, with the police perhaps visiting the parents to give them a warning.

The prejudices of middle-class judges and magistrates may mean that, when working-class people appear in court, they are more likely to be seen as 'typical criminals' and found guilty. The middle class are more likely to be found not guilty. Their offences may be seen more as a temporary lapse in otherwise good behaviour, and so are punished less severely than those of the working class.

Activity

Most judges and magistrates come from white, upper-middle-class and middle-class backgrounds.

1. Suggest ways this might influence judges and magistrates to give more favourable and sympathetic treatment to some groups and less favourable and unsympathetic treatment to others. Give examples of particular groups.
2. Imagine you are to appear in court on a shoplifting charge. You desperately want to get off lightly. Identify and explain four ways you might try to give a good impression to the judge or magistrate.
3. What might this activity suggest about the real pattern of crime in society?

Lower-working-class values
Miller has suggested that the values of the lower working class often carry with them risks of brushes with the law. These are discussed later in this chapter.

White-collar crime
White-collar crimes are offences committed by people in the course of their middle-class jobs. Such crimes are substantially under-represented in official statistics, giving the impression that the middle class commit less offences. However, there may be many white-collar criminals around who simply don't get caught or even have their crimes detected. The impression gained from the official statistics that most crime is committed by the working class may therefore be quite misleading.

White-collar crimes include offences such as bribery and corruption in government and business, professional misconduct, fraud, embezzlement, misrepresentation, industrial espionage, computer fraud, and breach of safety regulations. A typical case of such crime is that of Ernest Saunders, former chairman of Guinness, who in August 1990 was convicted of theft of £8 million, false accounting and conspiracy.

There are several reasons why white-collar crime is under-represented in the official statistics.

- Such crime is often 'without victims' and may benefit both the parties concerned. For example, in cases of bribery and corruption both parties stand to gain something. It is therefore hard to detect.
- There is often a lack of awareness that a crime has been committed and therefore it is not reported. For example, members of the public may lack the expertise to know if they are being misled or defrauded.
- Even if these crimes are detected, they are often not prosecuted. For example, violations of health and safety legislation often lead only to a reprimand. Crimes such as professional misconduct, medical negligence, industrial espionage, and computer fraud are rarely reported, to protect the interests or reputation of the profession or institution, and avoid the loss of public confidence which the surrounding scandal might cause. A typical example of this occurred in 1990, when it was reported that at least five British banks were being blackmailed by a group of computer hackers who had broken into their central computer systems. This was not reported to the police, but instead was investigated by a private security firm. This was so that the public would not find out about it, with the resulting damaging publicity to the banks' reputation and the loss of public confidence.

What's Wrong with the Official Crime Statistics?

The previous section outlined some explanations of the pattern of crime as revealed in the official crime statistics. However, the official crime statistics are not as factual as they might appear, and there is a large percentage of crimes which are not discovered or reported: the 'dark number' of undiscovered crimes. Figure 9.3 from the 1988 British Crime Survey shows a large gap between the amount of crime committed and that finally recorded by the police.

This survey estimated that overall about four times as many offences are committed as the number recorded by the police, though for some categories of crime, such as vandalism, theft from the person, and sexual offences, the number is much higher. Many burglaries, rapes, and crimes of domestic violence go unreported.

Activity

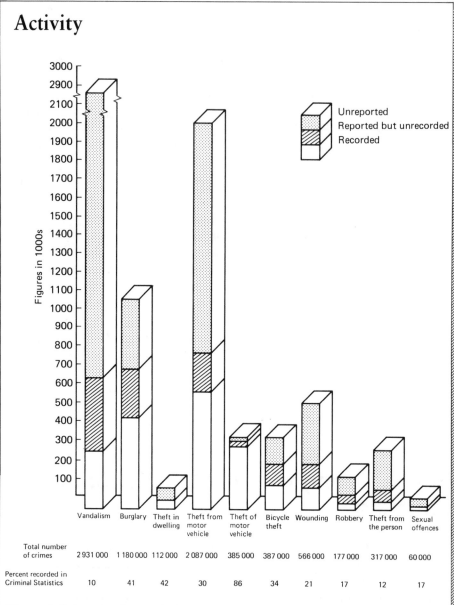

Total number of crimes	Vandalism	Burglary	Theft in dwelling	Theft from motor vehicle	Theft of motor vehicle	Bicycle theft	Wounding	Robbery	Theft from the person	Sexual offences
	2 931 000	1 180 000	112 000	2 087 000	385 000	387 000	566 000	177 000	317 000	60 000
Percent recorded in Criminal Statistics	10	41	42	30	86	34	21	17	12	17

Figure 9.3 Levels of recorded and unrecorded crime, Great Britain, 1987. Figures are British Crime Survey estimates.

Source: The 1988 British Crime Survey (HMSO 1989).

Study figure 9.3 and answer the following questions:

1. How many crimes of vandalism were there estimated to be in total in 1987?

2. Approximately how many thefts from motor vehicles were recorded in 1987?
3. Which type of crime was the most likely to be recorded in 1987?
4. Approximately how many bicycle thefts were reported but unrecorded in 1987?
5. According to the statistics above, a high percentage of crimes of vandalism, thefts from motor vehicles, wounding, robbery, theft from the person, and sexual offences went unreported. Suggest reasons for this for each offence.
6. Suggest, with examples, reasons why the police may decide not to record a crime:
    (a) Which has been reported to them.
    (b) Which the police themselves have detected.
7. Explain how the information given in figure 9.3 might be used to show that the official crime statistics give a misleading impression of the extent of crime in society. Is there any evidence for the opposite view? Be sure to give statistical evidence from the chart above.

Self-report studies and victim surveys

Sociologists know that the number of crimes is far higher than the official statistics suggest because of the use of self-report studies and victim surveys. Self-report studies are anonymous questionnaires where people own up to committing crimes, whether they have been discovered or not. Victim surveys involve people admitting to being the victim of a crime, whether or not they reported it. Table 9.1 shows an example of a self-report study.

Research from self-report studies and victim surveys suggests that the high proportion of young, urban, working-class males in the criminal statistics gives a misleading impression of the criminal population as a whole. In reality the ratio of working-class to middle-class crime and the ratio of male to female is much more equal than official statistics suggest. Therefore, the extent of crime and the type of people committing it are very different from those which the official statistics suggest. Why are the official crime statistics so inaccurate?

Table 9.1 Example of a self-report study

Acts of delinquency	Acts of delinquency
1 I have ridden a bicycle without lights after dark.	17 I have used a weapon in a fight, like a knife or a razor or a broken bottle.
2 I have driven a car or motor bike/scooter under 16.	18 I have drunk alcoholic drinks in a pub under 16.
3 I have been with a group who go round together making a row and sometimes getting into fights and causing disturbance.	19 I have been in a pub when I was under 16.
4 I have played truant from school.	20 I have taken things from big stores or supermarkets when the shop was open.
5 I have travelled on a train or bus without a ticket or deliberately paid the wrong fare.	21 I have taken things from little shops when the shop was open.
6 I have let off fireworks in the street.	22 I have dropped things in the street like litter or broken bottles.
7 I have taken money from home without returning it.	23 I have bought something cheap or accepted as a present something I knew was stolen.
8 I have taken someone else's car or motor bike for a joy ride then taken it back afterwards.	24 I have planned well in advance to get into a house to take things.
9 I have broken or smashed things in public places like on the streets, cinemas, dance halls, trains or buses.	25 I have got into a house and taken things even though I didn't plan it in advance.
10 I have insulted people on the street or got them angry and fought with them.	26 I have taken a bicycle belonging to someone else and kept it.
11 I have broken into a big store or garage or warehouse.	27 I have struggled or fought to get away from a policeman.
12 I have broken into a little shop even though I may not have taken anything.	28 I have struggled or fought with a policeman who was trying to arrest someone.
13 I have taken something out of a car.	29 I have stolen school property worth more than about 5p.
14 I have taken a weapon (like a knife) out with me in case I needed it in a fight.	30 I have stolen goods from someone I worked for worth more than about 5p.
15 I have fought with someone in a public place like in the street or a dance.	31 I have had sex with a boy when I was under 16.
16 I have broken the window of an empty house.	32 I have trespassed somewhere I was not supposed to go, like empty houses, railway lines or private gardens.

Table 9.1 (*Cont'd*)

Acts of delinquency	Acts of delinquency
33 I have been to an 'X'[1] film under age.	39 I have got money from someone by pretending to be someone else or lying about why I needed it.
34 I have spent money on gambling under 16.	
35 I have smoked cigarettes under 15.	40 I have taken someone's clothes hanging up somewhere.
36 I have had sex with someone for money.	41 I have smoked dope or taken pills (LSD, mandies, sleepers).
37 I have taken money from slot machines or telephones.	42 I have got money/drink/ cigarettes by saying I would have sex with someone even though I didn't.
38 I have taken money from someone's clothes hanging up somewhere.	
	43 I have run away from home.

[1] Now an '18' film.

Source: A. Campbell, *Girl Delinquents* (Basil Blackwell 1981).

Activity

1. Work through the self-report study in table 9.1. List any offences you and/or your friends have committed but have not been caught for (no matter how trivial or whether they're on the list or not). What conclusions might you draw from your findings about the levels of undiscovered crime in society? (For male students, point 31 of table 9.1 should be read as 'with a girl when I was under 16 or with a boy when I was under 21'.)
2. List five crimes which a victim might choose not to report to the police, and explain why in each case.
3. Have you or any of your friends ever been a victim of a crime (or suspected you might have been a victim) that you didn't report to the police? Explain the reasons why you didn't report it. What does this tell you about the real extent of crime in society?

The Failure to Report Crimes to the Police

The evidence suggests that a large number of people who are victims of crime don't bother to report it to the police. There are a number of reasons for this, which you can compare with your own findings in the previous activity.

- The victims may think that the incident is too trivial to report; for example, where the incident involved no loss or damage, or the loss was too small, such as losing a small amount of money.
- The victims may think there is little point in reporting the incident as they feel the police could not do anything about it, by either recovering their property or catching the offenders.
- The victims may fear embarrassment or humiliation at the hands of the police or in court. Groups working with rape victims such as the Rape Crisis Line estimate two out of three rape victims do not report it because of embarrassment, because they think the police won't take them seriously, or because they are made to feel it is their own fault they got raped. Recent rises in the number of reported rapes and crimes of domestic violence are often explained by changing police practice, and their growing willingness to treat such offences in a more serious way.
- People may not report offences because they will themselves be in trouble. Some crimes benefit both parties, and there is no obvious victim. The consequence of reporting such offences will harm all concerned. For example, offences such as the illegal supplying of drugs, under-age sex, or giving and accepting bribes involve an agreement between both parties, and both will lose out if the police find out. Similarly, the illegal drug user who gets ripped off is more likely to be charged with an offence than be shown sympathy by the police, and is therefore extremely unlikely to report the incident.
- The victim may fear reprisals if the crime is reported, for example the blackmail victim afraid of the consequences of reporting the blackmailer.
- Victims may feel it is a private matter they would rather deal with themselves. Examples might include offences such as theft or assault between friends.
- Victims may not be aware an offence has been committed. 'Lost' property may have been stolen, and while the media often reports cases of hoax gas meter readers and so on, there may be many people who never actually realize they have been the victim of such a hoax.

The Failure of the Police to Record a Crime

The police may decide not to record an offence because they may regard the matter as too trivial to waste their time on, such as the theft of a very small sum of money, or the vandalism of a car window.

They may regard the person complaining as too unreliable to take his or her account of the incident seriously, as in the case of complaints made by a tramp, a drug addict, or a drunk. The police may think that a report of an incident is mistaken, or that there is simply insufficient evidence to show that a crime has been committed.

In some cases, the police may regard an incident as nothing to do with them, even though an offence has been committed. This has traditionally been true in cases of domestic violence, such as wife-battering and rape within marriage, with such incidents being dismissed as a relatively unimportant 'domestic', and no offence being recorded or charges preferred.

Activity

The police often have a great deal of work to do, and every arrest they make involves considerable paper work. The police also have discretion over whether to arrest and charge someone for some offences. For example, pub closing-time may involve lots of trouble, but the police can choose to move people along rather than arrest them.

1. Suggest six examples of crimes which the police might turn a blind eye to. Give reasons for your answer.
2. Suggest six crimes the police would be forced to record and investigate. Give reasons for your answer.
3. Sometimes the police seem to take some offences more seriously than at other times, and this results in increasing numbers of arrests and prosecutions for these offences, for example drink-driving at Christmas. List, with examples, all the factors you can think of which might make the police occasionally increase their levels of activity against some offences.

Is the Crime Rate Increasing?

Much of what was said in the previous section suggests that the official crime statistics provide no real guide to the type or extent of crime, and must therefore be used with great care. Such care must also be applied to statistics which show increases in the amounts of recorded crime. In 1991, for example, much public concern was expressed at the increase in recorded crime, as shown in figure 9.4

Increases in the amount of recorded crime need not necessarily mean there are more crimes being committed, or that people are at greater risk of being victims of crime. The increases could be explained by a wide range of factors, which suggest more offences are being discovered, but not necessarily that more offences are being committed.

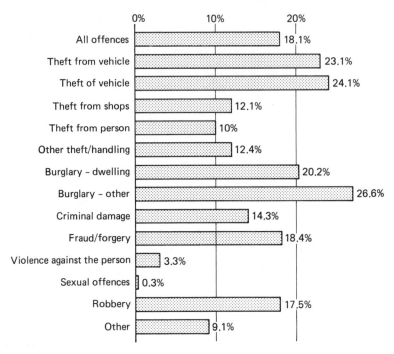

Figure 9.4 Changes in recorded crime, England and Wales: percentage change between the periods July 1989–June 1990 and July 1990–June 1991

Source: Home Office Statistical Bulletin 18/91 13 September 1991.

- More sophisticated police training and equipment, such as the use of computers, forensic science, and genetic fingerprinting, and higher policing levels all lead to increasing detection rates.
- A stronger desire by the police to prosecute certain offenders due to changing police attitudes and policies towards some offences, such as a crack-down on prostitution, drug-dealing, or drink-driving. This may give the impression of an increase in crimes of that type, when it is simply that the police are making extra efforts and allocating more officers to prosecute such crimes, and therefore catching more offenders.
- Changes in the law make more things illegal, such as rape in marriage.
- Easier communications make reporting of crime easier, such as mobile phones.
- Changing social norms – for example, changing attitudes to rape among the police and the public may have resulted in more rapes being reported, but not necessarily more being committed. The same might apply to crimes like domestic violence and child abuse, which are also statistically on the increase.

- People have more to lose today and more have insurance cover. Insurance claims for theft need a police report, so more crime is reported. For example, nearly all car thefts are reported today so people can claim the insurance money, and rising numbers of recorded burglaries may simply reflect more people with household contents insurance policies.

It is an irony of the official statistics that attempts to defeat crime by increased levels of policing, more police pay and resources, and a determination to crack down on offences, can actually increase the levels of recorded crime. The more you search for crime, the more you find...and the official crime rate rises.

Discussion

Do you think there are really more crimes being committed today, or do you think the reasons listed above explain the increased levels of recorded crime?

Explaining Crime and Deviance

Deviance covers very wide and varied forms of behaviour, and definitions of deviance and crime vary widely between societies and change over time. It is impossible to be born a criminal or a deviant because crime and deviance involve legal and social rules, and what counts as deviant or criminal will depend on how society defines these rules. No single explanation can possibly provide an adequate account of all forms of deviance. The following sections briefly cover some of the major theoretical explanations which have been offered by sociologists for deviance, particularly criminal deviance.

Anomie

Merton suggests in *Social Structure and Anomie* (American Sociological Review 1938) that all societies set goals which people are encouraged to achieve, such as making money and career success. Norms or social rules define the socially approved ways of achieving these goals, such as hard work and educational qualifications. Most people are what Merton calls conformists – they try to achieve society's goals in approved ways.

Merton argues deviance arises when the approved ways of achieving society's goals don't correspond with the actual situation individuals are in. In these circumstances, **anomie** results. This is a situation where the norms of society are weakened to some extent, and there are no clear rules for people to follow in their daily lives. For example, many disadvantaged groups such as the poor and the lower working class have little chance of achieving society's goals by acceptable means, because they face disadvantages in education or are stuck in dead-end jobs with no promotion prospects. A strain is therefore placed on these individuals – they want to achieve the goals but lack the opportunities for doing so by conventional means. Merton suggests people may respond to these difficulties in achieving society's goals by breaking the rules, for example turning to crime or other deviant behaviour. He identifies four different types of rule-breaking: innovation, ritualism, retreatism, and rebellion. Innovators, for example, break the accepted rules for achieving success and turn to illegal means of achieving society's goals, such as theft. The cartoon illustrates these four types of deviance.

Activity

Look at the cartoon on 'Merton's rule-breakers'.

1. Which one of the four types of rule-breaking would those who fiddled their income tax normally be considered as?
2. Explain in what way each of Merton's rule-breakers is deviant, and how each would have to change to become conformist.
3. Classify each of the following acts/groups according to Merton's ideas:

   Cheating in exams.
   A teacher who has lost interest in the job, but carries on teaching.
   A heroin addict.
   The IRA.
   A tramp.
   A lazy student who only pretends to do any work.

4. Suggest two examples of your own for each type of rule-breaking (or deviance), and explain how your examples show each type of deviance.

MERTON'S RULE-BREAKERS

INNOVATORS
Try to achieve success by illegitimate means e.g. theft

RITUALISTS
Continue to work within the system but give up trying for success e.g. office workers stuck in a rut and simply 'going through the motions'. No ambition.

RETREATISTS
Abandon both the goals and the means of achieving them, and become drop-outs, turning to drink, drugs or some other deviant behaviour.

REBELS
Reject society's goals and the accepted means of achieving them, and replace them with their own e.g. revolutionaries

Sub-cultural Explanations

A **sub-culture** is a smaller culture held by a group of people within the main culture of a society, in some ways different from the dominant culture, but with many aspects in common. Figure 9.5 illustrates, with examples, this idea of a sub-culture. Sub-cultural explanations of crime and deviance suggest that those who commit crime share some values which are to some extent different from the values of society as a whole.

Status frustration and the deviant sub-culture

While most lower-working-class young people accept the main goals of society, like wealth and educational success, they have little chance of attaining them. This is because they live in deprived areas, with poor schools and the worst chances in the job market. They therefore develop **status frustration**. This simply means they lack status in society, and feel frustration at being unable to achieve such status by accepted means.

Their response to this sense of status frustration is to develop a set of alternative, deviant values which provides them with alternative ways of gaining status – a deviant sub-culture. Delinquent acts are based on a deliberate reversal of accepted norms. At school, playing truant, messing about in class, and destroying school property may replace the values of studying and exam success. Stealing becomes a means of getting money,

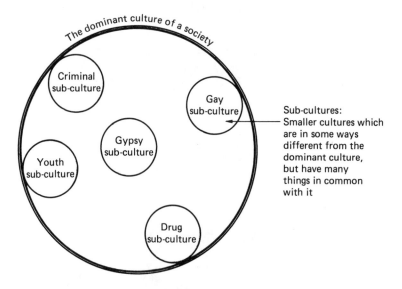

Figure 9.5 Culture and sub-cultures

replacing career success, and vandalism replaces respect for property. Such acts of delinquency enable some lower-working-class youth to gain a status in their peer group which the wider society has denied them. Delinquency also gives them a way of getting their revenge against the system which has condemned them to failure.

The lower-working-class sub-culture

Miller suggests that the values of lower-working-class male sub-culture can often lead to crime among young people. This sub-culture encourages men to demonstrate their toughness, their masculinity, and their 'smartness', and to pursue excitement and thrills. Miller argues that these features of working-class life can lead to clashes with the law. For example, the concern with 'toughness' might lead to offences like assault.

These values may become exaggerated in the lives of young males who want to achieve status in their peer group by engaging in delinquent acts to show how tough and smart they are. A 'good night out' might consist of a few drinks, a fight outside the pub, a rampage round the streets with mates, and a run-in with the police, with everyone competing to show they are more 'macho' than the rest.

Labelling Theory

Labelling theory is concerned with two main features:

- The process whereby some people committing some actions come to be defined or labelled as deviant, while others do not.
- The consequences which follow once a deviant label has been applied, and how this may create more deviance or crime.

The first of these issues was discussed earlier in this chapter, so here the emphasis will be on the consequences which follow once a deviant label has been applied.

The deviant 'master status'

Labelling theorists point out that most people commit crimes and other deviant acts at some time in their lives, but not everyone becomes defined as a deviant or a criminal. For labelling theorists, what is important in explaining crime is the consequences of being caught and labelled.

Once someone is caught and labelled as a criminal or deviant, the label attached may become the dominant label or '**master status**' which over-rides all other characteristics of that person – she or he becomes, not someone's wife/husband, mother/father, friend, or business associate, but an 'ex-con' or a 'hooligan'.

Once a person is labelled as 'mad' (mentally ill), as a football hooligan, as a thief, or as a failure at school, the label may have quite serious consequences for his or her life, as people are treated differently according to the label. Each label carries with it a range of prejudices and images – the football hooligan, for example, is often seen as irresponsible, violent, a drunkard, a racist, and a serious threat to society. A person with a conviction for theft may be seen as fundamentally untrustworthy and never to be left alone with valuables, and things that go missing may automatically reinforce suspicions that they have been stolen by the labelled thief. The bottom-stream pupil in school may be seen as a 'waster', and thoroughly untrustworthy and unreliable. Once labelled, a person's behaviour might be interpreted differently from that of a person not labelled as deviant. For example, teachers may treat some questions from bottom-stream 'delinquents' as red herrings, but regard the same questions from top-stream conformists as intelligent and worthy of discussion. Much the same could apply when different pupils offer excuses for not doing homework, missing games, and so on. Someone with a history of mental illness may have signs of eccentricity interpreted as evidence of his or her mental illness, but the same behaviour might pass unnoticed in a person not labelled as mentally ill.

Deviant careers

Labelling may lead to a **deviant career**. This simply means people start acting the way they have been labelled. For example, a man caught in an isolated act of stealing may be prosecuted, imprisoned, and labelled as a 'criminal' and later as an 'ex-con' – friends desert him, employers refuse to offer him jobs, and the man may then begin to see himself primarily as a criminal. Since alternative opportunities are closed off to him, and everyone treats him as a criminal anyway, he may then turn to crime as a way of life and follow a deviant career of crime.

In this way, labelling theory suggests that the attachment of a label can actually generate more deviance. For example, prisons and borstals play a key role in making the label of 'criminal' and, later, 'ex-con' stick. They immerse offenders in a criminal sub-culture, increase the opportunities to learn about crime, and make it extremely hard for them to go back to living a 'normal' life when they are released. More crime may therefore result as alternative opportunities are limited.

Activity

In each of the cases listed below:

1. Identify a possible label which may be attached to the person concerned as a result of her or his deviant behaviour.
2. Outline how a 'deviant career' might develop by describing the possible consequences of the labelling for the person's future life and relationships.
3. Suggest ways that a person might avoid being labelled even after she or he has committed the deviant act.

A young woman caught shoplifting.
A male teacher who publicly declares himself to be gay (homosexual).
A person who is temporarily admitted to a mental hospital as a result of a nervous breakdown.
An 18-year-old man who gets arrested during a fight at a football match.

Conclusion

This chapter has shown that the definition and explanation of deviance and crime are no simple matters. This is hardly surprising given the very wide range of behaviour that the term 'deviance' covers.

We must recognize that deviance, and even crime, are not by any means always harmful to society. Much crime remains fairly trivial, and the wide range of non-conformist behaviour, the quirks and oddities of behaviour, add a richness of colour and variety to what might otherwise be a drab existence.

Without deviance, even without crime, there would be no possibility of innovation and change. The rebels and the reformers, the heretics and the inventors, and campaigners for peace and justice have all been labelled as deviants or criminals at one time or another. Yet it is these non-conformists who have contributed to changes which many would regard as of benefit to all. Deviance should be treated with an open mind, for what is regarded as deviant today is often the accepted behaviour of tomorrow.

Chapter Summary

After studying this chapter, you should be able to:

- Define social control and explain how it is carried out formally and informally through agencies of social control.
- Explain the difference between crime and deviance.
- Explain how and why definitions of deviance vary.
- Explain the link between deviance and power.
- Describe and explain the pattern of crime shown in the official crime statistics.
- Explain why white-collar crime often goes undetected or unrecorded.
- Explain a range of reasons why the official crime statistics provide no accurate record of the full extent of crime in society.
- Explain why an increase in the official crime rate might not necessarily mean that there has been an increase in the real amount of crime.
- Provide a range of sociological explanations of crime, delinquency, and deviance.
- Describe and explain the ideas of labelling and deviant careers.

Project Suggestions

1. Using secondary sources, give an account of the pattern of crime in your own area, and compare it with the national crime statistics. Perhaps interview the local police for information.
2. Do a survey about attitudes to some deviant or illegal act, such as under-age drinking or drug abuse.
3. Carry out a case study of a Neighbourhood Watch scheme.
4. Carry out a self-report study (you might use the self-report study included in this chapter as a starting point) or a victim survey among a small sample in your school, college, or workplace, and try to discover how much undiscovered and/or unreported crime there is. Compare your results with those in the British Crime Survey.

Key Terms

anomie
deviant career
master status
status frustration
sub-culture

10 The Family and Marriage

Most people are raised in families, and so we might think we know all about them. We may make assumptions that people will fall in love with someone of the opposite sex and get married, start having children, and form their own family. We may have the impression that the typical family unit in Britain consists of parents and a couple of children, with Dad out working and Mum staying at home looking after the kids, but with both partners sharing a lot more jobs around the home. We may believe the family is the only place where children can be properly brought up, and that it is a source of unconditional affection – a place to retreat to whenever things get too much or go wrong in the outside world.

On the other hand, you may believe that the family is in decline, pointing to rising rates of divorce, extra-marital sex, and abortion, with rising numbers of single-parent families. You might point to rising levels of child abuse, violence against women, vandalism and crime, drug abuse, and homosexuality. You would not be alone in holding such a belief – the mass media, politicians, the police, social workers, teachers, and religious leaders have all at some time or another tried to 'blame the family' and lack of parental control for a wide range of problems in society.

There is, whatever way you look at it, a controversy over the family. This chapter will attempt to throw some light on some of these issues, and the variety of forms of marriage and the family. Four main issues will be examined:

- The major changes which have occurred in the family in Britain in the last century.
- Critical views of the family.
- Alternatives to the family.
- Whether marriage and the family are in decline.

What is the Family?

A family is a group of people who are related by **kinship** ties: relations of blood, marriage, or adoption. The family unit is one of the most important social institutions, which is found in some form in nearly all known societies. It is a basic unit of social organization, and plays a key role in socializing children into the culture of their society.

Different Forms of the Family and Marriage

Even though the family is found in nearly every society, it can take many different forms. Marriage and family life in earlier times in Britain, and today in many other societies, can be organized in quite different ways from family life in modern Britain. Sociologists use a number of different terms to describe the wide varieties of marriage and the family.

The Nuclear Family

The **nuclear family** means just the parents and children, living together in one household. It is sometimes called the two-generation family, because it contains only the two generations of parents and children. In Britain in 1990, 41 per cent of people lived in this type of family.

The Classic Extended Family

The **classic extended family** is made up of several nuclear families joined by kinship relations. The classic extended family is sometimes called a three- or four-generation family, because it contains the three generations of grandparents, parents, and children (or other relatives). The term 'classic extended family' is mainly used to describe a situation where many related nuclear families or family members live in the same house, street, or area and the members of these related nuclear families see one another regularly.

The Modified Extended Family

The **modified extended family** is one where related nuclear families, although they may be living far apart geographically, nevertheless maintain regular contact and mutual support through visiting, the phone, and letters: continuing close relations made possible by modern communications. This is probably the most common type of family arrangement in Britain today.

Activity

1. Do a brief survey among your friends or workmates and find out how many live in nuclear families, how many live in classic extended families, and how many have modified extended families. You will have to think of suitable ways of measuring the features of these families, such as how near relatives live, how often they see one another, what other relatives live in the household apart from parents and children, and so on.
2. Ask them what it is like living in these different types of family. On the basis of your findings and using also your own experience of family life, make a list of the advantages and disadvantages of living in each type of family.

The Single-Parent Family

The single-parent family is increasingly common in Western societies. In 1990, 10 per cent of people in Britain lived in this type of family. Although single-parent families can also arise from the death of a partner, they are today largely a result of the rise in the divorce rate. In 1990 almost 20 per cent of all families with dependent children were single-parent families, and nine out of ten of these single parents were women. Increasingly, single-parent families are arising from a simple lack of desire to get married – in 1990, one-third of single mothers fell into this category. About three-quarters of single-parent families receive income support.

The Reconstituted Family

The **reconstituted family** is a family where one or both partners have been previously married, and they bring with them children of a previous marriage. This 'reconstitutes' the family with various combinations of step-mothers, step-fathers, and step-children. Such families are increasingly common in Western societies, as a result of rising divorce rates and remarriages. In 1991 in Britain, nearly 40 per cent of all marriages involved remarriage for one or both partners, and at least one in ten children today live in step-families, with parents of one or more previous marriages.

The Symmetrical Family

The **symmetrical family** is one where the roles of husband and wife or of cohabiting partners have become more alike (symmetrical) and equal. There are more shared tasks within relationships rather than a clear division between the jobs of male and female partners. Both partners are likely to be wage earners. It remains a popular impression that most families in modern Britain are symmetrical, but evidence which will be discussed later in this chapter suggests this is not the case.

Monogamy

In modern Britain and the rest of Europe, the USA, and most Christian cultures, **monogamy** is the only legal form of marriage. Monogamy is a form of marriage in which a person can have only one husband or wife at the same time. Monogamy is not the most common form of marriage in the world, and it is found in only about 24 per cent of all societies. In a society where monogamy is the only form of legal marriage, a person who marries while still legally married to someone else is guilty of the crime of **bigamy** – a serious offence punishable by imprisonment.

Serial monogamy

In modern Britain, most of Western Europe, and the USA there are high rates of divorce and remarriage. Some people keep marrying and divorcing a series of different partners, but each marriage is monogamous. The term **serial**

monogamy is sometimes used to describe these marriage patterns. This form of marriage has been described as 'one at a time, one after the other and they don't last long'!

Arranged Marriages

Arranged marriages are those where the marriages of children are organized by their parents, who try to match their children with partners of a similar background and status. The arranged marriage is more a union between two families than between two people, and romantic love is not necessarily present between the marriage partners. They are typically found among Muslims, Sikhs, and Hindus. The arranged marriage is still common in the Asian community in Britain, where the custom is often more strictly enforced than in the Indian sub-continent. This is because the present generation of parents here often still stick to the customs which existed when they left India for Britain many years ago.

Discussion

What are the advantages and disadvantages of arranged marriages? How do you think arranged marriages might be changing in Britain, and what pressures do you think there might be on the survival of the custom in Britain?

Polygamy

While marrying a second partner without divorcing the first is a crime in Britain, in most societies it is perfectly acceptable to have more than one marriage partner at the same time. **Polygamy** is a general term referring to marriage between a member of one sex and two or more members of the opposite sex at the same time. According to Murdock, polygamy is found in about 76 per cent of all societies. There are two different types of polygamy: **polygyny** and **polyandry**.

Polygyny

Polygyny is the marriage of one man to two or more women at the same time. This is very common and is found in about 75 per cent of all societies. It is widely practised in Islamic countries such as Egypt and Saudi Arabia. It is also practised (illegally) among some Mormons in the state of Utah in the USA. The possession of several wives is often seen as a sign of wealth and success and generally only those men who can afford to support several wives practise polygyny. Because of this, even where polygyny is allowed, only a small number of men actually practise it. In any case, the numbers of men and women in most societies are usually fairly evenly balanced, and there are not enough women for all men to have more than one wife.

Polyandry

Polyandry is the marriage of one woman to two or more men at the same time. This is rare and is found in only about 1 per cent of all societies. Polyandry appears to arise where living standards are so low that a man can only afford to support a wife and child by sharing the responsibility with other men. It is found among the Todas of southern India and the Marquesan Islanders, and has been reported as occurring in parts of Tibet.

 Monogamy Polygyny Polyandry
Polygamy

Patterns of Family Inheritance

As well as the variety of marriage relations, there are also differences in the patterns of inheritance in the family. **Patrilineal descent** is the system where the inheritance of title, property, and position as family head is passed down through the male side of the family, from father to son. An example of this is the way the succession to the British throne is passed through the male side of the royal family. **Matrilineal descent** is the system where inheritance is through the female side of the family.

Patterns of Residence

Different societies have different traditions about where the newly married should live. **Patrilocal residence** is the system where a married couple lives by tradition with or near the husband's family. **Matrilocal residence** is the system where the couple lives with or near the wife's family. In modern Britain, families tend to be **neo-local,** in that couples are not expected to move near either the husband's or the wife's family.

Patterns of Authority

Patriarchy is a term used to describe the dominance of men over women. A patriarchal family is one where the father, husband, or eldest male is usually the chief authority and decision-maker. An example of this was the family in Victorian Britain, but many writers would argue the modern British family remains patriarchal. **Matriarchy** describes the dominance of women over men. Matriarchal families are where power and authority is held by the most senior woman. These are rare, but there is some evidence of them in rural Japan.

Table 10.1 Forms of marriage and the family

Forms of:	Description
Marriage	
Monogamy	One husband and one wife Found in Europe, the USA, and most Christian cultures
Serial monogamy	A series of monogamous marriages Found in Europe and the USA, where there are high rates of divorce and remarriage
Arranged marriage	Marriages arranged by parents Found in the Indian sub-continent and Asian community in Britain
Polygamy	Marriage to more than one partner at the same time. Includes polygyny and polyandry

Table 10.1 (cont'd)

Forms of:	Description
Marriage	
Polygyny	One husband and two or more wives Found in Islamic countries like Egypt and Saudi Arabia
Polyandry	One wife and two or more husbands Found in Tibet, among the Todas of southern India, and among the Marquesan islanders
Family Structure	
Nuclear family	Two generations: parents and children
Extended family	More than two generations: grandparents, parents and children, uncles, aunts, etc.
Classic extended family	An extended family sharing the same household or living close by
Modified extended family	An extended family living far apart but keeping in close touch by phone, letters, and frequent visits
Inheritance	
Patrilineal descent	Property and title passes through the male side of the family
Matrilineal descent	Property and title passes through the female side of the family
Residence	
Patrilocal	Married couple live with or near the husband's family
Matrilocal	Married couple live with or near the wife's family
Neo-local	Married couple set up home apart from either the husband's or wife's family
Authority	
Patriarchal family	Authority held by males
Matriarchal family	Authority held by females
Symmetrical family	Authority shared between male and female partners

Table 10.1 (cont'd)

Forms of:	Description
Results of marriage breakdown	
Reconstituted family	One or both partners previously married, with children of previous marriages
Single-parent family	Lone parent, most commonly after divorce or separation (though may also arise from death of a partner or unwillingness to marry)

Changes in the Family in Britain

The family in Britain has gone through a number of changes since the beginnings of industrialization, and it continues to change today. The extent of some of these changes thought to have occurred in the family has often been exaggerated, and misleading conclusions drawn. Each of these changes will be examined in turn. The key changes which have commonly been thought to have occurred are summarized in the box below.

Major changes in the family in Britain

- The changing role of the family in society, with the removal of some tasks once performed by the family to other social institutions, including the state.
- The change from the classic extended family to the privatized nuclear family as the most common form of the family.
- The emergence of the symmetrical family.
- A move to more child-centred families.
- A decline in average family size.
- A rising divorce rate and higher rates of remarriage.

Change 1: The Changing Role of the Family in Society

The family in Britain and most other societies has traditionally had a number of responsibilities placed upon it (its functions), primarily connected with its role in the preparation of children to fit into adult society. These tasks of the family, and how they've changed during the course of this century in Britain, are described below.

Traditional responsibilities	*How they have changed*
• *Reproduction of the population* – the reproduction and nurturing of children. Having children was often seen as the main reason for marriage, as a means of passing on family property and providing a future workforce.	• In Britain in the 1970s and 1980s, there has been a steady increase in the reproduction of children and sexual relations before and outside of marriage. In 1991, for example, nearly 29 per cent of children were born outside marriage. These changes might be explained as follows:

(a) The availability of modern methods of contraception and of safe and legal abortion reduces the risks of unwanted pregnancy.

(b) The decline of extended family life has meant less social pressure from relatives to maintain 'moral standards' and keep sexual relations within marriage.

(c) Growing **secularization** – the decline in importance of religious beliefs, practice, and institutions – means people are less concerned with conforming to religious moral beliefs as guides to their sexual behaviour.

(d) The welfare state has made it easier for a woman to support

- The family and kinship network traditionally played a major role in *maintaining and caring for dependent children* – housing, clothing, and feeding those children who were still unable to look after themselves. Before this century in Britain, most children were often poorly looked after because of poverty.

- The family provided most of the *help and care for the young, the old, the sick, and the poor* during periods of illness, unemployment, and other crises. Poverty often meant poor health and poor health care.

- The *primary socialization and social control of children*. The family is where society's new recruits first learn the basic values and norms of the culture of the society they will grow up in. For example, it is in the family that children first learn the difference between what is seen as 'right' and 'wrong', 'good' and 'bad' behaviour, the norms governing gender roles, and the acceptance of parental and other adult authority. These rules are reinforced by sanctions, such as praise and rewards.

- The family used to be one of the only sources of *education* for young people in Britain, and it still is in many less developed societies. Before compulsory

a child financially without a husband or help from relatives.

- Although the maintenance of children is still very important, the modern nuclear family is less dependent on relatives for this help and assistance, and relies more on the state. Welfare benefits like social security and child benefit, and the social services, including social workers working with families, all help parents to maintain their children.

- This has become shared with the state through the National Health Service and the social services. Old people's homes, hospitals, welfare clinics, GPs, old age pensions, unemployment benefit, and income support reduce the dependence on kin for money and support.

- The family still retains the major responsibility for the socialization of very young children, but the increase in the number of nurseries and playgroups has meant this is no longer restricted to the family. The state educational system now helps the family with the socialization of school-age children, and the mass media also play an important role.

- The education of children has been mainly taken over by the state, and is now primarily the responsibility of professional teachers rather than parents. All

Traditional responsibilities	*How they have changed*
schooling was provided by the state in Britain from 1880, many children from working-class families were very poorly educated by today's standards, and illiteracy rates were extremely high.	children between the ages of 5 and 16 now have to attend school by law. However, the family continues to play an important socializing and supporting role in preparing a child for school, and encouraging and supporting her or him while at school. The family still has a major effect on a child's level of educational achievement.
• Before industrialization and the growth of factory production in Britain, the family was a *unit of production*. This means that the family home was also the workplace, and the family produced most of the goods necessary for its own survival. Children would learn the skills needed for working life from their parents. An example of this was the domestic industry producing wool in eighteenth-century Britain. The whole family, including children, would work at home (hence the 'domestic system'), preparing, spinning, and weaving wool.	• Since the early nineteenth century in Britain, work has been mainly based in factories and offices, not in the home. Families do not generally produce the goods they need any more, they go out and buy them. The skills required for adult working life are therefore no longer learnt in the family, but at the place of work, at colleges or on government schemes like Youth Training.

Activity

1. Go carefully through the section above on the traditional responsibilities or functions of the family and how they have changed. Make a list summarizing these changes under two main headings:
   (a) The tasks traditionally performed by the family.
   (b) Who performs these functions today: family or government and state or shared between them.
2. Identify two ways that the family provides for the well-being of its members.
3. Do you think the changes that have occurred in the family's functions have made it more or less important in society today? Back up your viewpoint with evidence.
4. Imagine all families were banned by law tomorrow. What tasks currently carried out in your own family would someone else have to perform? Who would do these tasks, do you think?
5. Consider all the ways you can think of that the family a child is born into might affect the chances she or he gets in life, such as in health, education, and job opportunities. Be sure you explain the connection between family background and the life chances you identify.

Change 2: The Emergence of the Privatized Nuclear Family

A traditional view in sociology was that the main form of the family in Britain changed from the classic extended family before industrialization to the privatized nuclear family in the late twentieth century. However, research has shown that both nuclear and extended families were common in pre-industrial Britain, with the nuclear family perhaps being the most common. The family in Britain can be said to have developed through three basic stages.

The pre-industrial family

At this stage, the family was a unit of production which produced most of society's goods in small family workshops based in houses and farms (the domestic system), where family members would live and work together. The nuclear family was the most common form of the family.

The early industrial classic extended family

With industrialization in nineteenth-century England, factory production replaced the domestic system, and the family ceased to be a unit of production. People began to go outside the home to work in factories, offices, and mines. Early industrialization strengthened the extended family, especially in the working class. This was because in the new industrial towns wages were low, unemployment was high, housing conditions and health were very poor, and working-class poverty was widespread. Relatives often provided the only sources of help and support against the insecurity and hardship of poverty and unemployment, so most working-class people strengthened links with kin through the formation of extended families.

The late twentieth-century privatized nuclear family

Over about the last one hundred years, a traditional view has been that the extended family has largely disappeared in modern Britain, with the typical family form in Britain becoming the **privatized nuclear family**. This means the nuclear family is separated and isolated from its extended kin, and has become a self-contained, self-reliant, home-centred unit. Life for the modern privatized nuclear family is largely centred on the home – free time is spent doing jobs around the house and leisure is mainly home- and family-centred. DIY, gardening, watching television, or going out as a family to pleasure parks like Alton Towers are typical family activities. The modern nuclear family has thus become a very private institution, isolated from wider kin and often from neighbours and local community life as well.

The following explanations have been offered for this decline of extended family life and the process of privatization.

- Industrial societies require a geographically mobile labour force, with people able and willing to move to other areas of the country to find work, improve their education, or gain promotion. This often involves leaving relatives behind, thus weakening and breaking up traditional extended family life. The small size of the modern isolated nuclear family and its lack of permanent roots in an area (such as wider kin) means that it is geographically mobile, which some sociologists argue makes it ideally suited for life in an industrial society.
- Industrial societies have become more meritocratic – occupational status is mainly achieved on the basis of talent, skill, and educational qualifications, rather than whom you know. Extended kin therefore have less to offer family members, such as job opportunities, reducing reliance on kin.

- Educational success and promotion often involve upward social mobility and this leads to differences in income, status, lifestyle, and attitudes and values between kin. Kin have less in common, and this contributes to the weakening of extended family ties.
- With the development of higher standards of living and the provision of welfare services by the state for security against ill-health, unemployment, and poverty, people have become less dependent on kin for help in times of distress. This further weakens the extended family.

The modified extended family

While there is evidence that nuclear families have become the most common form of the family in industrial society, geographical separation does not necessarily mean all links with kin are severed. Often, in the age of mass communications and easy transportation, the closeness and mutual support between kin, typical of classic extended family life, are retained by letter writing, telephone, and visiting. It has therefore been suggested that the typical family today in Britain is not simply the isolated nuclear family, but a modified form of the extended family: the modified extended family.

The continued existence of the classic extended family

While the most common type of family found in modern Britain is the nuclear family or the modified extended family, there is evidence that the classic extended family still survives today in modern Britain in two types of community:

- Traditional working-class communities. These are long-established communities dominated by one industry, like fishing and mining, in the traditional working-class industrial centres of the north of England, and in inner-city working-class areas. In such communities, there is little geographical or social mobility, and children usually remain in the same area when they get married. People stay in the same community for several generations, and this creates a close-knit community life – it is the type of community shown in TV 'soaps' such as Coronation Street or EastEnders. Members of the extended family live close together and meet frequently, and there is a constant exchange of services between extended family members such as washing, shopping, and baby-sitting between female kin, and shared work and leisure activities between male relatives. Such extended family life is lessening in the 1990s, as traditional industries decline and people are forced to move away in search of new employment.

- The Asian community. There is evidence that the extended family is still very common in the Asian community in Britain – among those who came to this country in the 1960s and 1970s from India, Pakistan and Bangladesh. The extended family usually centres on the male side of the family, with grandfathers, sons, grandsons and their wives and unmarried daughters. Such a family life continues to be an important source of strength and support in such communities.

The return of the extended family?

Britain's ageing population (which is discussed in chapter 15) means that a growing number of people are reaching old age, and often living well into their eighties. This means that there is an increase in the number of extended three- and four-generation families, with more children growing up in extended families alongside several of their grandparents and even great-grandparents. In 1987, for example, 7 per cent of all people aged over 65, and 21 per cent of women over 80 years old, were living with their children. This return of the extended family can only be expected to increase with the growing numbers of the elderly.

The myth of 'cereal packet' families

The popular image of the family in Britain in the late twentieth century has been described as the 'cereal packet family'. This is the image often promoted in advertising, with 'family size' breakfast cereals, toothpaste, and a wide range of other consumer goods. This popular 'happy family' image often gives the impression that most people live in a 'typical family' with the following features:

- It contains two parents and about two dependent children.
- These parents are married to one another, and neither of them has been married before.
- The husband is the breadwinner, with the wife staying at home and primarily concerned with housework and childcare.

This 'cereal packet' image of the 'typical family' is very mistaken, and there is a wide range of family types and household arrangements in modern Britain.

Households and families

Figure 10.1 shows the different types of household in Britain in 1990, and the types of household people were living in (a household is simply either one person living alone or a group of people living together at the same address).

The 'cereal-packet' family

The 'cereal packet' family, with a working father married to a home-based mother caring for two small children, makes up only about 5 per cent of all households.

In 1990, only 25 per cent of households contained a married/cohabiting couple with dependent children, and only 41 per cent of people lived in such a family. This alone shows that the 'cereal packet' image of the nuclear family is not the typical arrangement in which most people in Britain live.

Families with dependent children

Figure 10.2 examines families with dependent children. This shows that in 1990, 20 per cent of such families were single-parent families, nearly nine out of ten of them headed by women. Although 80 per cent of families with dependent children were headed by a married or cohabiting couple, this doesn't mean that most of these families conformed to the 'cereal packet' image.

- A number of these families were reconstituted families, in which one or both partners were previously married. About 10 per cent of children under age 16 lived in such a family in 1991.
- Most of these families were dual-worker families, where both parents were working. In 1989, over half of married couples with children had partners who were both working. As figure 10.3 shows, large numbers of mothers with dependent children work in paid employment, with the

numbers increasing as children get older. In 1990, 60 per cent of all
women with dependent children were working.

- The 'cereal packet' 'happy family' stereotype, of a working father married
  to a home-based mother caring for two small children, in 1990 made up
  about only 5 per cent of all households.

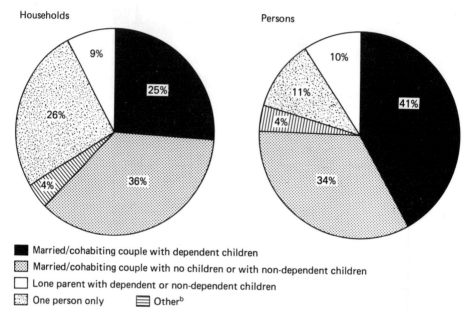

Households   Persons

■ Married/cohabiting couple with dependent children
▨ Married/cohabiting couple with no children or with non-dependent children
□ Lone parent with dependent or non-dependent children
▨ One person only   ☰ Other[b]

Figure 10.1 Households and people: by type of household,[a] Great Britain, 1990

[a]Households categorized by the type of family they contain. In the lone-parent and married-couple
households, other individuals who were not family members may also have been present.
[b]'Other' includes households containing two or more unrelated adults and those containing two or
more families.

Source: OPCS General Household Survey, 1990.

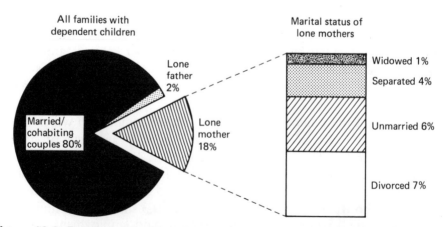

All families with
dependent children   Marital status of
lone mothers

Lone
father
2%

Married/
cohabiting
couples 80%

Lone
mother
18%

Widowed 1%

Separated 4%

Unmarried 6%

Divorced 7%

Figure 10.2 Families with dependent children: by family type and, for lone
mothers, by marital status, Great Britain, 1990

Source: General Household Survey, 1990.

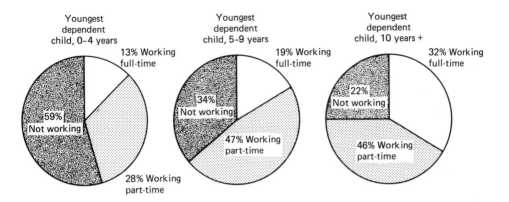

Figure 10.3 Working patterns of mothers with young children, Great Britain, 1990.

Source: Family Change and Future Policy (Family Policy Studies Centre 1990); OPCS General Household Survey, 1990.

Activity

Refer to figure 10.1

1. What percentage of households in 1990 consisted of one person only?
2. What percentage of people in 1990 were living in households consisting of a married or cohabiting couple with no children or with non-dependent children?

Refer to figure 10.2

3. In 1990, what percentage of all families with dependent children were lone-parent families?
4. What percentage of families with dependent children were headed by a lone mother who was widowed?
5. What was the main cause of lone motherhood?

Refer to figure 10.3

6. What percentage of mothers whose youngest child was aged 0–4 years was not working in 1990?
7. Identify two trends which occur as the youngest dependent child gets older.
8. What does figure 10.3 suggest might be the main restriction on mothers with young children going out to work? Suggest ways this restriction might be overcome.
9. Suggest reasons why so many people seem to believe that the 'cereal packet' family is the most common type of family.

Conclusion

This section has suggested that it is very misleading to assume that the 'cereal packet' image of the family represents the reality of family life in Britain. Only a small minority of families are of this type. It is much more realistic to recognize that there is a wide variety of family types in modern Britain, and future trends would suggest growing numbers of extended, dual-worker, reconstituted, and single-parent families.

Change 3: The Emergence of the 'Symmetrical' Family?

There is a common belief that the relations between male and female partner in the family in Britain have become more equal in the second half of the twentieth century. The assumption has been that there has been a change from segregated to integrated conjugal roles, and the emergence of a more 'symmetrical' or equally balanced family, with male partners taking more responsibility for housework and childcare. **Conjugal roles** are simply the roles played by male and female partners in marriage or in a cohabiting couple. There are said to be two main types.

- **Segregated conjugal roles,** where male and female partner play very different roles in the family, with a clear division and separation between the male's role and the female's role.
- **Integrated** (or joint) **conjugal roles,** where there are few divisions between male and female partner's roles.

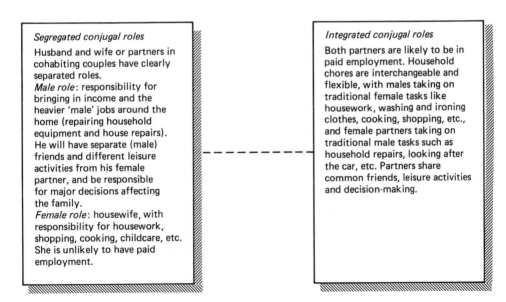

Segregated conjugal roles
Husband and wife or partners in cohabiting couples have clearly separated roles.
Male role: responsibility for bringing in income and the heavier 'male' jobs around the home (repairing household equipment and house repairs). He will have separate (male) friends and different leisure activities from his female partner, and be responsible for major decisions affecting the family.
Female role: housewife, with responsibility for housework, shopping, cooking, childcare, etc. She is unlikely to have paid employment.

Integrated conjugal roles
Both partners are likely to be in paid employment. Household chores are interchangeable and flexible, with males taking on traditional female tasks like housework, washing and ironing clothes, cooking, shopping, etc., and female partners taking on traditional male tasks such as household repairs, looking after the car, etc. Partners share common friends, leisure activities and decision-making.

Figure 10.4 Segregated and integrated conjugal roles

The change from segregated to integrated roles

This supposed change is thought to have occurred for a number of reasons.

- The improved status and rights of women have forced men to accept women more as equals and not simply as housewives and mothers.
- The increasing number of working women has increased women's independence and authority in the family – where the female partner has her own income, she is less dependent on her male partner, and has more power and authority. Decision-making is therefore more likely to be shared.
- The importance of female partners' earnings in maintaining the family's standard of living may have encouraged men to help more with house-work – a recognition that the women cannot be expected to do two jobs at once.
- Improved living standards in the home, such as central heating, TV, videos and stereos, and 'all mod cons', have encouraged men to spend more time at home, and share home-centred leisure with their female partners.
- The decline of the close-knit extended family and greater geographical mobility in industrial society have meant there is less pressure from kin on newly married or cohabiting couples to retain traditional roles – it is therefore easier to adopt new roles in a relationship. There are often no longer the separate male and female networks (of friends and especially kin) for male and female partner to mix with separately. This increases their dependence upon each other, and may avoid the teasing of men who adopt new roles from friends who knew them before they got married or began cohabiting.

The myth of integrated roles

Evidence from the 1988 British Social Attitudes Survey suggests that women still perform the majority of domestic tasks around the home, even when they have paid jobs themselves. Even among full-time working women, where one would expect to find the greatest degree of equality, cooking the evening meal, household cleaning, washing and ironing, and caring for sick children were still mainly performed by women (see figure 10.5). A *World in Action* TV documentary in June 1991 found that housework was the second largest cause of domestic rows after money.

There does seem to be evidence of some role integration in leisure activities and decision-making, but housework and childcare remain predominantly 'women's work'. While men are perhaps more involved in childcare than they used to be, this would appear to be in the more enjoyable activities like

Figure 10.5 Domestic division of labour: household tasks and female
employment status, Great Britain (*Respondents, married or living
as married with children aged under 16*)

Source: Family Change and Future Policy (Family Policy Studies Centre 1990), based on data from
British Social Attitudes Survey, 1988.

playing with the children and taking them out. The more routine jobs such as
bathing and feeding and taking children to the doctor still remain predominantly women's work. A survey by the Child Poverty Action Group in
1984 found that the time spent looking after children under the age of five
was about fifty hours each week, and mothers put in 87 per cent of this time.
It is still predominantly women who get the blame if the house is untidy or
children dirty or badly dressed.

While there does seem to be some evidence of husbands doing marginally
more around the home in recent years, this change would appear to have
been massively exaggerated. In a majority of marriages the traditional roles
of women and men remain.

Activity

How far is there equality between partners in your home? Are men pulling their weight in housework? Put the following questions, based on a *World in Action* programme in June 1991, to your (male) partner or your father:

1. Have you ever ironed your partner's blouse?
2. What foods do your children refuse to eat?
3. What do the following cost: a loaf, a jar of instant coffee, a packet of tea, a packet of butter, a tin of baked beans, a packet of soap-powder, and a packet of toilet rolls?
4. How does the washing machine work?
5. What would you use to clean the kitchen floor?
6. How do you empty the vacuum cleaner bag?
7. What days are the bins emptied?
8. What brand of washing powder do we use?
9. When did you last do the family shopping alone?
10. When did you last draw up the shopping list alone?
11. When did you last clean the loo?
12. What is the children's favourite meal?
13. How many hours a week do you spend on housework?
14. When did you last clean the bathroom or kitchen taps?
15. When did you last clean the bath or shower, or the kitchen/bathroom sinks?

Compare your findings with others in your group. What conclusions do your findings suggest about the apparent change to growing equality between men and women in the family?

Have conjugal roles really changed?

Change 4: The Changing Position of Children in the Family

Children and the family in the nineteenth century

In the nineteenth century, the father and husband was the head of the family, and often had a great deal of authority over other family members. He would have little to do with his children. In upper- and middle-class families, children might see relatively little of their parents, often being sent off to private boarding schools or being looked after by a nanny or governess. In working-class families, children in the early nineteenth century were seen as workers and an economic asset to the family, as they were able to work in the factories and mines and bring money into the house. Generally, children had low status in the family, and children were expected 'to be seen and not heard'.

Children and the family in the twentieth century

During the course of the twentieth century, families have become more child-centred, with family activities and outings often centred on the interests of the children. Parents are more involved with their children, spending more time with them, taking an interest in their activities, discussing decisions with them, and treating them more as equals. Often, the children's welfare is seen as the major family priority, frequently involving the parents in considerable financial sacrifice and cost.

The causes of child-centredness

- Families have got smaller this century, and this means more individual care and attention can be devoted to each child.
- In the nineteenth century, the working week was between 70 and 80 hours for many working-class people. Today, it is more like 39 hours and is continuing to get shorter. This means parents have more time to spend with their children.
- Increasing affluence, with higher wages and a higher standard of living, has benefited children, as more money can be spent on them and their activities.
- The social security system provides a wide range of benefits designed to help parents care for their children. The welfare state has increased demands on parents to look after their children properly: social workers, for example, have a wide range of powers to intervene in families on behalf of children, and have the ultimate power to remove children from families if parents fail to look after them properly.
- Paediatrics, or the science of childhood, has developed this century, with a wide range of research and popular books suggesting how parents should bring up their children to encourage their full development. For example, Dr Spock's childcare books have been sold to millions of parents.

Change 5: The Decline in Average Family Size

Over the last century, the birth rate has been declining in Britain. This has meant that average family size has been dropping, from around 6 children per family in the 1870s to an average 1.8 children per family in 1989. The reasons for this change are discussed in chapter 15 on population.

Change 6: The Rising Divorce Rate

One of the most startling changes in the family in Britain this century has been the general and dramatic increase in the number of marriages to end in divorce, as shown in figure 10.6. The number of divorces has risen from 29 000 in 1951 to 151 000 in 1989, with the number of divorces doubling during the 1970s. Britain has one of the highest **divorce rates** (numbers divorcing per thousand married people) in Europe, and an estimated 1 in 3 marriages in 1989 were likely to end in divorce. At the present rate of increase almost 40 per cent of marriages in England and Wales will ultimately end in divorce.

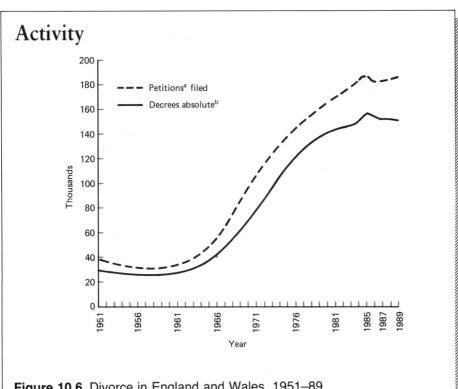

Activity

Figure 10.6 Divorce in England and Wales, 1951–89

[a]A request to a court for a divorce.
[b]The final divorce.

Source: Data from *Social Trends 12, 21* (HMSO 1982, 1991).

Study figure 10.6 and answer the following questions:

1. Approximately how many divorce petitions were filed in 1956?
2. How many decrees absolute were there in 1966?
3. In what year was there the highest number of decrees absolute?
4. How many more decrees absolute were there in 1981 than in 1971?
5. Figure 10.6 shows there is a large difference between the number of divorce petitions (requests to a court to grant a divorce) and the number of decrees absolute (the final divorce) granted. Suggest explanations for this.

Divorce and 'broken homes'

Divorce is the legal termination of a marriage, but this is not the only way that marriages and homes can be 'broken'. Homes and marriages may be broken in 'empty shell' marriages, where the marital relationship has broken down, but no divorce has taken place. Separation – either through choice or necessity (like working abroad or imprisonment) – may also cause a broken home, as may the death of a partner. So homes may be broken for reasons other than divorce, and divorce itself is often only the end result of a marriage which broke down long before.

Who gets divorced?

While divorce affects all groups in the population, there are some groups where divorce rates are higher than the average. Teenage marriages are twice as likely to end in divorce as those of couples married in their twenties, and there is a high incidence of divorce in the first five years of marriage and after about fifteen years (when the children are older or have left home). Childless couples and partners from different social class or religious backgrounds also face a higher risk of divorce.

Activity

Go through each of the groups above, and suggest explanations why each of these groups is more at risk of divorce than the rest of the population. Can you think of other groups who might have a higher risk of divorce than most people?

Explanations for the rising divorce rate

Rising divorce rates must be treated with considerable caution, and assessed against changing legal, financial, and social circumstances, if misleading conclusions about the declining importance of marriage and the family are to be avoided. The increase may simply reflect easier and cheaper divorce procedures enabling the legal termination of already unhappy 'empty shell' marriages rather than a real increase in marriage breakdowns. It could be that people who in previous years could only separate are now divorcing as legal and financial obstacles are removed.

There are two broad groups of reasons for the increase in the divorce rate. Firstly, there have been changes in the law which have gradually made divorce easier and cheaper to get. Each change in the divorce law has increased the divorce rate. However, legal changes alone do not explain the increasing divorce rate – legal changes often reflect changing social attitudes and norms. The second group of explanations is therefore made up of those changes in society which have made divorce a more practical and socially acceptable way of terminating a broken marriage.

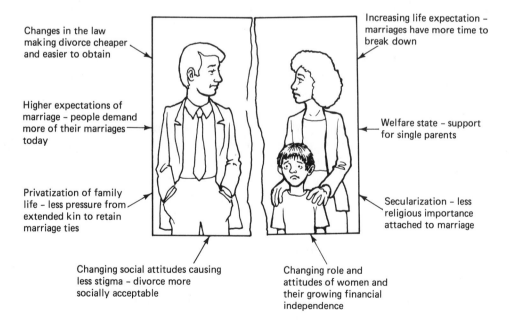

Figure 10.7 The causes of the rising divorce rate

Changes in the law

Before 1857, divorce could only be obtained by the rich, since each divorce needed a private Act of Parliament. As a result, there were very few divorces. Since that time, changes in the law have made it easier to get a divorce, particularly during the twentieth century.

The Matrimonial Causes Act of 1857 This made divorce procedure easier and cheaper, but still beyond the financial means of the lower middle class and the working class. Men had more rights in divorce than women, and divorce was only possible if it could be proved in court that a 'matrimonial offence' such as adultery, cruelty, or desertion had been committed.

The Matrimonial Causes Act of 1923 This gave women equal rights with men in divorce for the first time, and therefore gave more women the opportunity to terminate unhappy marriages.

The Legal Aid and Advice Act of 1949 This gave financial assistance with the costs of solicitors' and court fees, which made it far more possible for working-class people to cope with the costs of a divorce action.

The Divorce Law Reform Act of 1969 This came into effect in 1971, and was a major change. Before the 1969 Act, a person wanting a divorce had to prove before a court that his or her spouse had committed a 'matrimonial offence' such as adultery, cruelty, or desertion. This frequently led to major public scandals, as all the details of unhappy marriages were aired in a public law court. This may have intimidated many people whose marriage had broken down from seeking a divorce. Also, marriages may have broken down – become 'empty shell' marriages – without any matrimonial offence being committed.

The 1969 Act changed all this, and made 'irretrievable breakdown' of a marriage the only grounds for divorce. It is now no longer necessary to prove one partner 'guilty' of a matrimonial offence, but simply to demonstrate that a marriage has broken down beyond repair. After 1971, one way of demonstrating 'irretrievable breakdown' of a marriage was by two years of separation. This change in the law led to a massive increase in the number of divorces after 1971.

The Matrimonial and Family Proceedings Act of 1984 This allowed couples to petition for divorce after only one year of marriage, whereas previously couples could normally divorce only after three years of marriage. This led to a record increase in the number of divorces in 1984 and 1985.

Changes in society

The changing role of women This is a very important explanation for the rising divorce rate. As figure 10.8 shows, over 7 out of 10 (73 per cent) divorce petitions (requests to a court for a divorce) are presented by women. This suggests more women than men are unhappy with the state of their marriages, and are more likely to take the first steps in ending a marriage. This may well be because women's expectations of life and marriage have risen during the course of the twentieth century, and they are less willing to accept a traditional housewife/mother role, with the sacrifices to their own lives, independence, and careers this involves.

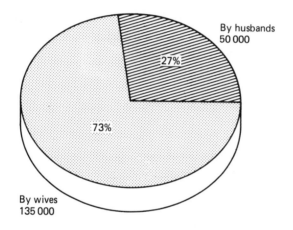

Figure 10.8 Petitions filed for divorce by husbands and wives, England and Wales, 1989

The employment of married women has increased this century. For example, in 1931, only 10 per cent of married women were employed, but this has gradually risen to about 70 per cent in 1991. This has increased their financial independence, and reduced the extent of dependence on their husbands. This makes it easier for women to escape from unhappy marriages, and in the event of marriage breakdown, there are a range of welfare state benefits to help divorced women, particularly those with children.

Higher expectations of marriage People's expectations of what marriage should be like have risen this century, and couples (especially women) expect and demand far more from married life today than their parents might have settled for. The mass media (especially television) often emphasize the romantic aspects of marriage, and they also provide us with images of and insights into other people's relationships which earlier generations didn't have. People therefore have come to expect more companionship, under-standing, and sexual compatibility in their marriage, rather than the financial security which seemed more important in the past. Consequently couples are more likely to end a relationship which earlier generations might have tolerated.

Changing social attitudes Divorce has become more socially acceptable, and there is less social disapproval and condemnation (*stigmatizing*) of divorcees. Divorce no longer hinders careers through a public sense of scandal and outrage. As a result, people are less afraid of the consequences of divorce, and are more likely to seek a legal end to an unhappy marriage rather than simply separating or carrying on in an 'empty shell' marriage.

Growing secularization Secularization – the decline in religious belief – has meant that divorce is not seen so much today as breaking solemn vows or morally wrong, and many people today probably do not attach much religious significance to their marriage.

Increasing life expectation People live to a greater age than they did in the early years of the twentieth century, and this means the potential number of years a couple may be together, before the death of a partner occurs, has increased. This gives more time for marriages to 'go wrong' and for divorces to occur. It has been suggested that the divorce courts have taken on the role in finishing unhappy marriages that the undertaker once did!

The growth of the privatized nuclear family This has meant that, during marital crises, it is no longer so easy for marriage partners to seek advice from or temporary refuge with relatives, and there is also less social control from extended kin pressuring couples to retain marriage ties.

Activity

1. Go through all the reasons suggested above for the rising divorce rate, putting them in the order which you think are most important.
2. Study television advertisements or television 'soaps' for a few days. What kind of overall impressions are given of married life today? Refer to particular advertisements or 'soaps' as evidence for your findings. Do you agree or disagree with the view that these create higher expectations of marriage today? Explain the reasons for your answer.
3. Of couples married in 1987, 58 per cent of men and 53 per cent of women said that they had lived with their partners beforehand, and

living together before marriage was seen as one of the major social changes of the 1980s. However, many of these people eventually marry. What social pressures are there that push people towards conforming to the norm of marriage? Write down all the reasons you can think of why so many people continue to marry eventually, despite the high divorce rate and previous experience of living together outside marriage. Discuss your reasons with others in your class.

Critical Views of the Family

The 'cereal packet' image of the 'typical family' has already been questioned earlier in this chapter, but the view of the warm and supportive 'happy family' which is often presented in the mass media has been questioned on a more fundamental level by many writers.

The 'Darker Side' of Family Life

Today the domestic household is isolated. The family looks inward upon itself; there is an intensification of emotional stress between husband and wife, and parents and children. The strain is greater than most of us can bear. Far from being the basis of the good society, the family, with its narrow privacy and tawdry secrets, is the source of all our discontents. (Edmund Leach in the 1967 BBC Reith Lectures)

While the family is often a warm and supportive unit for its members, it can also be a hostile and dangerous place. The growing privatization of family life can lead to emotional stress in the family. Family members are thrown together, isolated from and lacking the support of extended kin, neighbours, and the wider community. Tempers become easily frayed, emotional temperatures and stress levels rise, and – as in a pressure cooker without a safety valve – explosions occur, and family conflict is the result. This may lead to violence, divorce, psychological damage to children, perhaps even mental illness and crime.

The breakdown of marriages which leads to divorce is often the end result of long-running and bitter disputes between partners. The intense emotions involved in family life often mean that incidents that would appear trivial in other situations take on the proportion of major confrontations inside the family. The extent of violence in the family is coming to increasing attention, with rising reports of the physical and sexual abuse of children, the rape of wives by their husbands, and wife- and baby-battering. One in four murders takes place in the family. This is the darker side of family life.

Because of the private nature of the family, accurate evidence on the extent of violence and abuse inside the family is difficult to obtain, and fear or shame means that it is almost certain that most of such incidents are covered up.

The abuse of children

There are two kinds of abuse of children: sexual abuse and physical abuse. Sexual abuse refers to adults using their power to perform sex acts with children below the age of consent (16 for heterosexual and lesbian acts and 21 for male homosexual acts). Physical abuse refers to non-sexual violence. Much child abuse goes undiscovered, but social workers suggest it is far more common than we are led to believe.

Evidence suggests that 1 in 8 females and 1 in 12 males have had at least one sexually abusive experience before the age of 16, nearly always carried out by males (97 per cent), and much of it by relatives. Rape Crisis Centre figures suggest that the number of females under age 16 experiencing sexual abuse may be as high as 1 in 4.

The NSPCC in 1989 (see figure 10.9) estimated that there were at least 17 000 children under 16 facing physical or sexual abuse in England and Wales, with a further 19 000 at risk, including those facing neglect and emotional abuse. Between 1983 and 1989, the estimated number of children registered as at risk, neglected, or sexually, emotionally, or physically abused more than trebled from just under 12 000 to over 36 000.

Activity

Study figure 10.9 and answer the following questions:

1. About how many children in total under 16 were physically or sexually abused or at risk in 1985?
2. About how many children were sexually abused in 1989?

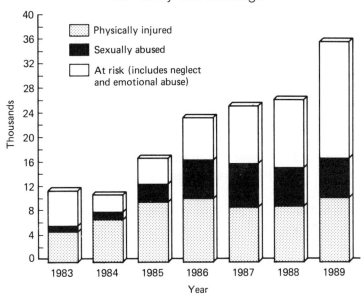

Figure 10.9 Physical and sexual abuse: estimated number of children aged 0–16, England and Wales, 1983–9

Source: NSPCC Research Briefing no. 11, 'Child abuse in 1989' (NSPCC 1990).

3. About how many more children under 16 were physically injured in 1989 compared to 1984?
4. Suggest reasons why the number of child abuse cases recorded in the NSPCC report might be inaccurate. Do you think that the large increase in the number of reported cases of child abuse means the problem is growing? What other explanations might there be for the increasing reporting of child abuse?

Violence against women

There is widespread evidence of violence by men against their female partners – battered wives. Such violence is often not taken very seriously by the police or courts, being dismissed as a 'domestic dispute' – which seems to suggest violence against women is seen in some quarters as an acceptable and normal part of a relationship! Certainly the type of physical violence women are subjected to by their male partners would quite probably result in prosecution and imprisonment if it was carried out against a stranger outside the family. The widespread growth of refuges for battered women since the 1970s reflects the extent and seriousness of the problem of violence against women in the home, much of which goes unreported and undiscovered.

Rape in marriage

Rape is when someone is forced to have sex against her or his will, often accompanied by the actual or threatened use of violence. A representative survey carried out in 1989 for Granada Television's *World in Action* programme reported that over one in four (28 per cent) of women had been raped, with most rapes being committed by husbands on their wives.

- One in seven women (14 per cent) in the survey had been raped by their husbands, compared with 12 per cent by acquaintances and boyfriends, and 2 per cent by strangers.
- Four out of five of the raped wives reported that rape by their husbands was a frequent occurrence.
- Nearly half (44 per cent) of the rapes within marriage were accompanied by the actual or threatened use of violence.
- One in five wives suffered physical injury.

Such sexual violence in the family, then, would appear to be disturbingly common, but only as recently as 1991 was rape within marriage confirmed as a criminal offence by the Court of Appeal.

A critical view of marriage

Feminist Criticisms of the Family

Feminist writers – those concerned with establishing equal rights for women – have been responsible for highlighting much of the violence against women in the family. However, they also have a range of other criticisms of the family, arguing that it is an institution that serves men's needs better than women's, and that it particularly oppresses and exploits women. Many of these criticisms are covered in other chapters, and the following is simply a brief summary of them.

- Far from the popular impression of growing equality between male and female partners in the family, inequalities continue. As seen earlier in this chapter, women still have most of the responsibility for housework, even when they are in full-time employment. Most women work both outside the home in paid employment, and inside the home as housewives and mothers. They have two jobs to the man's one.
- Feminists emphasize that housework is, in fact, unpaid labour. The value of the housework performed free by many women is illustrated by the Mercantile and General insurance company's 'Housewife's sickness income benefit', introduced in 1991. This paid benefits up to £10 000 per year or £192 per week to cover the costs of hiring help should a housewife be no longer able to perform domestic tasks such as food preparation, shopping, cleaning, and other household tasks (See chapter 6).
- It is still mainly women who give up paid work (or suffer from lost/restricted job opportunities) to look after children, the old, the sick, and male partners. Women still take most of the responsibility for child care and child rearing, and are most likely to get the blame from society if these tasks are not performed 'properly'.
- As seen in chapter 6, women's position in the family remains a primary source of discrimination and disadvantage in the labour market. Employers are often unwilling to employ or promote married women. Marriage poses no such problem for men.
- The family is a major source of gender role socialization, which causes women to underachieve (do less well than they are able) in a wide range of areas, and which keeps women in a secondary position to men in many areas of social life.

Looked at from these points of view, women have much to lose from the present organization of the family.

Discussion

Discuss the view that men have much to gain, and women much to lose, from marriage and the family.

Alternatives to the Family

Communes

Communes are self-contained and self-supporting communities. These developed in Western Europe, Britain, and the USA in the 1960s, among groups of people wanting to develop alternative lifestyles to conventional society because of the political or religious beliefs they held.

Communes often try to develop an alternative style of living and a kind of alternative household, with the emphasis on collective living rather than individual family units. A number of adults and children all aim to live and work together, with children being seen as the responsibility of the group as a whole rather than of natural parents. Many communes tended to be very short-lived, and only a few remain in Britain today.

The Kibbutz

The Israeli **kibbutz** is a form of commune, and is one of the most famous and successful attempts to establish an alternative to the family. Here, the emphasis is on collective child rearing, with the community as a whole taking over the tasks of the family. In the early kibbutzim, child rearing was separated as much as possible from the marriage relationship, with children kept apart from their natural parents for much of the time and brought up in the Children's House by metapelets. These were a kind of 'professional parent' combining the roles of nurse, housemother, and educator. The role of the natural parents was extremely limited, and they were only allowed to see their children for short periods each day. Children slept at the Children's House. The children were seen as the 'children of the kibbutz' – they were the responsibility of the community as a whole, which met all of their needs.

Children would move through a series of children's homes with others of the same age group until they reached adulthood.

In recent years, the more traditional family unit has re-emerged in the kibbutzim, with natural parents and children sharing the same accommodation, but the kibbutz remains one of the most important attempts to find an alternative to conventional family structures.

Are Marriage and the Family Declining Social Institutions?

The Case for Decline

In 1989, it was estimated that more than 1 in 3 marriages would end in divorce, and it was estimated almost 1 in 4 (24 per cent) children would experience a parental divorce by their sixteenth birthday. In Britain today, about 1 in 5 families with dependent children has just one parent. In 1991, nearly 29 per cent of births were outside of marriage. There are well over a million cohabiting couples who have refused to tie the marriage knot – 1 in 12 of all couples. Of couples married in 1987, 58 per cent of men and 53 per cent of women said they had lived with their partners beforehand, and living together before marriage was seen as one of the major social changes of the 1980s.

It is statistics like these which have made the state of the family a major battleground for politicians, with the suggestion that the very existence of the family is threatened by rising rates of divorce, cohabitation, single parenthood, and reconstituted families. This picture of the family in decline has been blamed for a wide range of social ills, such as declining moral standards, social disorder, drug abuse, rising crime rates, vandalism, football hooliganism, and increasing levels of violence in society. However, this view of the family in decline has to be treated with considerable caution: the causes of those social ills all too often blamed on the family are many and complex, and those who blame the family are often searching for simple solutions to complex problems.

The Case against Decline

Although the divorce rate has gone up, the evidence suggests that it is easier divorce laws, reduced social stigma, and more sympathetic public attitudes which have caused this, rather than more marriage breakdowns. In the past, many couples may have been condemned, by legal and financial obstacles and social intolerance, to suffer unhappy 'empty shell' marriages or to separate without divorcing. If the law were changed to make divorce harder to get, couples would continue to separate without divorcing.

Marriages today are more likely to be based on love and companionship rather than the custom and financial necessity of the past. Of all divorced people, 75 per cent remarry, a third of them within a year of getting divorced. This shows that what they are rejecting is not the institution of marriage itself, but a particular marriage partner – they divorce hoping to turn an unhappy marriage into a new, happier one. The marriages that exist today are therefore probably much stronger and happier than ever, since unhappy relationships are easily ended by divorce.

Many of those who cohabit eventually marry, and about 80 per cent of the population are married by the age of 50. It would appear that marriage remains an important social institution, even in the light of the high divorce rate and previous experience of living together outside marriage.

Despite the record numbers of children being born outside of marriage, over 73 per cent of those births in 1990 were registered jointly by the parents, and the same address was given by both parents in nearly three out of four of these cases. This suggests that most children are still being born into a stable relationship, and live in families with concerned parents who are simply reluctant to tie the legal marriage knot. Most dependent children still live in families headed by a married or cohabiting couple. In 1985, 78 per cent of children in Britain under the age of 16 were living with both natural parents who were legally married to one another.

What really seems to be happening is not so much that the family and marriage are in decline but that they are changing. There are more single-parent families, more reconstituted families, more experiments in living together before marriage, and fewer people being prepared to marry simply to bring up children. Nevertheless, marriage remains an important social norm, and strong pressures from parents, peer groups, and the responsibilities brought about by the birth of children continue to propel most people into marriage. The ideal of the family as a stable and supportive unit for one or two parents and children perhaps still remains intact.

Discussion

Is the family of less importance in society today than it used to be?

Chapter Summary

After studying this chapter, you should be able to:

- Describe the different forms of marriage and the family.
- Describe how the role of the family in society has changed.
- Explain the change from the classic extended family to the privatized nuclear family (or modified extended family) and provide evidence for the continued existence of the extended family.
- Explain the link between the nuclear family and industrial society.
- Explain why the 'cereal packet' image of the family is an inaccurate view of the family in modern Britain.
- Explain the apparent change from segregated to integrated conjugal roles, and criticize the view that marriages have become partnerships of equals.
- Explain why families have become more child-centred.
- Explain the reasons for the rising divorce rate and identify the groups most at risk of divorce.
- Criticize, with evidence, the view that the family is a 'happy' institution.
- Describe alternatives to the family.
- Explain the arguments and evidence for and against the view that the family and marriage are of declining social importance.

Project Suggestions

1. Investigate how far conjugal roles have really become more integrated, by carrying out a series of interviews with five or six families in the community to discover how work is divided between men and women in the home. Use equal numbers of middle-class and working-class families and/or different age groups and/or different ethnic groups to discover whether there are any social class, age, or ethnic differences. You might use the questions earlier in this chapter on equality of partners in your home as a basis for your research.
2. Using secondary sources, carry out a study of the variety of family types in Britain today. Alternatively, carry out a survey in your school, college, or workplace about the types of family people live in and how family life differs between nuclear and extended families. Take into account different class, ethnic, or religious backgrounds.
3. Carry out a survey of attitudes towards arranged marriages among different age groups or males and females in the Asian community.

4. Carry out a study among single-parent families, finding out the major problems they encounter.
5. Carry out a survey on attitudes to divorce among a small sample of people from different religious, ethnic, or age groups.

Key Terms

arranged marriage
bigamy
classic extended family
communes
conjugal roles
divorce rate
feminist
integrated conjugal roles
kibbutz
kinship
matriarchy
matrilineal descent
matrilocal residence
modified extended family
monogamy
neo-local residence
nuclear family
patrilineal descent
patrilocal residence
polyandry
polygamy
polygyny
privatized nuclear family
reconstituted family
secularization
segregated conjugal roles
serial monogamy
symmetrical family

11 Schooling in Britain

Education is a major social institution, and schools in Britain command a captive audience of virtually all children between the ages of 5 and 16. During this period of compulsory schooling, children spend about half of the time they are awake at school – about 15 000 hours of their lives.

The sociology of education covers a vast area, and it is impossible in this book to cover all aspects. This chapter therefore takes as its focus the school system, rather than further and higher education, and concentrates on two main aspects of this: the main changes which have occurred in the school system since 1944, and what the purposes of education are.

Photos: Michael Dyer LRPS.

Education in Britain before 1944

The pattern of free and compulsory state education we know today is a relatively recent phenomenon in Britain. It was only in 1870 that the state first began to provide free education, and this was only made compulsory in 1880. One of the major pressures for this came from the need for a numerate and literate population, who could learn the increasingly complex skills they required for adult working life in an industrial society.

The Forster Education Act of 1870 established free elementary schools, which provided a very limited and narrow education in the 'three Rs' of reading, writing, and arithmetic, with often a fourth 'R' of religion added as well. However, secondary education (which taught a much wider range of subjects, equipping people for middle-class jobs) remained restricted mainly to middle-class children because the schools were fee-paying.

Until 1944, most children attended only free and compulsory elementary schools to the age of 14, with their limited educational opportunities and narrow curriculum (a curriculum is a course of study). The education system was therefore divided along social class lines, with a fee-paying secondary education for middle-class children leading to middle-class jobs as adults, and a free and compulsory elementary education for the working class leading only to working-class jobs. Figure 11.1 illustrates this class-divided system of schooling.

The limited education of the majority of the population was shown when, in the Second World War (1939–45), many army recruits were found to be illiterate. Many had ability, but had not been able to receive a secondary education because their parents could not afford the fees. This wastage of human resources and talent made many people fear that Britain's industrial position would be threatened by such a poorly educated labour force.

Figure 11.1 The education system before 1944

It was against this background of the need for educational reform that the Butler Education Act of 1944 made secondary education free and compulsory for all to the age of 15.

Secondary Education for All: The Tripartite System

The 1944 Education Act introduced three stages of free state education: primary (age 5–11), secondary (age 11–15), and further education. All children were to go through the primary and secondary stages, with the secondary stage divided into three types of school. These three types of secondary school became known as the **tripartite system**. The 1944 Act was based on the principle of equality of educational opportunity.

> The principle of **equality of educational opportunity** is that every child, regardless of social class background, ability to pay school fees, ethnic background, or sex, should have an equal chance of doing as well as his or her ability will allow.

The 1944 Education Act tried to ensure equality of educational opportunity in three main ways:

- Secondary education was made free and compulsory for all.
- Three kinds of secondary school were set up to cater for children with three different types of ability, so all children would have a chance to develop to the full whatever abilities they had.

- These three types of school were all meant to be of equal status so no-one would have better or worse chances in life depending on the sort of school she or he went to. This idea of 'equal but different' was known as **parity of esteem.**

The 11+ Exam and the Three Types of Secondary School

The 1944 Education Act assumed children could be divided up into three categories, with three different types of ability and aptitude, that could best develop their potential in three different types of secondary school. It was thought these three different sorts of ability were fixed by the age of 11, were unlikely to change, and could be reliably and accurately measured at age 11 by a special intelligence quotient test (IQ test). This became known as the 11+ exam. According to how well they did in this exam, children went to one of three different types of secondary school, which were thought to provide the most suitable environment for pupils to develop to the full the different types of talent they had.

- The top 15–20 per cent of children passing the 11+ exam went to *grammar schools*, where they followed an academic curriculum preparing them for GCE 'O' and 'A' levels at ages 16 and 18.
- The 'less academic' pupils who showed more practical ability were sent to *technical schools*, aimed at occupations like technicians, engineers, and skilled manual work. Not many of these schools were developed.
- The large majority (about 60–70 per cent) who failed their 11+ were sent to *secondary modern schools*, which were thought to be more suited to lower-ability pupils.

This tripartite system, with three types of secondary school catering for children of three different types of ability, was based on the idea that it was possible to predict at the age of 11 the type of occupation children would be suited to as adults, and therefore select them for an appropriate form of education. Figure 11.2 illustrates the tripartite system, and the social class into which most pupils went from each type of school.

Criticisms of the Tripartite System

There were a number of criticisms of the tripartite system, which made many people question the fairness of the selection process and led them to doubt the claim that the system was offering real equality of educational opportunity.

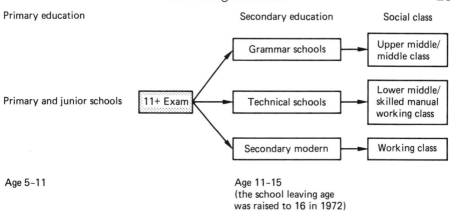

Figure 11.2 The tripartite system after the 1944 Education Act

Criticism	*Explanation*

- The 11+ exam was an unfair, unreliable, and inaccurate selection test.

- The 11+ IQ test proved to be very unreliable as an indicator of ability and future potential. Some very bright pupils failed the 11+, and the exam did not allow for late developers (children whose ability develops as they get older). A report as early as 1957 estimated at least 12 per cent of children were sent to the 'wrong' schools. It became clear that intelligence wasn't fixed at the age of 11 and could be improved with good teaching and encouragement.

- There was no parity of esteem between the three types of school. Grammar schools offered better life chances to their pupils.

- The grammar schools always had higher status than the technical or secondary modern schools, and were seen by parents, employers, and pupils themselves as better schools. They had better teachers and facilities, and only they provided the educational qualifications necessary for better-paid middle-class jobs. Not many technical schools were set up, and secondary modern schools were generally seen as inferior schools, with less qualified staff, poorer facilities, and limited educational and job opportunities for their

Criticism	*Explanation*
	pupils. There were no academic exams in secondary modern schools until the CSE was introduced in the 1960s, and more than 75 per cent of all pupils were leaving school without any academic qualifications, and so often only had access to lower-status and poorer-paid, working-class occupations.
• The system reinforced social class divisions.	• More middle-class children passed the 11+ exam and went to grammar school than working-class children. Working-class children were more likely to go to low-status secondary modern schools. The education system was therefore continuing to divide people along social class lines as it had done before the 1944 Education Act.
• The **self-fulfilling prophecy** meant that many pupils in secondary modern schools were almost guaranteed to fail in education.	• Much research has suggested that predicting whether a child will be a 'success' or 'failure' through testing or teachers' judgements, and labelling them as 'bright' or 'slow', can actually make that child a success or failure. Such predictions and labelling can affect an individual's view of him or herself – his or her self-esteem – and the individual will act in accordance with that prediction and labelling. This process of predicting that something will happen, and pupils acting the way teachers expect them to act in accordance with the label they have been given, is known as the *self-fulfilling prophecy*. Figure 11.3 illustrates this process. Teachers in secondary modern schools often had low expectations of pupils labelled as 'failures' and 'not very bright' after the 11+ exam. Such pupils often lowered their aspirations and, because of the self-fulfilling prophecy, were almost guaranteed to fail.

- There were geographical differences in the availability of grammar school places.

The opposite process occurred for many grammar school pupils.

- There were many more grammar school places available in some parts of the country than others. This meant children in some areas had a better chance of getting a grammar school place, so that where a child lived, rather than her or his ability, could affect whether she or he got a grammar school place or not.

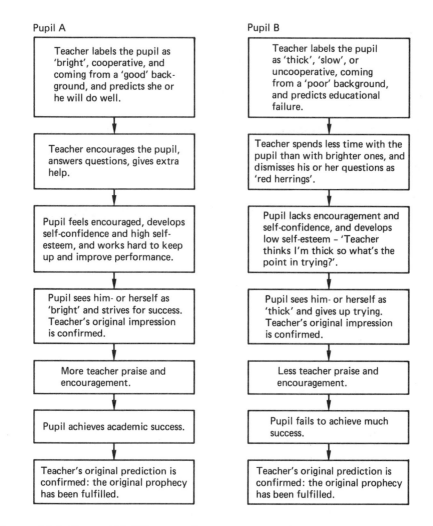

Figure 11.3 The self-fulfilling prophecy: two examples

Research in the 1950s and early 1960s suggested that the talent, ability, and potential of many children in the secondary modern schools were being wasted. It was felt that this wasted talent could be better developed in comprehensive schools, as these would enable more people to obtain qualifications and train for the skilled occupations which the economy desperately needed. As a result, in the 1960s the tripartite system began to be replaced in most of the country by comprehensive education.

Discussion

1. Do you think that the intelligence you are born with is fixed for all time? How do you think teachers and schools might improve the ability of people to think, develop their skills, and improve their intelligence?
2. Have you had any experience of the self-fulfilling prophecy in your own schooling? How do you know whether teachers think you are 'bright' or not, and how do you think this has affected your progress?

Comprehensive Schools

A comprehensive school is one which accepts pupils of all abilities. Comprehensive reorganization of secondary education was a further attempt to achieve equality of educational opportunity, and to overcome the basic unfairness and inequalities of the tripartite system and the self-fulfilling prophecy which it created.

Comprehensive education abolished both selection at age 11 by the 11+ exam and the three types of secondary school. Children in most areas now, regardless of their ability, generally transfer to the same type of school at the age of 11 (or 12), with no selection by examination (although parents have some choice over which school their children attend).

The Advantages of Comprehensive Schools

- The possibility of educational success and obtaining qualifications remains open throughout a child's school career, since moving between streams and classes within one school is easier and more likely to happen than moving between different types of school in the tripartite system.
- Late developers, whose intelligence and ability improve later in life, can be catered for better in the comprehensive system.
- Talent is less likely to be wasted, particularly among working-class children, and there is more opportunity for all children to reach their full potential and gain some educational qualifications.
- The large size of many comprehensive schools means there are more teachers teaching a wider range of subjects to meet the needs of pupils of all abilities, with a wide variety of equipment and facilities. This benefits all pupils and gives them greater equality of opportunity to develop whatever talents they may have. Fewer children leave school without any qualifications in the comprehensive system, and more obtain higher standards than under the tripartite system.
- If all children attend the same type of school, then children of different social classes are more likely to mix together, thus avoiding the social class divisions between grammar schools and secondary modern schools found in the tripartite system. This might promote better understanding between people from different social class backgrounds.

Criticisms of Comprehensive Schools

Comprehensive schools are not without their critics.

- Setting up comprehensive schools often involved merging several schools on different sites, and a lot of time may be wasted in moving between different buildings.
- Their large size may make it impossible for staff to know all pupils personally, and this may create discipline problems and the talents of individuals may not be noticed and developed.
- Where comprehensives draw their pupils from a certain neighbourhood, the social class pattern of that neighbourhood will be reflected in the school. For example, a working-class neighbourhood will have mainly

working-class pupils, so the aim of social mixing between children of different social classes is defeated.

- One of the major criticisms is that because they contain pupils of all abilities, brighter children are held back by the slower pace of learning of the less able. Critics argue this wouldn't have happened in the grammar schools which catered for 'high-flyers'.

Activity

Drawing on the material above and your own experiences at school, whether a comprehensive or grammar school, list the advantages and disadvantages of your particular school.

Streaming

One of the problems which remain in comprehensive schools is that of streaming. Streaming or banding is a system used in schools to separate pupils into different groups according to their predicted ability. Many comprehensives continue to stream pupils, and this has been shown to be unfair and harmful to the self-esteem and educational performance of bottom-stream pupils, particularly those from working-class and ethnic minority (especially Afro-Caribbean (West Indian)) backgrounds.

Evidence suggests that teachers' judgements of pupils' ability are influenced by factors other than ability alone. For example, teachers seem to take into account things like standards of behaviour, dress and speech. They also seem to be influenced by the social class background of pupils, with the assumption that pupils from middle-class backgrounds are 'brighter' than those from working-class homes. Streaming therefore seems to reflect the class divisions in society, with many children from lower working-class homes placed in lower streams.

Activity

1. In a streamed school, the best and most qualified teachers are often kept for the upper-stream classes. Why do you think this is the case?
2. List all the reasons you can think of to explain why pupils from lower working-class homes are more likely to be placed in lower streams than those from middle-class homes.

Once placed in bottom streams, pupils may become victims of the self-fulfilling prophecy discussed earlier – those pupils labelled as 'bottom-stream material' may take on the characteristics expected of them by teachers. Because more working-class children tend to be put into bottom streams by teachers, and middle-class children continue to dominate the higher streams, streamed comprehensives continue to divide pupils along social class lines in much the same way as the tripartite system did, except this time it is in the same school. Figure 11.4 illustrates this process.

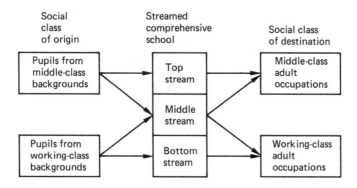

Figure 11.4 Social class divisions and streaming

The anti-school sub-culture

Most schools generally place a high value on things such as hard work, good behaviour, and exam success. One of the effects of streaming is to divide pupils into those in the top streams who more or less conform to these aims and therefore achieve high status, and those in the bottom streams who are labelled as 'failures' by the school and are therefore deprived of status. In response to this, bottom-stream pupils often rebel against the school and develop an alternative set of values, attitudes, and behaviour in opposition to the aims of the school. This is called an **anti-school sub-culture**, and provides a means for bottom-stream pupils to achieve some success and status in their peer group. Among such pupils, truancy, playing up teachers, messing about, breaking the school rules, and generally disrupting the smooth running of the school become a way of getting back at the system and resisting a schooling which has labelled them as 'failures' and denied them status.

The anti-school sub-culture

Activity

Study table 11.1 and answer the following questions:

1. What average change occurred in the test scores of children in a lower stream whose test score at 8 years of age was 55–7?
2. What average change occurred in the test scores of children in an upper stream whose test score at 8 years of age was 46–8?
3. Which ability group in which stream showed:
   (a) the greatest deterioration in test scores?
   (b) the greatest improvement in test scores.?
4. What does table 11.1 suggest about the effects of streaming on children's educational performance? List all the factors you can think of which might explain this, drawing on your own experiences at school.

Table 11.1 The effects of streaming on children's recorded ability
between the ages of 8 and 11 years

Measured ability at 8 years of age – test scores	Children in an *upper* stream	Children in a *lower* stream
	Average change in test scores between 8 and 11 years	Average change in test scores between 8 and 11 years
41–45	+ 5.67	– 0.95
46–48	+ 3.70	– 0.62
49–51	+ 4.44	– 1.60
52–54	+ 0.71	– 1.46
55–57	+ 2.23	– 1.94
58–60	+ 0.86	– 6.34

+ indicates improvements in score, – indicates deterioration in score.
Source: Adapted from J. W. B. Douglas, *The Home and the School* (Panther/Grafton Books 1967).

Mixed-ability Teaching

Many comprehensives use mixed-ability teaching to overcome the problems of streaming. This is where all pupils of the same age, regardless of their ability, are taught in the same classroom. Some see this as a disadvantage of comprehensive schools, since it is argued that 'more intelligent' pupils are held back by the 'less able'. Others, however, argue that in mixed-ability groups the more intelligent pupils can have a stimulating influence on the less able, and that the problems created by the self-fulfilling prophecy are easier to avoid. Mixed-ability teaching also helps to avoid creating divisions between pupils on the basis of home and social class background.

Activity

1. Make a brief summary chart in two columns comparing the advantages and disadvantages of comprehensive schools.
2. Suggest measures that could be taken to make comprehensive schools better for all pupils.

Discussion

Do you think streaming should be abolished in those schools where it is still found and replaced by mixed-ability teaching? Discuss the reasons for your views, drawing on your own experiences at school.

Recent Developments in Education

While the comprehensive system has succeeded in improving overall educational standards compared to the tripartite system, the education system came under increasing criticism in the 1980s for not reaching high enough standards and for not meeting the needs of employers and industry closely enough. As a result, attempts have been made to raise standards and to tie all parts of the education system more closely to the needs of industry.

Discussion

1. Do you think standards are falling in schools today? Make sure you are able to refer to evidence to back up your point of view.
2. What should the aims of schooling be? Should schools be concerned mainly with meeting the needs of industry and fitting people into the job market? Or should they be concerned with the development of individuals, allowing them to pursue and develop their interests?

Making Schools More Aware of Industry

Attempts here include:

- Sending teachers from schools (and further education) into industry to develop their understanding, which they can then apply in their teaching.

- Work experience programmes for fourth- and fifth-year pupils in schools to ease the transition from school to work.
- New educational courses which are more closely related to the world of work and concerned more with learning work-related skills. These include vocational courses such as CPVE (the Certificate in Pre-Vocational Education). The development of TVEI (the Technical and Vocational Educational Initiative) aimed to spread awareness of technology and industry across the whole curriculum.

Raising Standards

Activity-based learning

Teaching has become more student-centred and activity-based, with the aim of developing pupils' skills and understanding. This was reflected in the introduction of GCSE in 1988 as a replacement for GCE 'O' level and CSE exams. This is a more activity- and skills-based exam, and involves students doing more coursework. This has led to much better exam results among 16-year-olds. This approach is increasingly being adopted in 'A' level exams. The introduction of 'AS' levels aims to encourage 16–18 year olds to study a broader range of subjects, and make them more flexible and less specialized.

The National Curriculum

To improve standards across the country, the Education Reform Act of 1988 set up the National Curriculum – a range of subjects that must be studied by all pupils. All students have to study a Core Curriculum including English, Mathematics, and Science, and a series of Foundation subjects including History, Geography, Technology, a Modern Foreign Language, Physical Education, and Religious Education. There are set 'programmes of study' and 'attainment targets' (goals which all teachers are expected to enable pupils to reach), with testing at ages 7, 11, 14 and 16 to ensure these targets are met and standards maintained.

Local management of schools and 'opting out'

The 1988 Act gave more powers to individual schools to control their own affairs and finances (this is known as local management of schools or LMS) and increased the power of parents and local businesses on the governing bodies of schools. Schools may even choose to 'opt out' of local education authority control, after a ballot of the parents, and run their own affairs as Grant Maintained Schools. Parents can now choose which secondary school their children attend, and unpopular schools run the risk of losing pupils and therefore money. These are all attempts to make schools more responsive to the wishes of parents, and to the general community they are in.

The late 1980s was a period of frenzied change in education, and the impact of these changes – and how effective and successful they prove to be – will only be discovered throughout the 1990s and beyond. For example, it will be 2003 before the first child leaves school who has studied the entire National Curriculum.

The Parent's Charter

In 1991, the Conservative Government published 'The Parent's Charter', as part of its proposals to raise the standards in education. This announced government proposals:

- To oblige every school to provide a written report on their child's progress at least once a year.
- To ensure that every school is inspected regularly by government-approved inspectors, to identify the strengths and weaknesses of a school.
- To oblige every school to publish tables of exam results, National Curriculum test results, and truancy rates, and to report on what pupils do when they leave school.
- To oblige every school to publish a school prospectus, giving details of the aims of the school, the subjects and other activities offered, and their exam results compared with local and national results.
- To oblige every school to produce a governors' report to parents, including the standards achieved, the amount of truancy, and what school leavers do after they leave school. The 'Parent's Charter' is supposed to help parents to choose the 'best' schools and encourage schools to improve their performance.

Activity/Discussion

Many of the recent changes in education are very controversial, particularly as they may discriminate against schools in poorer working-class areas, and disguise schools which perform badly in well-off middle-class areas.

1. Do you think the recent changes in education will succeed in raising standards? Go through each of the changes, and explain in each case why it might or might not improve standards.
2. Discuss the advantages and disadvantages of 'The Parent's Charter'.
3. Do you think schools alone can be held responsible for exam results and truancy rates? What other factors might influence how good a school's exam results are, and whether pupils play truant or not?

The Purposes of Education

The provision of education is an incredibly expensive business, eating up about £20 billion a year and a twentieth of the total wealth of Britain. Why is such importance attached to the provision of education in modern industrial society? What does education contribute to society? Why are schools necessary in industrial societies and why is education to the age of 16 compulsory? The answer to these questions lies in the *functions* that education performs in society.

Activity

1. List all the reasons you go/went to school. What benefits (if any!) do you think going to school has brought you?
2. How do you think your life would differ if you didn't have/hadn't had to go to school?
3. Now read the following sections (to the end of the chapter) on the role that education plays in society, and compare them with your own reasons for going to school. Which do you think are the more important, from your point of view?
4. What problems might there be for individuals and society if compulsory education were to be abolished tomorrow?

Education and the Economy

In a complex industrial society, the education system plays an important role in preparation for working life in two respects:

- *Producing a labour force with the skills needed for working life.* A literate and numerate workforce is more or less essential in an industrial society, and there is the need for specific skills related to particular jobs, such as computing, engineering, technical drawing, car maintenance, typing, and science. The things learnt at school will generally affect the kind of job and training opportunities open to people after school.
- *Selecting people for different occupations.* Modern industrial societies are generally meritocratic, with most social positions being achieved on the basis of experience and exam qualifications. In schools, people are graded and receive different qualifications, which are used by employers and other educational institutions to select suitable people for work and further courses.

Through exams, schools sort pupils out, and decide the kinds of occupation they will eventually get – for example, who will become middle-class professionals or skilled or unskilled workers. Education will therefore influence the individual's eventual social class position as an adult. In a few cases, education can be a means of upward social mobility into the middle class for children from a working-class family. Figure 11.5 illustrates this link between education and the class structure.

Socialization

The school is an important agency of secondary socialization, continuing the process of socialization which begins in the family. Schools transmit from one generation to the next the culture of a society. For example, the school curriculum hands on knowledge about History, Geography, Science, English Language and Literature, and so on. Children also learn how to develop relationships with others and to adopt many of the norms of the society to which they belong. These are aspects of the hidden curriculum, which is discussed below. Society is therefore reproduced and each new generation integrated into society.

Figure 11.5 Education and the class structure

Social Control

Schools act as important agencies of social control, which encourage children to learn and conform to the values and norms expected by society. This is mainly carried out through what is known as the hidden curriculum – 'hidden' because there are no obvious, organized courses in 'obedience and conformity' as there are in Mathematics or English. Nevertheless, this hidden curriculum is present throughout schooling, and those who conform to it are likely to be rewarded, while those who don't are likely to be branded as non-conformists by the school and may find themselves getting into trouble. Some features of this hidden curriculum, and what is being taught, are listed below.

The hidden curriculum

Features of the hidden curriculum	What is being taught
Privileges and responsibilities given to older pupils.	Respect for elders.
School rules, detentions and suspensions, rewards like merit badges, prizes, good marks, etc.	Conformity to society's rules and laws, whether you agree with them or not.
School assemblies.	Respect for religious beliefs.
Males and females often playing different sports, having different dress rules, and being counselled into different subjects, further education courses, and careers. Many teachers having higher expectations of boys than girls and paying them more attention.	Males and females are expected to conform to gender stereotypes, with males as workers and 'bread-winners', and women working mainly in the home or in a narrow range of 'female occupations' which are often extensions of their domestic role.
Competitive sports and competition against each other in class rather than cooperating together. Students being tested individually – being encouraged to rely on themselves rather than others.	Workers have to compete for jobs and wages. Individuals should stand on their own two feet – not join with other workers.
Respecting authority of teachers regardless of what they say or do. Pupils always having to justify where they're going and why, and do as they're told.	Respect for those in authority, such as bosses at work and the police.
Punctuality/being on time – time belonging to the school, not the pupil.	Good time-keeping at work – the employer pays for the worker's time, so it belongs to the firm, not the worker.
Concentrating on schoolwork, whether or not it's boring and whether or not you want to do it.	Workers have to accept boring, menial, repetitive jobs.
Value being placed on hard work and getting on.	Everyone can make it to the top if they try hard enough.
Grading by ability and exam success/failure.	The differences in pay and status between social classes are natural and justified – those higher up are more intelligent and better qualified.

Features of the hidden curriculum   *What is being taught*

Different streams and bands.	Getting used to the different levels of the job market, such as professional, managerial, skilled, semi-skilled, and unskilled manual occupations.
Pupils' lack of power and control, about the subjects taught or how the school is run or the school day organized.	Workers lack power and control at work.
The authority hierarchy of the school involving pupils fitting into a complex organization of heads, deputies, heads of department, year heads, etc.	Learning about their place in the hierarchies of power and control in society and accepting it – for example, in the authority hierarchy at work.

Activity

1. Describe in detail five features of the hidden curriculum found in your school, or the one you once attended, which reflect the values of society outside school.
2. Drawing on your own experiences at school, what features of your education do you think prepared you/will prepare you most for life after school? Think of particular subjects studied and activities undertaken, and the features of the 'hidden curriculum' discussed above which were/are found in your school.

Implementing Government Policy

Schools have often been used as a means of carrying out government policies. For example, comprehensive schools were originally established by a Labour government in an attempt to create both more equal opportunities in society and greater social equality. Some schools in areas where there is widespread poverty have been given extra teachers and more resources than other schools in an attempt to relieve the disadvantages faced by the poor in education. Multi-cultural courses are also organized in many schools in an attempt to stop the spread of racist ideas, and encourage respect for people from different cultural backgrounds. Increasingly, attempts are being made to reduce the effects of gender stereotyping by encouraging girls to go into subjects like science and computing which have been traditionally dominated by boys.

Preparing for Social Change

As well as encouraging people to accept traditional ideas which will lead to order and stability in society, schools also prepare pupils for a rapidly changing industrial society. Since the 1970s there has been a massive increase in the use of computers in schools and the development of computer courses, in an attempt to prepare pupils for a world after school in which computer technology plays a central role. As discussed above, the Technical and Vocational Educational Initiative (TVEI) has attempted to increase awareness of technology and industry in schools. Attempts in the 1980s to make pupils more adaptable and aware of the world of work, and to make schools more closely related to the needs of the economy, are partly due to the demands of a rapidly changing industrial economy.

This chapter has shown that one of the most important consequences of education is the influence it has on people's life chances, and for most people it affects in a very direct way their occupational opportunities – and social class position – as adults. This important result of education has been reflected in the attempts to establish equality of opportunity in education, first in the tripartite system and then with comprehensive schooling, so that all children can have the best educational opportunities in life. However, despite these attempts, inequality in education remains. This continuing inequality in education is the theme of the following chapter.

Chapter Summary

After studying this chapter, you should bbe able to:

- Briefly outline the education system before 1944.
- Explain what is meant by equality of educational opportunity.
- Describe the tripartite system, explain how it tried to achieve equality of educational opportunity, and criticize its weaknesses.
- Explain what is meant by the self-fulfilling prophecy in education.
- Describe and explain the changes brought about by the comprehensive system, and explain how it tried to overcome the weaknesses of the tripartite system.

- Discuss the arguments for and against comprehensive schools.
- Explain what is meant by streaming and mixed-ability teaching, and the problems with each of them.
- Explain how the government has tried in recent years to improve standards in schools and make them more aware of the needs of industry.
- Outline some recent changes in the education system.
- Describe and explain the role of education in society.
- Explain what is meant by the 'hidden curriculum', and how it reflects the values of society outside schools.

Project Suggestions

1. Do interviews with a sample of people from three different age groups (such as 16–25, 35–50, and over 60) asking them about their views and experience of schools today compared to the past, and whether they think standards have fallen or not.
2. Do interviews with teachers asking them about stress in the teacher's job arising from recent changes in education (like the GCSE exam and the National Curriculum).
3. Do a study of work experience schemes in a local school, perhaps interviewing pupils and teachers about the aims and usefulness of such schemes.
4. Find a school that still has streaming, and interview a group of bottom-stream pupils to discover whether there is any evidence of the self-fulfilling prophecy at work. For example, find out whether they feel as valued and encouraged by teachers as those in higher streams.

Key Terms

anti-school sub-culture
equality of educational opportunity
parity of esteem
self-fulfilling prophecy
tripartite system

12 Inequality in Education

The 1944 Education Act, the tripartite system, and the comprehensive system which replaced it all aimed to secure equality of educational opportunity for all children, regardless of their social class, ethnic background, or sex. However, despite these efforts, sociological evidence has made it clear that not all children of the same ability achieve the same success in education, and inequalities in educational opportunity remain. The failure of pupils to do as well in education as they should, given their ability, is called **underachievement**. The evidence suggests that social class origins (the social class of a child's parents), ethnicity, and gender continue to have an influence on how well people do in education, even when they are of the same ability, and these factors appear to be more important than innate (inborn) ability in affecting the level of educational achievement or success. This chapter will look at the patterns of inequality remaining in education, and some of the explanations for them.

Ethnicity and Underachievement

The Facts

While children with Indian backgrounds tend to do as well and often better than many white children, children from Pakistani/Bangladeshi homes and males from Afro-Caribbean (West Indian) homes tend to do less well than they should given their ability.

- They tend to get fewer and poorer GCSE results than children of white or Indian origin.

- They appear to have below average reading ability.
- Male Afro-Caribbeans are over-represented (that is, there are more than there should be given their numbers in the population as a whole) in special schools for children with learning difficulties and special units for children with 'behaviour problems'.
- They are over-represented in lower streams and evidence suggests they get put in lower streams even if they get better results than pupils placed in higher streams.
- Relatively few obtain 'A' levels and go on to higher education at universities and polytechnics (though Afro-Caribbean females do much better than both Afro-Caribbean and white males).
- They are generally less qualified than those of white or Indian origin, as shown in figure 12.1.

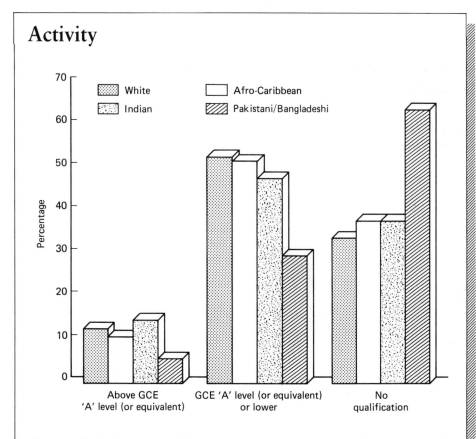

Activity

Figure 12.1 Highest qualification level of the population: by ethnic origin, Great Britain, 1987–9

Source: Department of Employment Labour Force Survey in *Social Trends 21* (HMSO 1991).

Study figure 12.1 and answer the following questions:

1. Which ethnic group has the highest percentage of people with a qualification above GCE 'A'-level (or equivalent)?
2. What percentage of Pakistani/Bangladeshi people have no qualification?
3. Which two ethnic groups are least likely to have a GCE 'A'-level (or equivalent) or lower qualification?
4. The category 'GCE "A"-level (or equivalent) or lower' is so broad it might hide wide inequalities in the qualifications held by different ethnic groups. Explain this statement.

Explaining the Underachievement of Some Ethnic Minorities

The pattern of underachievement of Pakistani/Bangladeshi and Afro-Caribbean children has a number of explanations.

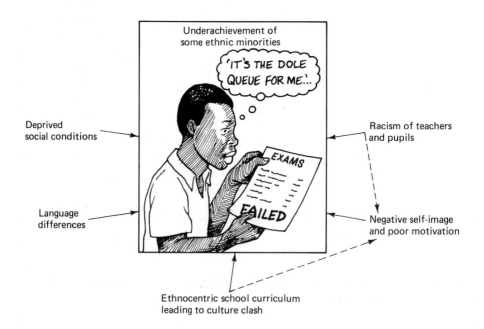

Figure 12.2 Ethnicity and educational underachievement

Social conditions

Such children often face a series of disadvantages in social conditions such as poor-quality housing, overcrowding, and higher rates of unemployment in their homes which contribute to difficulties in coping with school work. Many of the factors discussed below explaining working-class underachievement also affect these ethnic minorities, as they tend to be mainly working class.

Racism

Racism is as widespread among teachers and pupils as it is in the rest of society, and Afro-Caribbean male pupils, in particular, are more likely to fight it and form anti-school peer groups, leading to labelling by teachers as 'trouble-makers'. Research in 1990 found that Afro-Caribbean children, unlike whites and Asians, are often punished not for any particular offence but because they have the 'wrong attitude'. Teachers often expect black pupils to be trouble-makers and so they take swift action against them. Teachers themselves may be racist, and therefore may have low expectations of non-white pupils – they may label them as 'stupid' or 'difficult to control' and therefore the self-fulfilling prophecy may come into effect, and lead to a lack of interest in schoolwork, disruptive behaviour, being put in lower streams, and poorer exam results than they are capable of achieving.

An ethnocentric curriculum

Because of racism both in the school and the wider society, many Afro-Caribbean children in Britain may grow up with a negative self-image – a lack of self-respect and confidence because they feel they are in some ways rejected. The school curriculum tends to be ethnocentric, which may contribute to this low self-esteem. **Ethnocentrism** means that school subjects concentrate on a particular society and culture – in this case white British society and culture – rather than recognizing and taking into account the cultures of different ethnic communities. This may cause a culture clash between home and school for Afro-Caribbean pupils. Textbooks still frequently carry degrading stereotypes of people from non-white races. This may lead to low motivation in school and poor educational achievement.

Activity/Discussion

1. What evidence can you think of from your own experiences at school which suggests that the cultures of ethnic minorities are either ignored or treated in a degrading way? Think about the subjects you studied, the textbooks you used, and the kinds of activity you undertook.
2. Many schools today are trying to include the cultures of the ethnic minorities in school subjects and activities. What evidence is there of this happening in your experience? Give examples.
3. It has been suggested that the cartoon below, while clearly intending to put forward an anti-racist message, may in fact be itself racist, as it portrays an inaccurate and racist stereotype of Afro-Caribbean male youth. What do you think?

Afro-Caribbean males generally achieve less at school than Afro-Caribbean females. They are more likely to resist and fight racism at school

Source: Case Con, Summer 1974.

Language

Some Afro-Caribbean children speak a different dialect of English, 'creole' or 'Caribbean English', and children from other ethnic groups may have a language other than English used in their homes. This language difference may cause difficulties in doing some school work and communicating with the teacher, and may create disadvantages at school. Teachers may mistake language difficulties for lack of ability, and because Caribbean English is non-standard English, it may be unconsciously penalized in the classroom, because most teachers are white and middle class. Such cultural difficulties may present obstacles to motivation and progress at school.

Activity

1. Go through the explanations above for the underachievement of some ethnic minorities, putting them in the order which you think might be the most important. Give reasons why you have put them in that order.
2. For each of the explanations, suggest changes that could be made in both school and society which might help to improve the educational performance of these ethnic minorities.

Gender Differences in Education

The Facts

There are marked differences between the sexes in education. As figure 12.3 shows, while females tend to do better than males up to GCSE, and as well as males at 'A' level (in two subjects), women are less likely to go on to higher education, and women as a whole are more likely than men to lack any formal qualification.

The major differences between men and women in education are:

- Females tend to do different subjects to males, which influences future career choices. Females have traditionally tended to do arts subjects (like English Literature, History, foreign languages, and Sociology) and to

Figure 12.3 Educational qualifications, and students in higher education: by sex, United Kingdom, 1988

Source: Department of Education and Science statistics; Department of Employment Labour Force Survey.

study Home Economics, Commerce, and Typing, which prepare them more for jobs in health, caring, and communication and information. Males have traditionally been more likely to take scientific and technical subjects – such as Physics, Chemistry, and CDT – which are more likely to lead to higher-status, more skilled, and better-paid occupations after school. The National Curriculum may in time change these gender divisions between subjects at school (see chapters 5 and 11). Figure 12.4 shows this pattern in 1988–9 in GCSE results. This subject difference is also found at 'A' level and, as table 12.1 shows, in higher education.

- While males and females are equally likely to get two or more passes at 'A' level, males are more likely to get the three 'A' levels required for university entry.
- More males than females go onto higher education after school.
- On training courses in colleges, females are more likely to enter lower-level courses such as catering, secretarial and hairdressing courses,

whereas males are more likely to enter courses leading to more skilled, and better-paid, work.

Activity

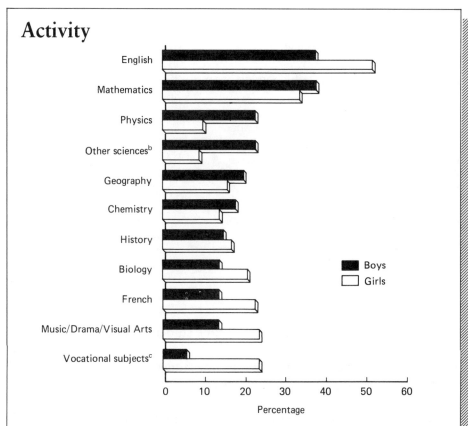

Figure 12.4 Percentage of school leavers with higher-grade results[a] at GCSE by subject and sex, Great Britain, 1988–9

[a]Includes GCSE/GCE/SCE levels/grades A–C and CSE grade 1
[b]Includes metalwork, woodwork, and technical drawing
[c]Includes business and domestic subjects

Source: DES Statistics 1990 (HMSO 1991).

Refer to figure 12.4

1. In which subject did girls receive the highest number of higher-grade results at GCSE?
2. In which subject did girls receive the lowest number of higher-grade results at GCSE?
3. In which GCSE subjects did girls get more higher-grade results than boys?
4. Which *three* GCSE subjects show the greatest differences between the girls and the boys?

Table 12.1 Subjects studied by full-time students (home and overseas), 1987–8

	Females (%)	Males (%)
Education	69	31
Medicine, dentistry, and health	67	33
Engineering and technology	11	89
Agriculture, forestry, and veterinary science	32	68
Science	34	66
Administrative, business, and social studies	57	43
Architecture and other professional and vocational subjects	63	37
Languages, literature, and area studies	67	33
Arts other than languages	53	47
Music, drama, art, and design	57	43
GCE, GCSE, SCE, and CSE	54	46
Other	53	47

Source: Calculated from *Annual Abstract of Statistics 1991*, table 5.9.

Refer to table 12.1.

5. Which *two* subjects studied by full-time students show the greatest difference between females and males?
6. Which *two* subjects studied by full-time students show the smallest difference between females and males?
7. How might the differences between the subjects studied by males and females at GCSE and by full-time students affect the kinds of jobs that they enter after studying? Illustrate your answer with examples of particular subjects and occupations.

Explaining Gender Differences in Education

Socialization

As seen earlier in chapter 5 on gender socialization, males and females are socialized differently into the 'breadwinner'/housewife roles. Schools re-inforce the gender socialization process begun in the family. Sue Sharpe in *Just Like a Girl* (Penguin 1976) has suggested that as a result of this girls have different priorities to males, and put 'love, marriage, husbands, children, jobs and careers in that order'. Because of this socialization, females often make job choices which do not require 'A' levels or higher qualifications, such as routine office work. Parents' expectations of boys and girls often differ, and they are more likely to support males rather than females staying on at school or going to college after school-leaving age, especially if money is short.

The hidden curriculum

The hidden curriculum, which was discussed in the previous chapter, also contributes to gender differences in achievement. Teachers have been

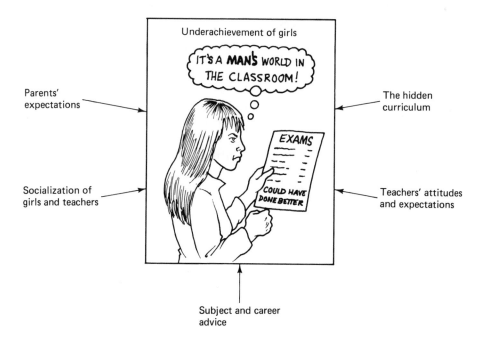

Figure 12.5 Gender and educational underachievement

socialized into gender roles too, and there is evidence suggesting that teachers place more emphasis on boys' progress than girls', since boys are expected to be the future 'breadwinners'. Research into teachers' attitudes and expectations suggests that teachers:

- Have higher expectations of boys than girls.
- Ask boys more questions.
- Give boys more help and encouragement (especially in sciences and computing).
- Allow boys to dominate discussions and let girls sit quietly.
- Are less likely to know girls' names.
- Often under-estimate girls' abilities and ambitions.
- Give boys more of their time.
- Are more tolerant of disruptive, unruly behaviour from boys than the same behaviour from girls.

Girls soon learn that 'it's a man's world' in the classroom, with the consequence of lower self-esteem, ambition, and motivation, and the self-fulfilling prophecy may then come into effect.

This hidden curriculum is also found, for example, in science textbooks, which often show more pictures of males doing physics or chemistry; by contrast, home economics or childcare textbooks usually show females doing these subjects. Such imagery helps to reinforce the 'masculinity' or 'femininity' of different subjects.

Subject and career advice

In giving subject and career advice, teachers often counsel girls into different subject options to boys (which has important effects on future educational and career opportunities), and provide different career advice. For example, girls are often counselled into taking traditional female subjects, and to apply for traditional female occupations such as catering, nursing, and secretarial and clerical work, which generally require fairly low qualifications. Boys are likely to be advised about a much wider range of careers.

Discussion

Think about your own experiences at school, and what has been said above about the hidden curriculum and subject and career advice at school. Do you think schools stereotype girls, and that 'it's a man's world in the classroom'? What evidence do you have of this in your own experience? How might gender differences in schooling be overcome?

Social Class and Underachievement

The Facts

There are major differences between the levels of achievement of the working class and middle class and, in general, the higher the social class of the parents, the more successful will a child be in education. The degree of social class inequality in education begins in the primary school and becomes wider as children move through the education system, with the higher levels of the education system dominated by middle-class students.

Working-class children, compared to middle-class children of the same ability:

- In the tripartite system were far more likely to fail the 11+ exam and go to secondary modern schools.
- Are more likely to start school unable to read.
- Are more likely to be placed in lower streams.
- Generally get poorer exam results.
- Are more likely to leave school at the minimum leaving age of 16.

In addition, a high proportion of 'A' level students and sixth-formers, and those entering further and higher education, are from the middle class: a much higher proportion than is justified by the proportion of the middle class in society as a whole. Even when the working class do enter further education, they are more likely to take lower-status courses than students from middle-class backgrounds, such as job training courses rather than 'A' levels leading to higher education.

The working class is under-represented in higher education. As figure 12.6 shows, in 1990 81 per cent of university students came from middle-class backgrounds, even though only about 45 per cent of the population was middle class. Figure 12.7 shows the type of educational establishment last attended full-time by people who are no longer in full-time education. It shows very clearly that education is closely linked to social class. For example, of people with fathers in professional occupations, 26 per cent had a university education compared to only 1 per cent whose fathers were unskilled manual workers.

Activity

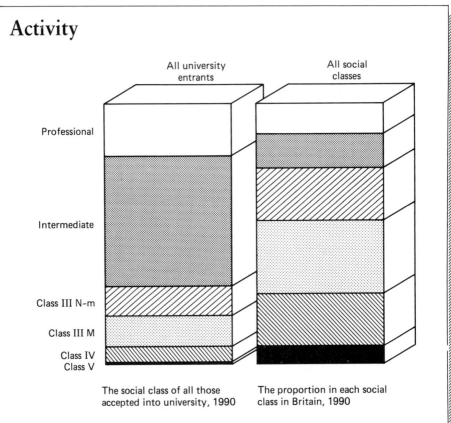

Figure 12.6 The social class of university students (home applicants accepted) UK, 1990

Source: UCCA Statistical Supplement, 1991.

Look at figure 12.6

1. Which social class had the largest share of university places in 1990?
2. Which social class had the most generous share of university places compared to its proportion in society as a whole?

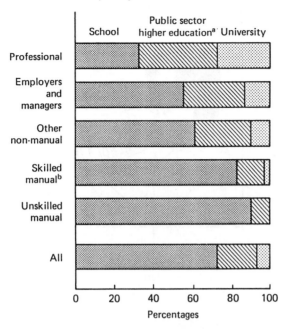

Figure 12.7 Educational establishment last attended full-time: by socio-economic group of father, Great Britain, 1987–8

[a]Includes paramedical and nursing.

[b]Includes semi-skilled manual.

Source: Social Trends 21 (HMSO 1991).

Look at figure 12.7

3. What percentage of people whose fathers were employers and managers last attended full-time a public sector higher education establishment?
4. From which social class did the highest proportion of people come whose last education establishment was a school?
5. What is the difference between the percentage of those whose fathers were professionals who last attended school full-time and those whose fathers were skilled and semi-skilled manual workers?
6. Explain how figures 12.6 and 12.7 show social class inequality among those who attend public sector higher education and university.

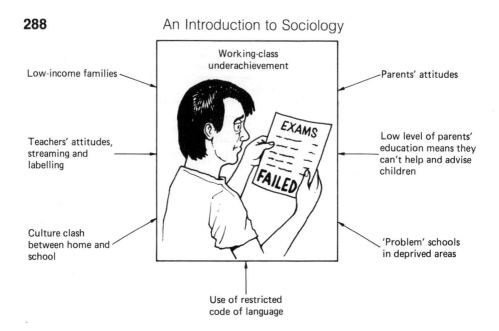

Low-income families

Teachers' attitudes, streaming and labelling

Culture clash between home and school

Working-class underachievement

Parents' attitudes

Low level of parents' education means they can't help and advise children

'Problem' schools in deprived areas

Use of restricted code of language

Figure 12.8 Social class and educational underachievement

Explaining Working-class Underachievement

Home circumstances

Poverty and low wages are concentrated among the semi-skilled and unskilled levels of the working class, and can have an important effect on school performance. Poor housing conditions such as overcrowding or poor heating can make study at home difficult, and a higher level of sickness in such homes may affect school attendance and mean falling behind with lessons. Low wages or unemployment may mean that educational books and toys are not bought, which may affect a child's educational development before and during her or his time at school. There may also be a lack of money for school trips, sports equipment, geometry sets, pocket dictionaries, calculators, and the other hidden costs of free state education. It may be financially difficult for lower-paid parents to support children in education after school leaving age, no matter how bright their prospects. In such circumstances, children may be encouraged to leave school as soon as possible and get a job or go onto a Youth Training scheme, to support themselves and bring some money into the house.

Parents' attitudes to education

Middle-class parents on the whole seem to place a higher value on their children's education and take more interest in their progress at school than working-class parents. Evidence suggests middle-class parents visit the school more frequently to discuss how their children are getting on, and this interest grows as the children reach the 'more important' stages of education as they get older , when exam options are selected and career choices loom. Middle-class parents are also more likely to encourage their children to stay at school beyond the minimum leaving age. This difference between working-class and middle-class parents, however, may not necessarily indicate that working-class parents have a 'poor attitude' to education, but just that working-class parents are more likely to work longer hours, doing shift-work and overtime, and are less likely than the middle class to get paid for time off work. This may mean it is more difficult for working-class parents to visit schools, rather than that they don't care about their children's progress. Middle-class parents also, of course, can more easily afford to continue to support their children in education after the age of 16. The interest shown by middle-class parents may be due to the importance of educational qualifications in obtaining their own middle-class occupations. By contrast, working-class parents may see education as of less importance because they may have found their own education had little relevance to their working-class jobs. This may lead to poor motivation of some working-class children in school and therefore lower levels of achievement, regardless of ability. Parental attitudes can also affect the child's learning by the lower value placed on books or educational toys in many lower-working-class homes.

Parents' level of education

Because they are generally themselves better educated, middle-class parents tend to understand the school system better than working-class parents: they know more about schools, the examination system, and careers and so are more able to advise and counsel their children on getting into the best subjects and courses. They can hold their own more in disagreements with teachers (who are also middle class) about the treatment and education of their child. They know what games and books to buy to stimulate their children's educational development both before and during schooling (and have the money to buy them) and can help their children with school work generally. As a consequence, even before they get to school, middle-class children may have learned more as a result of their socialization in the family. These advantages of a middle-class home may be reinforced throughout a child's career at school.

The catchment area

Catchment areas are the areas from which primary and secondary schools draw their pupils. Schools in deprived areas, where there may be a range of social problems such as high unemployment, poverty, juvenile delinquency, crime, and drug abuse, are more likely to have 'discipline problems' owing to the accumulated effects of the environment on children's behaviour, and hence a higher turnover of teachers. This may mean that children from the most disadvantaged backgrounds have the 'worst' schools. In contrast, schools in middle-class neighbourhoods will probably have fewer 'discipline problems', and have a better learning environment. Additionally, schools in middle-class areas will have more active and wealthy Parent Teacher Associations able to provide extra resources for the school. This was confirmed by a survey in November 1991 by the National Confederation of Parent Teacher Associations. This found that parents were contributing more than a quarter of the money spent on books and equipment in primary schools. Parents in poorer areas may find it difficult to make such contributions to school funds, and therefore the schools in such areas may lack the resources found in schools in wealthier middle-class areas.

Language use: the restricted and elaborated codes

Success at school depends very heavily on language – for reading, writing, speaking, and understanding. Bernstein has argued that there is a relationship between language use and social class, and that the language used by the middle class is a superior instrument for success at school compared to the language used by the working class. He argued that the language used by the lower working class has a **restricted code** while the language used by the middle class has an **elaborated code**.

The restricted code
The restricted code of language is used by both middle-class and working-class people, but is more characteristic of working-class people. It is the sort of language which is used between friends or family members – colloquial, everyday language, with limited explanation, sometimes ungrammatical and limited in vocabulary. This form of language is quite adequate for everyday use with friends because they know what the speaker is referring to – the context is understood by both speakers and so detailed explanation is not

required. Bernstein argues that lower-working-class people are mainly limited to this form of language use.

The elaborated code

The elaborated code of language is used mainly by middle-class people. It is the language of strangers and individuals in some formal context, where explanation and detail are required – like an interview for a job, writing a business letter, writing an essay or examination answer, or in a school lesson or textbook. It has a much wider vocabulary than the restricted code.

Bernstein argues that the language used in schools is the elaborated code of the middle class, and that it is the middle-class child's ability to use the elaborated code that gives her or him an advantage at school over working-class children. The elaborated code of the middle class is more suited to the demands of school work, since understanding textbooks and writing essays and examination questions require the detail and explanation which is found mainly in the formal language of the elaborated code. Middle-class children who are used to using the elaborated code at home will therefore find school work much easier and learn more in school than those working-class children whose language is limited only to the restricted code. In addition, the teacher may mistake the working-class child's restricted use of language for lack of ability, and therefore expect less from the child. The self-fulfilling prophecy may then come into effect.

The 'culture clash'

Schools are mainly middle-class institutions, and they stress the value of many features of the middle-class way of life, such as the importance of hard work and study, making sacrifices now for future rewards, the 'right' form of dress, behaviour, manners, and language use, 'good' books, good TV programmes, 'quality' newspapers, and so on. This means that middle-class children may find that school greets them almost as an extension of their home life, and they may start school already familiar with and 'tuned in' to the atmosphere of the school, such as the subjects that will be explored there, seeking good marks, doing homework, good behaviour and a cooperative attitude to teachers, and other features of middle-class culture. Consequently, they may appear to the teacher as fairly intelligent and sophisticated.

For the working-class child, the atmosphere and values of the school may be quite unfamiliar and different to those of his or her home. This is likely to result in a culture clash between her or his home and social class background and the middle-class culture of the school. This culture clash may partly explain working-class underachievement.

Teachers' attitudes, streaming, and labelling

Teachers are middle class, and children from middle-class homes who share the same standards and values as the teacher are often likely to be seen by teachers as 'more intelligent'. Teachers' judgements of children's ability are often influenced by the types of home children come from. Even if children really are of equal ability, teachers are more likely to think working-class children are less intelligent because of the assumptions they hold about their home backgrounds. This may explain why working-class children tend to be found more in the lower streams of comprehensive schools. As shown in the previous chapter, the evidence suggests that teachers expect less from children in lower streams and give them less encouragement than those in higher streams. Teachers may label lower-stream pupils as 'low achievers', and such pupils are then almost guaranteed to fail – victims of the self-fulfilling prophecy.

Because of all the factors discussed above causing the underachievement of working-class pupils in schools, bottom-stream pupils are very often working class and such pupils will often form the anti-school sub-culture which was discussed in the previous chapter. They then themselves reject the school which has already rejected them as 'failures' and 'thick'. They look forward to leaving school at the earliest possible opportunity, often before taking any GCSEs or other formal qualifications.

The double test for working-class children

Taken together, the factors in the home, social class background, and the school discussed in this chapter help to explain why working-class children do less well at school than middle-class children of the same ability. Schools test all pupils when doing subjects like Mathematics, English, or Sociology. However, for the working-class child there is a double test. At the same time as coping with the academic difficulties of schoolwork which all children face, working-class children must also cope with a wide range of other disadvantages and difficulties.

These problems on top of the demands of academic work explain working-class underachievement in schools. These disadvantages start in the primary school and become more and more emphasized as children grow older, as they fall further and further behind and become more disillusioned with school. In this context, it is perhaps not surprising that a large majority of those who leave school at age 16 every year, with few or no qualifications, come from working-class backgrounds.

Activity

1. Put the following explanations for working-class underachievement in what you think is their order of importance: home circumstances; parents' attitudes to education; parents' level of education; the catchment area; language use; the culture clash; teachers' attitudes, streaming, and labelling.
2. In the light of your list, suggest ways that schools and teachers might improve the performance of pupils who face social class disadvantages in education.
3. Do you think schools can make up for problems that begin outside of school, such as in the home and the neighbourhood? Give reasons for your answer.

Compensatory Education

Because of the disadvantages in education arising from social class background, **positive discrimination** has been attempted as a solution to working-class underachievement. This means that schools in deprived areas, where home and social class background are seen as obstacles to success in education, are singled out for more favourable treatment. They are given more resources than schools in other areas, in terms of better-paid teachers and more money to spend on buildings and equipment. This is an attempt to compensate for the problems of disadvantage faced by the poorer sections of the working class in schooling (hence the term **compensatory education**).

The idea of positive discrimination is based on the idea of equality of opportunity, since it is argued children from disadvantaged backgrounds and poor homes can only get an equal opportunity in education to those who come from non-disadvantaged backgrounds if they get unequal and more generous treatment to compensate.

The policy of positive discrimination and compensatory education is put into practice by the government setting up **Educational Priority Areas**. These are areas where unemployment is high, where there is poverty, overcrowding, many children whose home language is not English, and large concentrations of unskilled and semi-skilled working-class people. Schools in these areas are given extra money and teachers. However, compensatory education hasn't really succeeded, and schools have not been able to overcome or compensate for the disadvantages arising from home and social class background.

Do schools make a difference?

Michael Rutter, Barbara Maughan, Peter Mortimore and Janet Ouston, in their book *Fifteen Thousand Hours: Secondary Schools and their Effects on Children* (Open Books 1979) reported research they had carried out in twelve schools. This study attempts to show, in the face of much previous research suggesting the opposite, that 'good' schools can make a difference to the life chances of all pupils. Rutter et al. suggest that it is features of the school's organization which make this difference. These features are summarized below.

- Teachers are well prepared for lessons.
- Teachers have high expectations of pupils' academic performance, and set and mark classwork and homework regularly.
- Teachers set examples of behaviour, for example they are on time and they use only officially approved forms of discipline.
- Teachers place more emphasis on praise and reward rather than blame and punishment.
- Teachers treat pupils as responsible people, for example by giving them positions of responsibility, looking after school books and property.
- Teachers show an interest in the pupils and encourage them to do well.
- There is an atmosphere or ethos in the school which reflects the above points, with all teachers sharing a commitment to the aims and values of the school.
- There is a mixture of abilities in the school, as the presence of high-ability pupils benefits the academic performance and behaviour of pupils of all abilities.

Activity/Discussion

1. Explain how you think each of the features of a 'good' school which Rutter describes above might help pupils of all backgrounds and abilities to make more progress.

2. Are there any other features that you would expect to find in a 'good' school?
3. List at least six characteristics, based on your own opinions, of a 'good teacher'. How important do you think the role of the teacher is in the educational progress of pupils compared to the home, the neighbourhood, and the pressures of friends?

Private Education: The Independent Schools

A final problem for the principle of equality of educational opportunity in Britain is the continued existence of a fee-paying private sector of education – the independent schools. Pupils at these schools are largely the children of wealthier upper-middle- and upper-class parents who have decided to opt out of the free, state-run comprehensive system and can afford to pay for a private education.

Founded in 1495, Loughborough Grammar School is one of the oldest schools in the independent sector

There are many poor-quality schools in the private sector of education, but the public schools are a small group of all the independent schools. These are long-established private schools, many dating back hundreds of years, which charge fees often running into thousands of pounds a year. According to the Independent Schools Information Service, in 1991 the average boarding fee in boys' public schools was £6600, and well over £4500 for day pupils at some schools. The two most famous boys' public schools are probably Eton and Harrow, and many of the 'top people' in this country have attended these or other public schools. A public school education means parents can almost guarantee their children will have well-paid future careers bringing them power and status in society.

The Case for Independent Schools

The defenders of private education point to the smaller class sizes and better facilities of the public schools than those found in the state system, so children have a better chance of educational success. Many teachers are paid more, examination results are often better, and pupils have a much higher chance of getting into university. Many defend private education on the grounds that parents should have the right to spend their money as they wish, and improving their children's life chances is a sensible way of doing so.

The Case against Independent Schools

Many remain opposed to private education, arguing that most people do not have the money to purchase a private education for their children, and it is wrong that the children of the well-off should be given more advantages in education than the poor. Many of these schools have charitable status, which entitles them to receive various tax benefits on gifts of money and reduced rates. This means they are effectively subsidized by the taxpayers, the vast majority of whom can't afford to attend them. The taxpayer also pays the cost of training the teachers in these schools, since thay attend state-run institutes of higher education. The existence of private schools undermines the principle of equality of educational opportunity, because social class background rather than simply ability becomes the key to success in education. Not all children of the same ability have the same chance of paying for this route to educational success.

The quality of teaching in independent schools is no better than in state-run comprehensives. However, their pupils may obtain better results because classes tend to be smaller than in comprehensives, allowing more individual attention, and the schools often have better resources and facilities. The opponents of private education argue more money should be spent on improving the state system so everyone has an equal chance in education.

Research has shown that even when children who go to private schools, especially the public schools, get worse examination results than children who go to comprehensive schools, they still get better jobs in the end. This suggests that simply the fact of attending a public school is itself enough to secure them good jobs, even if their qualifications are not quite as good as those of pupils from comprehensives.

Elite Education and Elite Jobs

A public school education remains an essential qualification for the elite jobs in society – that small number of jobs in the country which involve holding a great deal of power and privilege. Although only about 7 per cent of the population have attended independent schools (and public schools are only a proportion of these schools), most of the top positions in the Civil Service, the courts, the Church of England, industry, banking, and commerce are held by ex-public school pupils, as shown in table 12.2.

In many cases, even well-qualified candidates from comprehensive schools will stand a poor chance of getting such jobs if competing with public school pupils. The route into the elite jobs is basically through a public school and Oxford and Cambridge Universities (where about 50 per cent of students come from public schools). This establishes the 'old boys' network', where those in positions of power recruit others who come from the same social class background and who have been to the same public schools and universities as themselves. This shows one aspect of the clear relationship which exists between wealth and power in modern Britain, and how being able to afford a public school education can lead to a position of power and influence in society.

Table 12.2 Public school educated holders of some elite jobs in Britain in the 1980s

Category	Percentage who attended public schools
Pupils at school in UK	7 (all independent schools)
Labour MPs	14
Conservative MPs	70
Conservative Cabinet	90
50 most senior army officers	80
Directors of 40 leading industrial firms	66
Directors of clearing banks	70
Directors of major life insurance companies	92
Senior civil servants (under-secretary and above)	50
High court judges	83
Ambassadors	69
Church of England bishops	59

Source: Devised from M.Moran, *Politics and Society in Britain* (Macmillan 1985); C. Leys, *Politics in Britain* (Heinemann 1983); *Social Trends 20* (HMSO 1990); I. Reid, *Social Class Differences in Britain* (Fontana 1989); *The Guardian*, 29 November 1990.

Discussion

Should private education be abolished? It might be useful to think at the same time about whether private medicine should be abolished – there are many similarities.

Is Equality of Educational Opportunity Possible to Achieve?

Despite the efforts of first the tripartite system and now the comprehensive system to secure equality of educational opportunity, children of equal ability but from different social classes, from different ethnic backgrounds, and of different sexes are still not achieving the same success in education. Compensatory education has not overcome the disadvantages faced by many pupils in education.

We live in an unequal society, where different groups and classes do not start the educational race on equal terms. In such a society, the combined effects of socialization, home and social class background, teachers' attitudes, the white, male-dominated, middle-class language and culture of the school, and the continued existence of a privileged private sector of education will mean the realization of the ideal of equality of educational opportunity will remain an impossible dream.

Discussion

It has been suggested that reforming schools is as worthwhile an exercise as rearranging the furniture on the *Titanic* – the luxury liner that sank on its first voyage. This is because in terms of improving life chances, schools often do not make much difference to social class, gender, or ethnic inequalities in society as a whole, so reforming schools is basically a pointless exercise. Do you agree?

Chapter Summary

After studying this chapter, you should be able to:

- Explain what is meant by educational underachievement.
- Describe, and give a range of explanations for, the differences in achievement in relation to ethnicity, gender, and social class.
- Explain what is meant by positive discrimination and compensatory education.
- Discuss the arguments for and against the existence of the private sector of education.
- Explain the obstacles to the achievement of equality of educational opportunity.

Project Suggestions

1. Observe classroom activities and try to see if boys and girls behave differently in class and are treated differently by teachers. For example, do they sit separately? Are boys asked more questions? Are boys more troublesome? Does this vary in different subject classes and between male and female teachers? Draw conclusions about the hidden curriculum and gender socialization in schools.
2. Make a study of class, ethnic, or gender differences in educational achievement in a local school or college. For example, examine subject choices and exam results.
3. Interview a sample of school students from different class or ethnic groups, and/or of different sexes, asking them what the major influences are on their subject choices and whether they stay on at school after 16 or not.

Key Terms

compensatory education
educational priority area
elaborated code
ethnocentrism
positive discrimination
restricted code
underachievement

13   Religion

Sociologists are not generally concerned with whether religious belief is 'true' or not. In many ways this does not matter, for the fact is that millions of people hold religious beliefs, and these beliefs have given rise to powerful movements and institutions. In modern Britain, there are millions of followers of the main religions of Christianity, Islam, Hinduism, and Sikhism. Religious belief is therefore certainly real enough in its consequences. Sociologists are mainly interested in these consequences, or the role and significance of religion in society.

A Definition of Religion

There is no single agreed definition of religion, but organized religions and religious beliefs are likely to include all or some of the following features:

- A belief in the supernatural (some sort of belief in God or gods) or in symbols which are in some way regarded as sacred, such as a cross or totem pole.
- A set of teachings and beliefs (theology), usually based on some holy book, such as the Bible or the Koran.
- A series of rituals or ceremonies to express these beliefs, either publicly or privately. For example, most religions contain rituals such as getting on your knees to pray, church services, singing, fasting, or lighting candles.
- Some form of organization of the worshippers/believers, such as priests, churches, mosques, and temples.
- A set of moral values which guide or influence the everyday behaviour of believers, such as the Ten Commandments in Christianity.

The Role of Religion in Society

The role of religion in society can be broadly categorized under three headings: individual support, social integration, and social control.

Individual Support

Religion can play an important role for individuals in a number of ways.

- Religion can provide a source of comfort, explanation, and meaning for individuals when faced by strains and crises in their lives, such as war, death, accidents, and natural disasters. Funeral services, for example, act as a source of comfort for the bereaved – either with beliefs in life after death, or through the support gained in such moments of stress through the gathering of friends and relatives. Church attendances soar during wartime.
- Religious ceremonies can give believers a feeling of identity and security and a sense of belonging to a group that cares about them, and unite them around a shared moral code of behaviour.
- Religion can provide a source of explanation and understanding of questions such as the meaning of life and death, or an explanation or justification for an individual's social position. For example, in the Indian caste system (see chapter 2), the Hindu religion provides an explanation for an individual's position in the social hierarchy.
- Religious groups still carry out some important welfare roles for individuals, even though many of these have been taken over by the welfare state. For example, the Salvation Army remains the largest provider of sleeping accommodation for homeless single men in the country, and its work with 'down and outs' is renowned.

Social Integration

Religion is part of the culture or way of life of a society, and it helps to maintain cultural traditions. Society can only survive if people share some common beliefs about right and wrong behaviour. Durkheim, writing in the nineteenth century, saw religion as a kind of social glue, binding society together and integrating individuals into it by encouraging them to accept basic social values. For example, he saw worshipping together as a means of reinforcing a sense of solidarity in a social group, and it is partly through religion that an individual is socialized into the values of a society. The dominant Christian culture of Britain maintains traditions like Christmas, baptism, and monogamous marriage, and tries to encourage conformity to society's norms. For example, monogamous marriage is seen as 'God-given', and the Ten Commandments, with their rules about stealing, murder, adultery, and so on, in many ways reinforce society's norms.

This set of moral beliefs and values may have been so deeply ingrained through socialization that it may have an effect on the everyday behaviour of believers and non-believers alike. For example, if the rules about killing, stealing, adultery, and extra-marital sex are broken, most individuals will experience a guilty conscience about doing something 'wrong', and this is a powerful socializing and controlling influence over the individual.

In ethnic minority communities in Britain, religious beliefs and customs are often a means for these groups to maintain their own cultural identity and traditions. Sikh and Hindu temples and Muslim mosques often play an important role in integrating such communities, acting as focal points of community life as well as religious life.

Social Control

Religion is the sigh of the oppressed creature, the heart of a heartless world, and the soul of soulless conditions. It is the *opium* of the people. (Karl Marx, 1844)

Karl Marx, writing in the nineteenth century, described religion as the 'opium of the people'. This is because he saw religious belief as an illusion – an hallucinatory drug – attempting to justify existing arrangements in society and encouraging people to accept them. He saw religion doing this in two ways.

Firstly, religion justifies existing inequalities in income and power in society, by explaining the position of the rich and poor as 'the will of God'. For example, the Hindu religion provides a religious justification for the inequalities of the Indian caste system, and the Bible is riddled with quotations such as 'It is easier for a camel to pass through the eye of a needle, than for a rich man to enter the Kingdom of Heaven.' Poverty and resignation to it therefore become, in themselves, virtues. As a result, the poor are more likely to accept their position in society.

> The rich man in his castle,
> The poor man at his gate,
> God made them, high or lowly,
> And ordered their estate.
>
> (the third verse of the traditional hymn 'All Things Bright and Beautiful')

Secondly, Marx believed religion provided comfort for the poor, and drew their attention away from their present misery and the inequalities and injustices of this world with promises of a future golden life after death. In this way, the poor are encouraged to put off the pursuit of personal happiness and rewards in this life for some future reward in heaven. These two aspects of religion, Marx believed, could only benefit the privileged and powerful, since the poor are encouraged to find 'salvation' through religion rather than challenging the position of the rich and powerful.

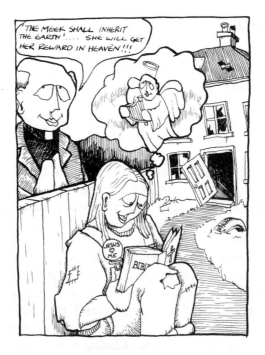

Religion: the opium
of the people?

Activity

1. Explain what point the cartoon is making.
2. Religion mainly encourages people to accept the way things are. Suggest evidence both for and against this view.

Religion, Social Conflict and Social Change

As well as acting as a stabilizing and integrating force in society, religion can also be a source of social change and conflict, causing divisions and instability in society. For example, in Northern Ireland, competing religious beliefs between Catholics and Protestants have been partly responsible for massive social unrest for centuries. The present round of 'the troubles' there has involved armed conflict with the British Army since 1969. In the Indian sub-continent, warfare between Muslims and Hindus was in part responsible for the division of a once united India into two separate countries, India and Pakistan. In the 1980s and 1990s, these divisions have been added to by conflicts between Hindus and Sikhs.

Religion has been responsible for major social change. For example, in South America, Roman Catholic priests – followers of a doctrine mixing Communism and Catholicism called **liberation theology** – have played major roles in fighting against political dictatorships and poverty. In Iran, an Islamic revolution led to the overthrow of the monarchy (the Shah) and the establishment of an Islamic Republic in 1978–9. Islam has become a major international force for social change in the late twentieth century, and the spread of Islamic **Fundamentalism** (a return to the literal words of holy texts) has attempted to forge social changes in much of the Islamic world based on literal interpretations of the Koran. This generally involves the removal of 'decadent' Western cultural influences, changes in the position of women (such as the wearing of veils, being banned from driving and going out in public unaccompanied, and being refused access to some education and occupations), and the establishment of legal punishments which to most Western eyes are barbaric, such as public flogging or the amputation of the hands of persistent thieves.

The Secularization Thesis

The word 'secular' means 'non-religious', and the secularization thesis is simply the suggestion that religion and religious beliefs are of declining importance both in society and for the individual. Wilson gives the following definition of secularization in *Religion in a Secular Society* (C. A. Watts 1966):

> Secularization is the process whereby religious thinking, practice, and institutions lose social significance.

Using Wilson's definition, secularization can then be examined in terms of three aspects: religious thinking – the influence of religion on people's beliefs and values; religious practice – such as the levels of church membership and church attendance; and religious institutions – the extent to which churches and other religious institutions have maintained their social influence and wealth.

Activity

1. Take each of the three aspects of secularization – religious thinking, religious practice, and religious institutions – and suggest four ways in each case you might measure whether secularization is occurring (apart from those given above).
2. Using the 'measures' you have just drawn up, suggest how, in each case, the indicators may not necessarily provide reliable evidence of a decline of religion in society.

The Problem of Measuring Secularization

The previous activity may have shown you that the main difficulty with deciding whether secularization has taken place is how religion and religious belief are defined and measured. For example, is church attendance a good way of measuring how much religious belief there is in a society? Does going to church mean you really believe in God? Can you be religious without attending religious ceremonies?

Church membership figures are very unreliable as sources of evidence for secularization because different denominations have different ways of defining membership. For example, the Catholic Church decides membership on the basis of those who are baptized as Catholics, but this tells us nothing about their beliefs as adults. The Methodists decide on the basis of those attending a membership service, while the Church of England may use indicators such as baptisms, confirmations, or those attending key services such as Easter Communion.

Table 13.1 shows the results of a survey on people's religious beliefs in Great Britain in 1985. Sociologists would want to ask what the indicators used actually mean. For example, what do people mean by 'God', 'sin', the 'soul', and that 'God is important in my life' (in what ways?)? If people say they believe in God, does this mean it influences their everyday behaviour?

Because of these problems of interpreting and measuring the extent of religious belief and practice, there is no clear agreement among sociologists over whether and to what extent secularization has occurred.

Activity/Discussion

Refer to table 13.1.

1. List the ten most important indicators of religious commitment in table 13.1 which, in your opinion, show that Britain has become a secular society. Explain the reasons why you think these indicators are important.
2. Are you a religious person? How many of the forty eight indicators in table 13.1 would you answer 'yes' to? How many would you answer 'no' to?
3. Study the 'indicators of moral values'. Do you think these are necessarily good indicators of religious commitment? Do religious people have to support them? Does not supporting them mean a person is not religious? Discuss this with others if you are in a group.

Despite the problems in measuring secularization, there does seem to be a general decline in participation in organized religion in modern Britain. Table 13.1 suggests that while many people claim to continue to hold some orthodox religious beliefs and religiously based moral values, most people do not have much attachment to religious institutions. In a supposedly Christian country, only 14 per cent of the population are members of a Christian church, and in 1989, only 52 per cent of all marriages involved a religious ceremony.

Table 13.1 Indicators of religious commitment, Great Britain, 1985

Indicators of religious disposition	% of sample	Indicators of orthodox belief	% of sample
Often think about meaning and purposes of life	34	Believe in personal God	31
Never think life meaningless	50	(Believe in a spirit or life force)	39
Often think about death	15	Believe in:	
Often regret doing wrong	8	God	76
Need moments of prayer, etc.	50	Sin	69
Define self as a religious person	58	Soul	59
Draw comfort/strength from religion	46	Heaven	57
God is important in my life	50	Life after death	45
Have had a spiritual experience	19	The devil	30
		Hell	27
		Personally fully accept Commandments demanding:	
		No other gods	48
		Reverence of God's name	43
		Holy Sabbath	25

Indicators of moral values		Indicators of institutional attachment	
Absolute guidelines exist about good and evil	28	Great confidence in church	19
Personally fully accept commandments prohibiting:		Church answers moral problems	30
Killing	90	Church answers family problems	32
Adultery	78	Church answers spiritual needs	42
Stealing	87	Attend church monthly	23
False witness	78	Denomination:	
Agree with unrestricted sex	23	Roman Catholic	11
Terrorism may be justified	12	Protestant (established)	68
Following acts never justified:		Free church/Non-conformist	6
Claiming unentitled benefit	78	Believe religion will become:	
Accepting a bribe	79	More important in future	21
Taking marijuana	81	Less important in future	40
Homosexuality	47	Believe in one true religion	21
Euthanasia	30	Religious faith an important value to develop in	
Political assassination	77	children	14
Greater respect for authority: good	73		
Willing to sacrifice life	34		

Source: Adapted from M. Abrams, D. Gerard and N. Timms, (eds), *Values and Social Change in Britain* (Macmillan 1985).

The reasons for growing secularization

The apparent growth of secularization would seem to be the result of the combination of a number of factors.

- Advances in science and technology now provide scientific explanations for questions traditionally answered by religion, such as the origin of the universe and the causes of famine and disease. The 'miracles' of yesterday have become today's scientific discoveries. The growing development of scientific knowledge and explanation tends to undermine religious belief.
- The growth of the welfare state has removed many of the tasks that used to be performed by religious institutions, such as the provision of education, and financial aid in times of distress. This reduces the significance of religion in people's lives.
- The development of the mass media, particularly television, has replaced the church as the main source of authority and knowledge for many people. People are now more likely to form their opinions on the basis of what they read in the newspapers or watch on TV rather than what religion or the church has to say.

Religious beliefs have been
replaced by scientific explanations

Activity

1. Explain in your own words the point being made in the cartoon on the previous page.
2. Look at the following religiously based explanations. Suggest a scientific explanation for each event.
   (a) God made the walls of Jericho come tumbling down.
   (b) 'Mad' people are possessed by evil.
   (c) AIDS is God's vengeance for immorality.
   (d) Witches cure people by casting magic spells.
   (e) 'And the Lord sent a sign...and all the land of Egypt was corrupted by a swarm of flies.'
   (f) 'And the Lord appointed a set time...and all the cattle of Egypt died: but of the cattle of the children of Israel died not one.'
   (g) Lazarus was dead, and 'when Jesus came, he found that he had lain in the grave four days already...it was a cave and a stone covered the entrance...Jesus said 'Take ye away the stone'...and 'Lazarus, come forth'. And he that was dead came forth, bound hand and foot with grave-clothes.' Christ had made Lazarus rise from the dead.

Competing Evidence on Secularization

Much of the secularization debate has been focused on the Christian religion in Britain, and there would appear to be little evidence of secularization occurring in the ethnic minority religions. On the contrary, such religious belief is perhaps growing in strength, particularly in the Muslim community. The following section, therefore, primarily concentrates on some of the competing arguments and evidence both for and against the view that secularization is occurring in the Christian religion in modern Britain.

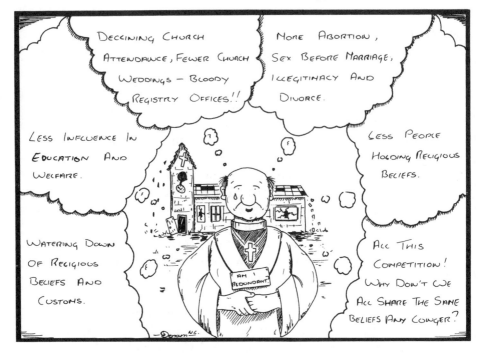

Some indicators of secularization

Evidence for secularization

The decline of religious thinking

Religious beliefs have become less important to individuals in guiding their morals in everyday life. The British Social Attitudes Survey of 1989 found that 1 in 3 Britons claimed to have no religion at all. Various churches' traditional disapproval of divorce, contraception, abortion, sex outside of marriage, illegitimacy, and homosexuality appears to have little impact on people's behaviour. The rising number of divorces, single-parent families, and illegitimate children, couples living together without getting married, extra-marital sex, the growing acceptance of homosexuality, the widespread use of contraception among Catholics in direct opposition to Catholic teachings, and rising levels of drug abuse, pornography, and violent crime might all be used as evidence for the declining importance of religious morals and beliefs in people's lives.

The decline of religious practice

There has been a decline in church membership and church and Sunday school attendance in all the major Christian denominations. Traditional churches have lost one member every six minutes since 1975.

MORI and Social and Community Planning Research surveys in 1989 found that only 15 per cent of the population attended church once a week or more, compared to about 40 per cent in 1851. Only 20 per cent went at least once a month and only about half of the population goes to any religious service at all each year. This makes Britain one of the most irreligious countries in the Christian world. Many of those who attend may do so for reasons other than religious belief, such as family pressure or because friends or relatives are being buried or married. The picture may, therefore, be even worse for religious practice.

While many people do still make use of religious ceremonies for the 'rites of passage' marking significant stages in life – such as baptism, marriage, and funerals – these may only be used to give a sense of occasion, and for most people they may have little religious significance. Most people never attend a church apart from these occasions, and in any case the numbers of these ceremonies are declining. For example, nearly half of all marriages in 1989 were civil marriages (held in registry offices).

The decline of religious institutions

The power and influence of the church in society has declined. The status of the clergy is steadily declining, they are hard to recruit, and they often have lower pay than unskilled manual workers. Church buildings are closing and crumbling today, with over 1250 churches being closed since 1970 and only 390 opened. In the much poorer society of the past they were built, expensively decorated, well maintained, and repaired.

The church used to have great influence in the state and society, in terms of law-making (such as on divorce and abortion), education, politics, and social welfare. Today, the welfare state has taken over many of these roles, with free state education, the social services, the NHS, state benefits, old people's homes, and so on to care for the sick, the poor, the unemployed, and other disadvantaged groups.

Religion is fighting a losing battle to survive, by uniting in the **ecumenical movement**. This is a movement which seeks to achieve greater unity between different Christian churches, such as the Church of England, the Roman Catholic and the Methodist Churches. This could be seen as a classic example of religion – drowning in a sea of apathy, indifference, and empty churches – desperately clutching at straws trying to save itself. Ecumenism might therefore be interpreted as a sign of the weakness of the churches, as they are no longer able to stand on their own feet.

Table 13.2 Membership of churches and other religions, UK, 1975–90

Church or religion	1975	1983	1990
Trinitarian churches[a]: thousands			
Protestant:			
Anglican	2270	2083	1820
Presbyterian	1646	1430	1290
Methodist	615	529	510
Baptist	270	235	240
Other Protestant	728	759	650
Total Protestant	5529	5036	4510
Total Roman Catholic	2535	2215	1950
Total Trinitarian	8063	7251	6460
Percentage of adult population	18.6	16.0	14.0
Non-Trinitarian churches: thousands			
Mormons	100	125	150
Jehovah's Witnesses	80	95	110
Spiritualists	57	52	50
Other non-Trinitarian	97	107	130
Total	334	379	440
Other religions: thousands			
Muslims	400	750	1000
Sikhs	115	160	220
Hindus	100	130	170
Jews	111	109	110
Others	88	176	240
Total	814	1325	1740

[a]Trinitarian churches are Christian churches which believe God consists of three persons: Father, Son, and Holy Spirit.

Source: Social Trends 19, 21 (HMSO 1989, 1991).

The growing number of competing religions, churches, and sects means there is no longer one main church or body of shared religious belief around which people are united. Religion can no longer attract people without packaging itself in many different guises, to appeal to a whole variety of consumer tastes. Religion has become like washing powder on supermarket shelves, with all the rival manufacturers competing desperately to sell the same product to a declining market.

Religion itself is becoming secularized. It no longer provides a lead for people and seems to follow trends rather than set them. The only way

Activity

Study table 13.2 and answer the following questions:

1. How many people belonged to Anglican churches in 1990?
2. By how many did the membership of the Roman Catholic Church decline between 1975 and 1990?
3. What percentage of the population belonged to a Trinitarian church in 1983?
4. Identify two trends shown in the membership of non-Trinitarian churches in table 13.2.
5. How might the evidence in the table be used to show that religion is not necessarily declining in the United Kingdom?
6. There has been a decline in the number of religious marriages in Britain, and about half of all marriages today are civil ceremonies, held in registry offices. Do you think this necessarily means there is a decline in religious belief? What other explanations might there be?

religion can maintain any support is by repackaging itself and watering down or abandoning traditional beliefs and customs – by itself becoming 'less religious'. For example, pop music in churches, the acceptance of easier divorce laws and allowing divorced people to remarry in churches, the growing acceptance of abortion, the abolition of Latin in Catholic services, the ordination of women priests, and a growing acceptance of homosexuality might all be seen as evidence of this collapse of traditional beliefs.

Evidence against secularization

The continuing importance of religious thinking

Religious belief of various kinds remains very widespread. Surveys show that, although 70 per cent of the population thinks religion is losing its influence, 76 per cent of people still claim to believe in God, 69 per cent in sin, and 57 per cent in heaven (see table 13.1 earlier in this chapter). A 1991 survey by the Times Mirror Center of Washington, USA, found that as many as 58% of people in the United Kingdom claimed never to have even doubted the existence of God. There is still widespread belief in the supernatural; many remain superstitious and believe in horoscopes, ghosts, and so on.

Activity/Discussion

Read the spoof article from *Viz* magazine in figure 13.1. The article is intended to be amusing, but how far do you think it highlights the kinds of thing that are happening to religious institutions today?

1. Do you think religious institutions are becoming less religious in the face of competing demands from DIY superstores, garden centres, and the lure of television? What evidence can you think of to back up your view?
2. Do you think religious institutions should follow some of the suggestions (somewhat adapted!) of the 'Rev. Randall', and water down traditional beliefs and practices in order to get 'more arses on pews'?
3. Make a list of your own suggestions for ways religious institutions might attract more people.

Rising rates of crime, divorce, illegitimacy, and so on have a wide range of causes, and cannot be explained as simply arising from declining religious beliefs. Religious beliefs still play an important role in underpinning many social values and social welfare policies. Table 13.1 shows that many people in Britain still support religiously based moral values, such as attitudes to stealing, killing, and adultery.

The widespread acceptance of religiously based beliefs such as the importance of caring for the poor may have forced the state to take over many of the social welfare responsibilities formerly carried out by the church.

The strength of religious practice

Believing in God does not necessarily mean going to church, and going to church does not necessarily mean believing in God. In the past many people may have attended church regularly only because church-going was seen as necessary to achieve respectability in the community. The decline in church attendance today therefore may not necessarily mean that there has been a decline in belief, only a decline in the social pressure to attend church.

The desire for religious belief and commitment is still very strong today. People are simply disillusioned with the traditional churches and are expressing their beliefs in different ways. For example, declining church attendance may simply mean that people prefer to practise their religion more in the privacy of their own homes, in 'house groups', or with services on TV and radio, rather than going to church.

ARSES ON PEWS!

A controversial vicar is calling for dramatic changes in the way churches operate. For unless drastic steps are taken, he fears we could soon be witnessing the end of Christianity itself.

And vicar Dennis Randall believes that unless Holy men are prepared to move with the times, they will soon be left preaching to rows of empty pews.

PACKED

Christmas has traditionally meant big business for the churches, with standing room only in packed houses throughout the country. But all that is changing, and this year vicars are bracing themselves for record low attendances.

FALL

Over the last few years there has been a dramatic fall in the number of people going to church. And religious chiefs fear that unless action is taken to stop the rot, thousands of churches around Britain could soon go under.

STEEPLES

Rev. Randall believes several factors are responsible for the fall in attendances. 'There's been a lack of investment' he told us. 'Too much money has been spent on steeples, and not enough on the churches themselves. We're stuck with old, outdated buildings. Most of them lack even basic toilet facilities.'

FORMAL

'Hymns are also outdated. Some of them are literally hundreds of years old. And I'm sure many young people are put off by the formal dress code. For instance, a church is probably the only place in Britain where you aren't allowed to wear a hat.'

'That's what churches need' says controversial vicar

Could churches like this soon be closing their doors for the last time. (Inset) Rev. Randall yesterday.

SHORTCOMING

Failure to compete in an increasingly competitive Sunday morning environment has been another major shortcoming, according to Rev. Randall. 'DIY superstores and Garden Centres are pulling in the punters in their thousands', he told us.

'They offer shopping, refreshments, play areas for the kids and free car parking. An all we have to offer is a cold seat, a couple of hymns and a few stories about God you've probably heard a hundred times before. It's no wonder we're losing out.'

OUTSKIRTS

Among many suggestions he has put forward is the construction of new, out-of-town 'super-churches'. 'The whole idea of the little church on the corner is completely outdated. We should be building big, new churches on the outskirts of town, with late opening, seven nights a week, and free car parking.'

SPACE

Steps should also be taken to attract people to church. 'Prime land is wasted on cemeteries. We could use this space to have attractive garden displays, fun fairs for kids, and car washes. Everyone washes their car on a Sunday.'

FINAL

Rev. Randall believes a huge commercial opportunity exists in the form of Sunday lunches. 'If we served up good, basic, traditional nosh, at reasonable prices, we'd have the punters queuing up for it', he told us.

The Reverend also dreams of the day when churches will be granted drinks licenses. 'It's ridiculous', he told us. 'You can buy a drink in any pub in the country. But if you're in a church you can't. Britain must be the only country in the world that has such outdated licensing laws. God only knows what tourists make of it all.'

FRONTIER

Rev. Randall believes the key to future success will be attracting young people back to church. 'We must try to get families back. It's all well and good the old folks turning up – they're always welcome – but a lot of them are only interested in the free cup of tea afterwards. And they're not exactly the most generous people in the world when the collection plate comes round.'

BISHOP

So far Rev. Randall's suggestions have met with a cautious response from the Archbishop of Canterbury. 'He hasn't actually replied yet', Rev. Randall admitted, 'but he's been very busy lately.'

ROOK

Meanwhile, the Reverend tells us that he hopes to attract a bumper congregation to his church on Christmas Day, by lining up a troup of exotic dancers to top the bill. 'There's nothing in the Bible to say thou shalt not have strippers on', he joked yesterday. 'And besides, anything that puts arses on pews is good business in my book.' To overcome the drinks ban Rev. Randall will be inviting parishioners to bring along their own bottle of wine.

Figure 13.1 Article from *Viz*
Reproduced with permission of JBP/House of Viz.

As table 13.2 shows, there has actually been an increase in membership of other Christian groupings, such as the Mormons and the Jehovah's Witnesses, and of other religions.

Evangelical 'born again' Christianity is recruiting and converting many people, and is expected to double regular English church-going to 18 per cent of adults by 2015 – four million new churchgoers (see box).

Despite an overall decline in church attendance, that many people continue to make use of religious ceremonies for the 'rites of passage' such as baptism, marriage, and death may show they still believe it is important for religion to 'bless' the important stages in their lives. About 90 per cent of funerals involve a religious ceremony.

The decline in the number of people marrying in churches and the increase in registry office weddings could be because many involve second marriages for one or both partners, or because of the cost, not because of a lack of religious belief. Of first marriages, 69 per cent for both partners still involve a religious ceremony.

Evangelical christianity

The fastest growing Christian movement in Britain in the 1980s and 1990s is evangelical Christianity, part of a worldwide revival of Christianity. **Evangelicalism** is a broad collection of Christians sharing a fundamentalist belief in the Bible – accepting that the Bible is God's literal word and should be strictly followed. Many evangelicals believe in the Second Coming of Christ, faith healing, speaking in tongues, miracles, casting out of demons, and possession by evil. They campaign against witchcraft, satanism, black magic, any form of occult activity, smoking, drinking, sexual promiscuity, and homosexuality.

More than half of all new Anglican priests in 1990 were evangelical 'born again' Christians, and nearly one-quarter of Anglican bishops, including the Archbishop of Canterbury, Dr. George Carey, are evangelicals.

The year 1990 saw 200 000 people taking part in March for Jesus rallies throughout Britain, and a Decade of Evangelism was launched in 1991. This is a ten-year campaign in Britain (with supporters from all the major churches) to win new recruits to Christianity. This new evangelicalism appears to be reviving the religious passion and commitment lacking in the traditional churches, and looks set in the 1990s to halt and even reverse the decline in religious belief and church attendance which has been going on throughout much of the twentieth century.

The continuing influence of religious institutions

Although the power and influence of religious institutions, particularly the Church of England, may have declined compared to last century, they remain important in a number of ways.

- Church of England bishops have seats in the House of Lords (the 'Lords Spiritual').
- The monarch must be a member of the Church of England, is crowned by the Archbishop of Canterbury, and since the time of Henry VIII, has been Head of the Church of England, and 'Defender of the Faith'.
- The Church of England remains the established (or 'official') church in England.
- The Church of England is extremely wealthy, with investment funds of an estimated £3 billion in 1991, and it is one of the largest landowners in the country.
- Since the 1944 Education Act, all schools have been legally obliged to hold a religious ceremony each day, and the 1988 Education Reform Act reaffirmed and strengthened the requirement to hold Christian assemblies and teach Christian beliefs in schools.
- Religious institutions still provide many schools, such as Catholic and Church of England 'maintained schools'.
- There remains a religiously defined 'day of rest' on Sundays, and religious groups have proven, so far, to be extremely effective in fighting off attempts to change the Sunday trading laws (in order to allow all shops to open on Sundays), despite widespread opposition to them. (However, towards the end of 1991, it looked as though such groups were finally losing this battle, as major supermarket chains, like Tescos and Sainsburys, began to defy the Sunday trading laws by opening on Sundays, with the Attorney-General announcing he would not prosecute them for doing so.)
- Religious groups can still act as powerful pressure groups influencing those in positions of power in society. For example, LIFE and SPUC (The Society for the Protection of the Unborn Child) are mainly Catholic organizations seeking to make abortion completely illegal, and have been very effective (though unsuccessful) in raising the issue of abortion in the House of Commons. In Northern Ireland, the Presbyterian Church (in its various forms) and the Catholic Church play major political roles.
- Religion remains very important in the ethnic minority communities. Mosques, temples, and synagogues are often a focus of social and cultural life as well as religious life.

It is unrealistic to expect religion not to change with the times, and the wide variety of churches today simply represents different ways of expressing belief. Evangelical Christianity is the fastest growing form of Christianity in Britain, and the religious fundamentalism this involves cannot be regarded as 'watered down' religion.

Conclusion

This chapter has shown that, while religion can play an important role for the individual and in society, there does seem to be evidence that religion is of declining significance in Britain. However, whether secularization is judged to have taken place or not will be influenced by the indicators of religious commitment which are used. While many people in Britain still claim to hold religious beliefs and to support religiously based moral values, there is little evidence of their showing much participation in religious activities. Nevertheless, evangelicalism looks set to be a major force for Christian revival in the 1990s, and may reverse or at least halt the decline of the Christian churches which has been continuing throughout the twentieth century.

Discussion

Has religion a future in Britain?

Chapter Summary

After studying this chapter, you should be able to:

- Give a definition of religion.
- Explain, with examples, the role of religion for the individual and society.
- Explain how religion can act as an agency of social control.
- Explain, with examples, how religion can influence social change and conflict.
- Explain what is meant by the term 'secularization'.
- Explain some of the problems with measuring religious belief, particularly the difficulties of using church membership and attendance statistics.

- Explain the reasons why society may have become more secular.
- Provide a range of arguments and evidence both for and against the secularization thesis.

Project Suggestions

1. Carry out a study of church attendance figures over time in some local church(es) – are people becoming less religious as measured by church attendance? Try to discover some reasons for this.
2. Interview some local clergy from a variety of denominations and faiths – or members of the public – about whether and in what ways religion is or is not becoming less important.
3. Study the role of a church/mosque/temple in the local community, including interviews with religious leaders.
4. Ask a sample of people of different ages about what, if any, religious beliefs they hold. Table 13.1 in this chapter may give you some ideas for a questionnaire. Relate your findings to the secularization debate.
5. Investigate a local evangelical group, exploring their beliefs, the commitment required, and the occupations (social class), sex, and ages of those involved.

Key Terms

ecumenical movement
evangelicalism
fundamentalism
liberation theology

14 Work and Leisure

Without work, it is difficult to see how society could survive in the form to which we have grown accustomed. The building of roads, houses, hospitals, schools, shops, and factories, the education of children, the production of food and consumer goods, the provision of services, health, welfare, and leisure activities all involve people working. Even when most of us relax from work by watching television, going to a sports centre or a cinema, going out for a meal or to the pub, someone else is working to provide these services.

When we meet someone for the first time, one of the first things we usually find out about them is what they do for a living. In fact, it is quite likely that most people we do meet as adults are a result of contacts made through work. The kinds of leisure pursuit we follow and the time and money available to enjoy them are all related to our work. For this reason, work is central to both society and the lives of the individuals who make it up.

In this chapter, the major issues covered are the importance of work, the factors which influence whether or not work may be an enjoyable experience, and the role of trade unions in the workplace. The changes that have occurred in employment patterns in modern Britain, the changing nature of technology and its consequences for the individual and society, and the patterns of leisure are other key themes.

The Importance of Work

Work is the production of goods or services that usually earns a wage or salary or provides other rewards, though some work, like housework, remains unpaid. Work is an important element in occupying, directing, and structuring the individual's time – the demands of working life involve a high degree of discipline if jobs are to be kept. It is, for most people, the single biggest commitment of time in any week, and it is perhaps one of the most important experiences affecting people's entire lives. Work influences:

- *Status and social class.* The work a person does is generally the most important single factor deciding status in modern societies – most people categorize themselves and others by the job they do. Work is therefore central to the individual's sense of identity and self-esteem. For most people, the work they do provides their sole or major source of income and a person's occupation is a major factor deciding her or his social class.

- *Life chances.* How money is earned, how much, in what working conditions, and how long it takes decide in many ways the kind of life a person will lead. For example, income from work – and future possibilities for promotion and therefore increasing income – will affect the kind of housing and mortgage a person can afford, and therefore the residential area he or she will live in. The hours worked and whether working conditions are good or bad can have major effects on health. Shift-work, nightwork, long hours of overtime, and work carrying risks of industrial disease, accidents, and stress can have serious consequences for a person's health and life expectation.

- *Friendship and community life.* Work is a major place for meeting people and for making friends. The nature of the work situation can affect how much 'social mingling' there is at work and therefore how easily friendships can be made. In the case of traditional working-class communities which are dominated by one industry for generation after generation, such as traditional coal mining and fishing communities, relationships formed at work are likely to be the basis for community life, as workmates are often neighbours, kin, and childhood friends.

- *Values and attitudes.* Work is an important socializing experience that shapes the individual's values and attitudes. Attitudes to trade unions, for example, are likely to be formed by people's experiences at work and the solidarity which develops there. The extent to which people can adopt future planning will frequently depend on how secure their employment is, and whether they can look forward to promotion and increased pay.

- *Family life.* Work will affect the amount of money and time available for family life. Full-time working married or cohabiting women generally have less time for leisure, as they are often expected to do two jobs – their paid work and unpaid housework inside the home.

- *Leisure activities.* The number of hours spent at work and the income earned will obviously affect the time available for leisure activities and the money available to enjoy them. However, a person's occupation and her or his experiences at work can have a direct effect on how leisure time is spent. Parker, *The Sociology of Leisure* (Allen and Unwin 1976), saw the relationship between work and leisure falling into three main patterns, which he called the opposition, neutrality, and extension patterns (see table 14.1).

Attitudes to work

The extrinsic or instrumental attitude to work is one in which the most important thing about a job is high wages. This attitude is usually found in boring, uninteresting, and repetitive jobs such as assembly line work, where high wages are a means of compensating for otherwise boring work, and achieving satisfaction outside work in leisure time.

The intrinsic attitude to work is one in which the most important feature of a job is the amount of pleasure, fulfilment, and satisfaction it offers. High pay is not seen as the only, or most important, reason for doing the job. This attitude is found in professional jobs such as nursing and teaching, and among craft workers.

Figure 14.1 The importance of work

Table 14.1 Patterns of relationship between work and leisure

Work–leisure pattern	Nature of work	Typical occupations	Nature of leisure
Opposition	Physically hard and dangerous male-dominated occupations	Steelworkers, miners, deep-sea fishermen	Opposition to work: escape from hardships of work through drinking and gambling with workmates
Neutrality	Boring and routine work, leading to apathy and indifference	Routine clerical workers, shop assistants	Nothing much to do with work (neutral): leisure for relaxation with home and kin, like DIY and going out with the family
Extension	High levels of personal commitment, involvement, and job satisfaction	Professionals and managers – doctors, teachers, social workers, and business executives	Because work is so interesting or demanding, leisure is work-related – work extends into leisure time; for example, business executives playing golf or eating out with clients, teachers using their own time to run school trips/ holidays with pupils

Unemployment

Nothing shows the importance of work more than the loss of a job, or not being able to find one. Being made redundant is nearly always a shattering experience for the individual, particularly for older people who stand poorer chances of finding another job than those who are younger. Throughout the 1980s, unemployment was a major problem in Britain, and it shows every indication of being a depressingly permanent feature of life for the foreseeable future.

The Causes of Unemployment

The causes of unemployment are varied.

- The development of new technology, with fully automated work processes using computers and microelectronics, requires fewer workers.
- The increase in the working population, including more married women working and more people working to retirement age, reduces the number of unfilled job vacancies.
- Foreign competition from manufactured goods, such as Japanese cars and electrical goods, and the decline of older manufacturing industries has led to many factory closures.
- A depression in the economy, and the unwillingness of governments to invest in job creation schemes, such as road and house building programmes to create employment opportunities, has kept the number of jobs down.
- The skills workers possess may become redundant or obsolete, and they may lack the skills required for the jobs available. This may mean that, despite unemployment, those job vacancies that are available may remain unfilled. It is also possible job vacancies may not be in the same area of the country as the unemployed.

Activity

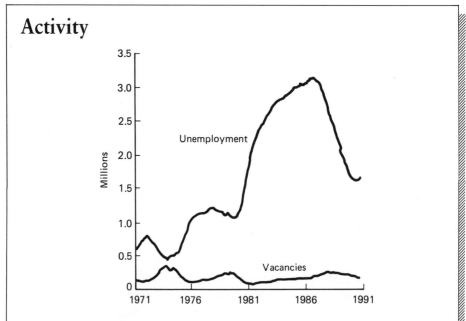

Figure 14.2 Unemployment and vacancies, United Kingdom, 1971–91

Source: Social Trends 21 (HMSO 1991).

Study figure 14.2 and answer the following questions:

1. In approximately which years were there 2 million unemployed?
2. In which year was unemployment at its highest?
3. Approximately how many vacancies were there in 1986?
4. Identify two trends shown in figure 14.2
5. How might the evidence in figure 14.2 be used to challenge the view that 'the jobs are there if people really want them'?
6. Suggest as many reasons as you can for the fact that, even during periods of high unemployment, job vacancies may remain unfilled.

Attempts to Reduce Unemployment

Attempts to reduce unemployment have involved schemes such as job sharing, where two people working part-time share a full-time job. Trade unions have been pressing for a reduction in the working week and longer paid holidays, both of which would, they say, reduce unemployment. Other measures which might be taken include extending the period of compulsory full-time education by raising the school leaving age, reducing the retirement age, and more state investment in job creation schemes.

One method which has been used to reduce the numbers of people appearing in the unemployment statistics has been the development of government job training schemes for the unemployed, such as Employment Training and Youth Training. Those on such schemes are not counted as unemployed as far as the official unemployment statistics are concerned. However, while some of the unemployed find work after being on such schemes, many are only temporarily removed from the unemployment figures and do not find jobs.

Who is Most at Risk of Unemployment?

Neither all groups in the population nor those in different areas of the country face the same risks of unemployment. Some groups and areas are far more likely to face unemployment than others.

* Young people (18–24), because they need training and cannot compete with those already trained.

Figure 14.3 Unemployment rate by region (percentage of workforce unemployed), October 1991

Source: Data from Department of Employment.

- Older people (over 55), as they have a limited working life. Employers are reluctant to retrain them if they have redundant skills, or to offer them jobs if unemployed.
- Non-white people more than white people – an effect of racism and educational underachievement. Between 1987–1989, about 9 per cent of white people were unemployed, compared to 11 per cent of Indians, 16 per cent of Afro-Caribbeans, and 25 per cent of Pakistanis/Bangladeshis.
- Semi-skilled and unskilled manual workers more than skilled manual and non-manual occupations, since they are more disposable and more easily replaceable. In 1990, unemployment among manual workers was twice as high as it was among non-manual workers.
- Men are at a higher risk than women, because men are more likely than women to be in higher-paid, full-time employment in the manufacturing industries which are hardest hit by unemployment.
- As figure 14.3 shows, in October 1991, Northern Ireland had the highest rate of unemployment in the United Kingdom, followed by the North and North-West. The northern areas of Britain are generally hit harder by unemployment than the more prosperous South (this is sometimes referred to as the North-South divide).

The Consequences of Unemployment

The importance of paid work for individuals and society is shown by the effects of its loss – unemployment.

Consequences for individuals

- The loss of the identity, status, and self-esteem which are obtained through work may undermine a person's self-confidence. The endless search for work and the stigma of dependence on welfare benefits and social services are likely to undermine self-esteem further and contribute to growing demoralization and despair.
- Poverty, mounting debts, and hardship arising from the loss of an adequate regular income may create stress and anxiety in coping

Consequences for society

- More discipline at work, with declining influence and membership of trade unions and fewer strikes, as people worry about their jobs.
- An increase in political unrest. The high levels of unemployment in the 1980s in Britain were accompanied by periodic outbreaks of rioting in many of the inner cities.
- More racism and scapegoating, as people try to find easy answers to their unemployment and try to lay the blame on vulnerable groups

Consequences for individuals   *Consequences for society*

with daily life. The loss of a home may result for home-owners or tenants if mortgages or rent cannot be paid.

- Social isolation, with the loss of friendships formed through work, particularly as there is little money to spend on leisure activities, such as going to the pub with friends. More free time, but with little money to enjoy it, may result in boredom.
- More ill-health, brought on by a poorer diet and stress.
- Increasing stress in the family. There may be confusion over roles in the family, for example the 'role swapping' which may occur with working wives and unemployed husbands. 'Getting under one another's feet' may be a problem, particularly if both partners are unemployed.

such as black people and youth.

- More social problems such as poverty, homelessness, mental illness, and rising rates of crime, suicide, alcoholism, and drug abuse.
- Rising levels of stress in the family may cause more family breakdowns, higher divorce rates, and increases in wife- and child-battering.

Activity

Imagine you were to lose your job, or left school or college and were unable to find work while your friends were working. List all the ways this would affect or change your life. What conclusions can you draw about the importance of work in the lives of individuals?

Industrialization, Mechanization and Automation

Craft Production

Before industrialization, work was mainly agricultural but with some small-scale **craft production** based in the home. In craft production, a worker has full control of the production process, and makes a complete product from start to finish using manual skills and hand tools. An example would be hand-making and finishing a pair of shoes.

The Division of Labour

In industrial society, work becomes factory-based, and the **division of labour** develops very rapidly. This is a term referring to the way work is divided up into a large number of specialized tasks, each of which is carried out by one worker or group of workers. In modern industrial society, the division of labour has been developed so highly that most jobs have been reduced to a few simple tasks requiring very little skill – they have been deskilled. Today, most workers make only one small part of a finished product. This often leads to little satisfaction and pride for the worker, compared to the craft worker who used to make an entire product, and many craft skills have been taken over by machinery today.

Industrial society

An industrial society is one which has the following features:

- The production of goods is mainly carried out by machines rather than using craft skills.
- The workforce is urban-based, in industrial towns and cities, rather than rural-based, in agriculture in the countryside.
- Work is based in factories and offices, rather than the home.
- The workforce is dependent for its livelihood on earnings gained through working for others, rather than self-produced goods and foodstuffs.

Mechanization

Mechanization involves the production of goods by machines, which take over the manual skills involved in craft production. *Assembly line production* is a further development of mechanization. Here, as products travel along a moving conveyor belt, each worker uses machines to carry out the same small task until the product is finished at the end of the line. Because the tasks required of each worker are so routine and simple and require little skill or training, such work is often boring, repetitive, and unsatisfying.

From the employer's point of view, assembly line production is fast, cheap, and efficient, because workers can be cheaply and quickly trained, as there are so few skills involved in the work, and they can easily be replaced. Henry Ford, founder of the Ford Motor Company, was one of the first to use assembly lines for the mass production of cars at the beginning of this century. This soon became the model for the production of cars internationally, and the assembly line is widely used in many manufacturing industries today.

craft   mechanization   assembly line   automation
production   production

Automation

Automation is the process where machinery and computers not only make goods, but also control the speed of production, the input of raw materials, and the correction of any mistakes, with very little human supervision. Automation has become very widespread in the late twentieth century in many industries because of the development of the microchip and computer technology. It is most obvious in the production of cars today using robot technology. However, computer technology such as word processors has also transformed many aspects of routine clerical work, such as record keeping, monitoring sales and orders, and mailshots to customers. Many aspects of routine management work have also been largely automated, for example with the application of computer spreadsheets to accounting tasks.

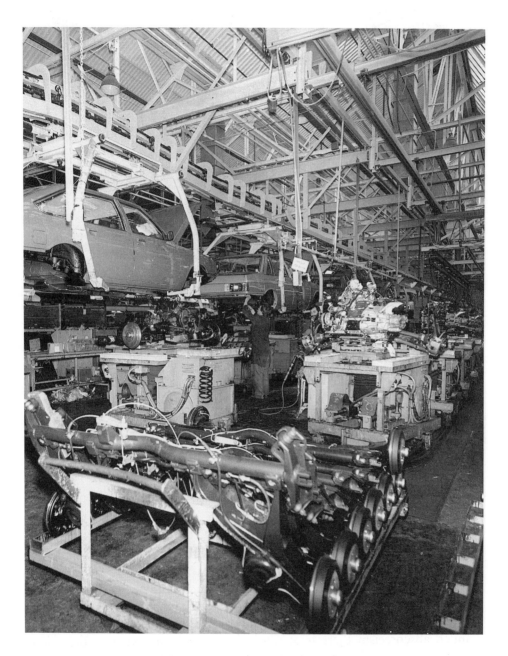

Car assembly line production

Source: Peugeot Talbot.

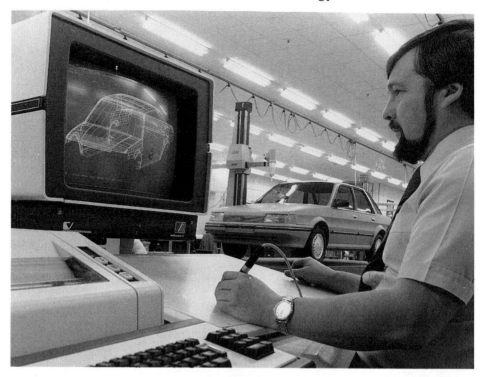

Computers play a key role today in car design and engineering development

Source: Rover Group.

Alienation and Job Satisfaction

- **Job satisfaction** is concerned with how much enjoyment, involvement, and pleasure people get from their work. Sociologists have attempted to measure the degree of job satisfaction by looking at factors such as how much absenteeism there is at work, how much involvement there is in work-based social clubs and similar activities, and how many strikes there are.
- **Alienation** is the condition where workers have no job satisfaction or fulfilment from their work. Work becomes meaningless and workers have an extrinsic or instrumental attitude to their job.

Two Views of Alienation

The Marxist view

Karl Marx believed alienation came about because the workers lacked power and were exploited at work. The workers have little control over the work they do, and they own neither the products they produce, nor the means of producing them, with all the products and the profits going to the factory owner – the capitalist. In many cases, the workers cannot even afford to buy the products they spend all day producing. Marx believed that only in a communist society, where industry was owned by all the people rather than private individuals, could work be really satisfying and fulfilling. (see chapter 3 for a fuller discussion of Marx's ideas.)

Blauner's view

Blauner described four main aspects of alienation.

- *Powerlessness*. The worker has no control over decisions that are made at work; for example, a lack of control over working conditions or management decisions.
- *Meaninglessness*. Work is seen as pointless and boring, as it often involves making only one small part of a finished product.
- *Isolation*. The worker feels isolated from fellow workers. Friendships are hard to form and the worker feels like a cog in a machine.
- *Self-estrangement*. The worker feels his or her full potential is not being fulfilled, with no personal creativity or self-expression in the work – a feeling that anyone could do the job.

The type of technology used and the way it is used can have an effect on how much alienation or job satisfaction workers derive from their work. For example, craft production often involves a high level of job satisfaction. This is because the craft worker is responsible for the production of a complete product, and the work involves a high level of skill in using hand tools, and demands creativity and judgement. The skills of craft workers often give them independence, responsibility, and control in the work situation. By contrast, assembly line work often involves high levels of alienation. Here, the speed of the assembly line decides how fast the worker must work, and each worker makes only a small part of the finished product. Such work requires little skill and is very boring and repetitive. The worker lacks control over the speed of work, and the speed and noise of the assembly line often prevent the development of any real social contact with other workers.

Figure 14.4 illustrates the range of factors which can influence the amount of satisfaction found in work.

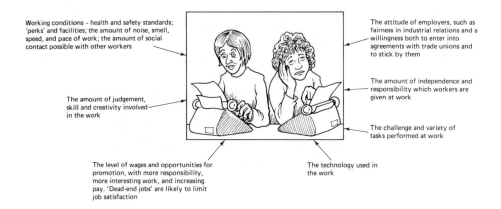

Figure 14.4 Factors influencing job satisfaction and alienation

Activity

1. Study figure 14.4 and look at the following list of jobs. Based on your own opinions, mark each of them as having either 'high', 'medium' or 'low' levels of job satisfaction. In each case identify the features of each job which explains your answer.

Nurse
Refuse collector
Car assembly line worker
Police officer
Teacher
Airline pilot
Pub/bar worker
Shop assistant

Social worker
Office worker (clerical work)
Painter and decorator
Bricklayer
Senior company manager
Housewife
Taxi driver
Fire fighter
Receptionist

2. It is often thought that people in non-manual work are more likely to have higher levels of job satisfaction than those in manual jobs. Explain, with reference to particular jobs, why this might be the case. How and why do you think this might be changing?

Responses to Alienation

Workers do not take alienating work lying down, and there is a wide range of methods used to resist it. Some typical responses of workers to alienating work include:

- Producing poor quality, faulty goods.
- Taking unofficial breaks ('going to the toilet'), and extending official ones to get some relief.
- High levels of absenteeism and 'skiving off', with large numbers of workers 'off sick'.
- Leaving the job because it is so boring. A high turnover of workers is common in alienating work.
- Conflict with management, with workers using trade unions to 'get back' at management, through actions such as lack of cooperation, strikes, and working to rule.
- Attempts to achieve more creativity outside work in leisure time to compensate for the lack of meaning in work, such as DIY activities or gardening.
- Industrial sabotage. This concerns actions aimed at destroying the workplace, machinery, or goods produced – literally putting a spanner in the works – to get some temporary relief from alienating work. Laurie Taylor and Paul Walton describe this process graphically:

They had to throw away half a mile of Blackpool rock last year, for, instead of the customary motif running through its length, it carried the terse injunction 'Fuck Off'. A worker dismissed by a sweet factory had effectively demonstrated his annoyance by sabotaging the product of his labour. In the Christmas rush in a Knightsbridge store, the machine which shuttled change backwards and forwards suddenly ground to a halt. A frustrated salesman had demobilized it by ramming a cream bun down its gullet. In our researches we have been told by Woolworth's sales girls how they clank half a dozen buttons on the till simultaneously to win a few minutes rest from 'ringing up'. Railwaymen have described how they block lines with trucks to delay shunting operations for a few hours. Materials are hidden in factories, conveyor belts jammed with sticks, cogs stopped with wire and ropes, lorries 'accidentally' backed into ditches. Electricians labour to put in weak fuses, textile workers 'knife' through carpets and farmworkers cooperate to choke agricultural machinery with tree branches. (Laurie Taylor and Paul Walton, 'Industrial sabotage: motives and meanings' in Stanley Cohen (ed.), *Images of Deviance* (Penguin 1971))

Attempts to Reduce Alienation

In the face of declining work satisfaction and the consequences of this for the efficient running of industry, a number of attempts have been made to overcome feelings of alienation among the workforce and increase their involvement in their work.

Teamwork, job rotation, and job enlargement involve a group of workers carrying out a complete operation, swapping around jobs to vary the skills used and the routine of work, and making each particular job cover a wider range of activities. These changes may make otherwise boring jobs more interesting, and lead to more responsibility and control at work, and more social contact among workmates. This method has been successfully used at the Volvo car factories in Sweden.

Attempts have been made to increase the workforce's sense of control at work through worker participation in management decision-making and 'worker directors'. With flexitime, workers have to work the normal total hours each week, but can work some long days and some short ones at their own discretion, as long as they are completed between certain hours each day, for example between 8 a.m. and 7 p.m. This gives the worker more independence and choice at work. This practice is more likely to be found in office work than factory work, as there are less pressures to keep machinery running.

To encourage workers to identify themselves as having a stake in the firm's success, profit-sharing schemes have been developed. These are an attempt to motivate the workers by a promise of a share in the firm's profits if they work harder.

Who Gets Job Satisfaction Today?

Industrialization, changing technology, and the division of labour have meant that most jobs today require little skill or creativity, and work for many people has become a boring, mind-numbing experience. There are probably only a minority of people today who really enjoy their work. Craftworkers, artists, and those in professional and managerial occupations are likely to find some intrinsic job satisfaction. Professional caring jobs such as those in medicine, nursing, social work, and teaching are often personally satisfying jobs because of the responsibility and commitment involved in caring for people. However, many workers lack the independence and responsibility found in such occupations, and it is likely that the majority of workers have an instrumental attitude to work. It is not something they enjoy or identify with. Work is primarily and simply a means of getting the money to enjoy 'real life' outside work, rather than an enjoyable and satisfying activity in its own right.

Discussion

Do you agree that most work today is basically unsatisfying? What could be done to make work a more fulfilling experience for people?

The Effects of Changing Technology on Society

The development of technology has had important effects in deskilling work, and has generally had negative consequences on the way people experience their work. But there are wider effects.

- As technology changes, new skills are needed and old skills become redundant, and retraining of workers is becoming increasingly important. Educational institutions are more and more concerned with providing people with new qualifications to meet the demands of industry for changing expertise, and the emphasis now is on the adaptability of workers to adjust to rapidly changing technology.

- Many of the dirtier physical aspects of work have disappeared, as have some of the more repetitive tasks, as machines have taken over jobs formerly done by people. As a consequence, the numbers of unskilled and semi-skilled workers have been reduced.

- A long-term rise in under-employment and unemployment is a real possibility, especially among less qualified workers, as machines take over jobs. Even skilled manual jobs have been wiped out by new technology, such as robot technology taking over the jobs of car workers and computerized desk-top publishing and typesetting reducing the need for printers. In the High Street today, for example, cash dispensers outside every bank and computerized bar-code checkouts at supermarkets have led to hundreds of redundancies among bank and shop staff.

- While new technology threatens existing jobs, it also creates new ones. More skilled manual and white-collar supervisory jobs are created, such as technicians, engineers, computer programmers, and administrators, which are necessary for maintaining and servicing the new technology, and administering and organizing production. However, it remains to be seen whether these will be enough to make up for the job losses.

- If enough new jobs are not created, and unless there is a substantial increase in spending by the welfare state, one consequence of technological change might be even more widespread poverty.

Does automation threaten all jobs?

- New technology is likely to generate changing work patterns, with more shift-work, nightwork, six-day working, and overtime to keep complex automated processes running twenty-four hours a day. At the same time, automation can produce cheaper and better-quality products in a shorter space of time. As industry becomes more productive and efficient, there is the possibility of a shorter working week, earlier retirement, and more leisure time.
- The 1980s saw a massive expansion of DIY activities of various kinds, as people sought to fill expanding leisure time and find some satisfaction and creativity from exercising skills which were increasingly denied at work.

Discussion

Do you think that technological change will have good or bad effects on society and the individual's experience of work?

The Changing Occupational Structure

The themes which have been discussed in much of this chapter so far have contributed to quite dramatic changes in the pattern of employment in Britain over the past two centuries. The key changes, which are all related to each other, are outlined below.

Change 1: The Service Economy

The pattern of work has shifted from a predominantly agricultural economy before industrialization, when most people were working in agriculture (this is often referred to as the *primary sector* of the economy). With the beginning of the Industrial Revolution about two hundred years ago, most people began to move into manufacturing industries (known as the *secondary sector*) in the nineteenth century, concerned with the production of goods. The second half of the twentieth century has seen a decline in manufacturing, with most people working in the service sector (or *tertiary sector*) of the economy. The service sector is concerned with administration, information, communication, catering, the leisure industry, sales, finance and insurance, transport and distribution, and the running of government services such as the health, welfare, and education services. This shift in employment patterns between the three sectors of the economy is often referred to as the change to a service economy. Table 14.2 illustrates this change between 1971 and 1991.

Table 14.2 Employees in employment (by industry)

Industry	1971	1991	% change
Agriculture, forestry, and fishing	450 000	269 000	− 40
Manufacturing	8 065 000	4 886 000	− 39
Services	11 627 000	15 436 000	+ 33

Source: Derived from Social Trends 21 (HMSO 1991) and Employment Gazette, May 1991.

This change has meant that the numbers of people employed in different industries has changed, as figure 14.5 shows.

Activity

Study figure 14.5 and answer the following questions:

1. How many people were employed in metal goods, engineering, and vehicles in 1971?
2. Which industry employed 1 336 000 workers in 1971?
3. Which industry employed the most workers in 1989?
4. How many people were employed in banking, finance, and insurance in 1998 compared to 1971?
5. Which industry employed the smallest number of workers in 1989?
6. Which two industries showed the greatest percentage decline between 1971 and 1989?
7. How many more women employees were there in 1989 than in 1971?
8. What percentage change was there between 1971 and 1989 in the number of male employees?
9. Classify each of the following jobs as either 'manufacturing' or 'services':

Bank clerk   Carpenter
Car assembly line worker   Teacher
Assistant in burger bar   Shipbuilder
Lorry driver   Shop assistant
Tool maker   Baker

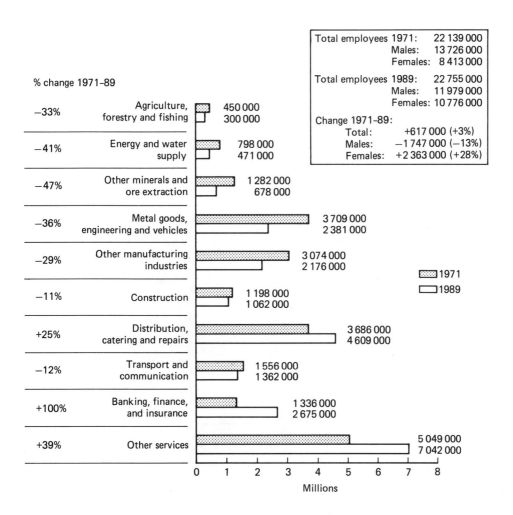

Figure 14.5 Employees in employment: by industry and sex, United Kingdom, 1971–89

Source: Adapted from *Social Trends 21* (HMSO 1991).

Change 2: The Decline of Manual Occupations and the Increase in Non-manual Occupations

The change towards a service economy has meant there has been a decline in the proportion of the labour force working in manual occupations, and a rapid increase in the percentage engaged in non-manual occupations, especially in routine clerical and sales work, and in managerial and professional work. This is illustrated in Figure 14.6.

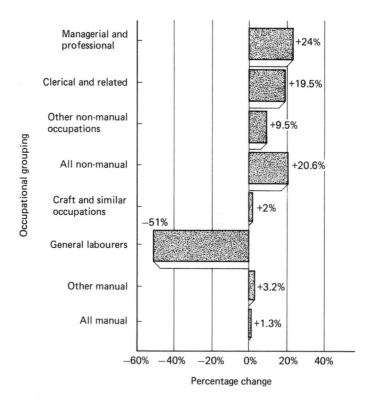

Figure 14.6 Percentage change in occupations of people in employment, Great Britain, 1984–90

Source: Department of Employment Labour Force Survey 1990.

Change 3: The Decline of Semi- and Unskilled Manual Work and the Increase in Skilled Manual Work

Traditional industries such as shipbuilding, mining, and the iron and steel industries have declined. These employed many semi- and unskilled workers. This, combined with the speed of technological change, has meant that many semi- and unskilled manual jobs have disappeared, as machinery has taken over tasks that were previously carried out by labourers. New, skilled workers are required to operate new machinery and to maintain computerized industries. Figure 14.6 shows this change quite dramatically between 1984 and 1990.

Change 4: The Growing Employment of Women

There has been a large increase in the numbers of women working in paid employment, contrasting with a decline in the numbers of men employed. There are several points worth noting about the employment patterns of women.

- A large proportion of the increase in the numbers of women working outside the home has been among married women. Far more women work part-time than men, as table 14.3 shows, and in 1989 just over half of married women in employment were in part-time work compared with about a quarter of non-married women.
- Women generally work in different types of jobs to men.

  — They are more likely than men to be in non-manual work, though this is usually in the more 'menial' non-manual occupations, such as routine clerical work and sales assistants. Even those women in the professions are most commonly found in the lower professions such as teaching, nursing, and social work.
  — They are most likely to be employed in the service sector of the economy.

The position of women in paid employment was discussed extensively in chapter 6. You should refer to this for further detail on the employment patterns of women, and explanations for it.

Table 14.3 People in employment, by sex and full- or part-time status, 1971–90

	1971	1981	1990
Women in employment[a] of which:	8 413 000	9 331 000	10 535 500
Full-time	5 216 060 (62%)	5 318 670 (57%)	5 873 600 (56%)
Part-time	3 196 940 (38%)	4 012 330 (43%)	4 661 900 (44%)
Men in employment[b] of which:	13 726 000	12 562 000	11 643 600
Full-time	13 588 740 (99%)	12 185 140 (97%)	10 692 800 (92%)
Part-time	137 260 (1%)	376 860 (3%)	950 800 (8%)

[a]Women aged 16–59
[b]Men aged 16–64

Source: Adapted from the *Employment Gazette* and *Social Trends 21* (HMSO 1991).

Activity

Study figure 14.3 and answer the following questions:

1. How many women were in employment in 1990?
2. How many women were in part-time employment in 1981?
3. By how many did the number of part-time women workers increase between 1971 and 1990?
4. According to table 14.3, state whether each of the following statements is true or false:

    (a) There were more men in employment in 1971 than in 1990.
    (b) Between 1971 and 1990, the numbers of women working full-time increased more than the numbers of women working part-time.
    (c) The numbers of men working part-time increased by 642 500 between 1971 and 1990.
    (d) The numbers of women in full-time employment increased between 1981 and 1990.
    (e) The table might be misleading because the men included come from a wider age range than the women.

5. Suggest reasons why women are more likely to work part-time than men.

Trade Unions

Trade unions are organizations of workers formed for the protection of their members' interests. A trade union is an example of a protective pressure group. Most larger workplaces today will have a shop steward or convenor – a union representative elected by union members in a particular workplace – to advise and assist union members. The strength of trade unions lies in the fact that they represent the interests of large numbers of workers, who can act together as one force to negotiate with management. The unity of workers is the union's strength.

The trade union movement in Britain began in the nineteenth century, and today trade unions play an important part in the working life of the nation. About 40 per cent of the employed workforce belonged to a trade union in 1991. Growth in trade union membership has been greatest among white-collar workers in recent years, partly due to the expansion of these occupations. However, the process of proletarianization of white-collar workers, which was discussed in chapter 3, has certainly contributed to their turn to trade unionism.

What do Trade Unions Do?

Individuals have little power on their own to improve or change things in the workplace, and uniting together with other workers is the most effective way for workers to defend their interests. Individuals join unions to benefit from the wide range of activities which unions carry out. These activities include:

- Bargaining with employers for better wages, overtime rates, and bonuses.
- Improving the working hours and terms and conditions of employment of their members. These might include a shorter working week, longer paid holidays, maternity benefits, better pension and sick pay schemes, improved promotion prospects and training schemes, improved health and safety at work, and better canteen and sports facilities.
- Fighting against unfair dismissal and reducing the risks of redundancy, and protecting and promoting the rights of workers in areas such as health and safety at work and employment law.
- Providing legal and financial assistance to members, such as taking an employer to court for causing injury due to negligence in safety standards, and providing strike pay.
- Acting as pressure groups, putting pressure on those with political power in society to reform industrial and employment legislation, and campaigning on other general issues of interest to their members, such as unemployment or declining standards in the NHS.

The Methods Unions Use to Protect their Members' Interests

Negotiation with management is one of the most common everyday activities of unions. Elected representatives of the workforce, such as shop stewards or convenors, play an important role in discussing grievances and improvements in wages and working conditions with employers. Negotiation may go on at the level of the individual workplace or of the area, or at the national level with employers' organizations.

Legal action is sometimes taken against employers; for example, because the employer is to blame for an industrial accident or disease, or because the employer has broken the employment laws in some way.

Overtime bans, 'going slow' or working to rule are frequent forms of industrial action used by trade unions to put pressure on an employer during an industrial dispute. By banning overtime and doing the minimum necessary by working strictly to the employer's rulebook and agreements reached between a trade union and the employer, workers can slow down production and therefore bring pressure to bear on an employer by eating into his or her profits.

By refusing to work at all, by going on strike, workers can bring production to a standstill. The strike weapon is generally used by unions only as a last resort when all negotiations with employers have broken down. Official strikes are those approved by the union leadership; unofficial strikes are not.

The Declining Membership and Influence of Trade Unions

In recent years the power and influence of trade unions in both society and the workplace have declined. As shown in figures 14.7 and 14.8 both the number of trade union members and the percentage of the employed labour force belonging to trade unions have declined since their peaks in 1978.

There are three broad explanations behind the decline in the influence and membership of trade unions.

Changes in the law

Laws have been passed limiting the power of trade unions, such as the Trade Union Act of 1984 and the Employment Acts of 1980, 1982, 1988, and 1991. These have reduced the power of unions in a number of ways.

- It is now necessary for a secret ballot of the membership to be held before industrial action such as strikes and overtime bans can be taken, with the threat of court action if the unions fail to comply. This can limit the speed with which a trade union can bring a dispute to an end, as well as allowing workers who are not familiar with the issues to vote.
- The right to picket has been limited (picketing is trying to persuade fellow workers not to work during a strike by meeting them outside the workplace). This restricts the ability of a trade union to bring pressure to bear on an employer by disrupting the everyday routine of the workplace, and to spread a strike to other areas.
- It is now a legal requirement to hold a secret ballot before union funds can be used to support political parties or campaigns.

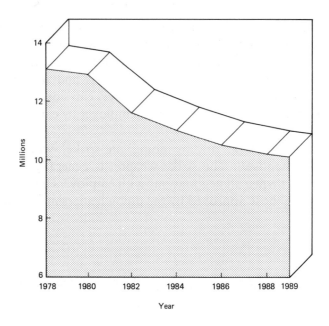

Figure 14.7 Trade unions in decline: membership figures, United Kingdom, 1978–89

Source: *Employment Gazette*, Department of Employment, May 1990 and June 1991.

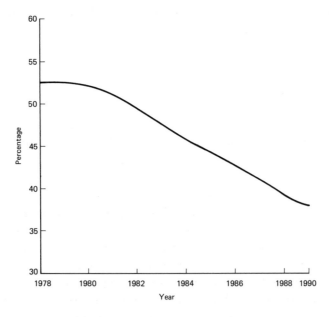

Figure 14.8 Trade union members as a percentage of the employed workforce, United Kingdom, 1978–90

Source: *Employment Gazette*, Department of Employment, May 1990 and June 1991.

- The closed shop has been made illegal. (In a closed shop, all the workers must belong to the trade union, and a refusal to join will result in dismissal.) This weakens the power of the union to represent all those in the workplace.

Activity

1. According to figure 14.7, approximately how many trade union members were there in 1982?
2. In what two-year period was there the steepest drop in trade union membership?
3. According to figure 14.8, what percentage of the employed workforce belonged to trade unions in 1982?
4. Describe the trend shown in figure 14.8 (giving figures).

Higher levels of unemployment

Higher levels of unemployment, especially in older manufacturing industries where trade unions have traditionally been well represented, have reduced union membership and power, and made those in employment unwilling to take industrial action in case they lose their jobs. The decline in industrial stoppages (strikes) as unemployment rises is shown in figure 14.9.

The decline in the traditional working class

There has been a reduction in the numbers of the traditional working class employed in the declining heavy industries concentrated in the north of England, such as mining and shipbuilding, and dock-labour forces. Such workers have traditionally been committed trade union supporters. The 'new' working class found in the newer lighter industries mainly in the south of England are less likely to be union members. (See chapter 3 for a discussion of the 'traditional' and 'new' working classes.)

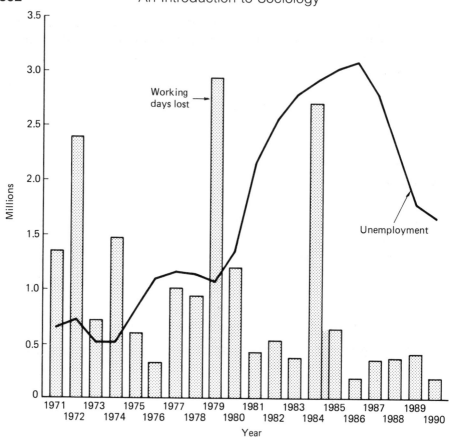

Figure 14.9 Industrial stoppages and unemployment: working days lost due to industrial disputes, 1972–90. The high level of strikes in 1972 was due to the miners' strike, that of 1979 was due to the 'winter of discontent', and that of 1984 was due to the miners' strike.

Source: Department of Employment.

Activity/Discussion

1. What does the cartoon opposite suggest might be some of the causes of strikes?
2. Suggest other issues at work which might provoke trade unions into taking strike action.

3. Discuss the following statement: 'Workers should have the right to join together in trade unions to protect their interests, and should be allowed to take any non-violent action they choose in order to do so, provided the majority of the members support it. Any attempts by the government to limit the power of trade unions undermines workers' rights and can only benefit the employer.'

Do employers and workers have different interests?

Leisure

What is Leisure?

Leisure time is not simply time not spent at work, because activities like travelling to work, personal care, housework, shopping, childcare, and sleeping are all essential commitments of time which most people would not regard as leisure. Leisure time and activity generally involve:

- Time free of practical commitments, such as work and study.
- Activities which are self-imposed and freely chosen.
- Activities which the individual considers to be personally enjoyable.

The distinction between 'work time', 'committed time', and 'leisure time' is sometimes difficult to make, and some activities are not easy to separate. For example, cooking for a family every day may be seen as a real work chore by a housewife, but it might be seen as an enjoyable leisure pastime by those who are not compelled to do it every day. The same activity may be work for one person and yet not work for another. The following examples illustrate this.

- Decorating your own home yourself is not generally seen as work, but would be for the painter you employed to do it for you. Similarly, some people may not see this as 'committed time' but as an enjoyable leisure activity.
- Watching a professional football match would be leisure for most people, but not for the newspaper reporter who has to write a report on the game, nor for the players.
- People in professional and managerial work might use their leisure time to carry out work-related activities, such as business people entertaining clients at home or playing golf with them, or teachers going on school trips with pupils.
- Some jobs involve work-related responsibilities at all times, as in the case of doctors or the police.
- Some people may enjoy their work so much that they take it up as a leisure activity, such as professional musicians.

Activity

1. Keep a record for one week of the time you spend on all your various activities. Classify them under the headings 'work time', 'committed time', and 'leisure time'. (Count studying as 'work time' if you are in full-time education.) Keep a record of those activities which you find difficult to classify under any of these headings.
2. Present your findings in the form of a pie chart (there are 168 hours in a week), with a category 'other' for activities which don't really fit under the main headings.
3. Explain why you found the activities in 'other' difficult to classify.
4. What do your findings tell you about:
    (a) the amounts of real leisure time you have?
    (b) the restrictions on expanding your leisure time?
    (c) the difficulties of distinguishing between work and leisure?

The Changing Pattern of Leisure

In pre-industrial Britain, the division between work and leisure was more blurred than it is today. People worked in the family home, which was a unit of production, and people had greater control over when to work and when to enjoy their leisure. Work and leisure were also more closely linked. For example, people might mix business and pleasure, by going to a country fair not only to enjoy themselves but also to sell a few of their goods.

With industrialization, work moved outside the home to factories, and people lost control over their work and leisure time: people had to work for employers who decided the length of the working day and the length of holidays. Leisure therefore became clearly separated from work.

This century the basic working week has been shortened, reduced to about 39 hours a week in 1989, as shown in figure 14.10. This means people have more time for leisure today.

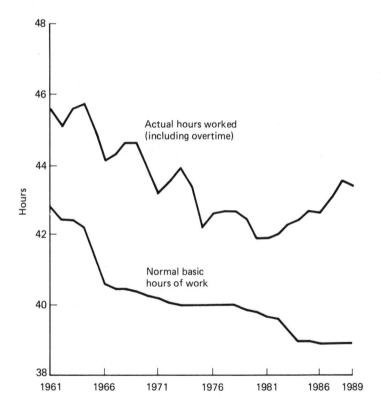

Figure 14.10 Weekly hours of work: full-time manual employees, United Kingdom, 1961–89

Source: Social Trends 21 (HMSO 1991).

Paid holidays have increased, and higher incomes have raised standards of living. This has enabled people to take advantage of increased leisure time to pursue more varied and ambitious activities. Widespread car ownership, for example, has opened up a range of leisure activities, and more working-class people have access through package holidays to places like Greece and Spain that were once only available to the rich.

Rapid changes in technology have occurred this century, which have affected the nature of leisure activities. Increased alienation at work, with deskilling through new technology, has meant that many people are trying to achieve satisfaction and creativity outside work through creative leisure pursuits. The massive growth of the DIY industry and the prolific spread of garden centres illustrates this.

Leisure has itself become a highly organized and commercialized business. The mass production methods employed in manufacturing industry have been applied to leisure activities, such as the mass production of stereo systems and video recorders to cater for the products of the record and music industries. Mass entertainment such as spectator sports, television, the cinema and video, the package holiday industry, the DIY industry, and the spectacular (and expensive) developments such as Alton Towers and Disneyland are very big business indeed. Fewer people make their own entertainment today, and large businesses make huge profits organizing leisure activities for the 'masses'.

Factors Influencing the Choice of Leisure Activity

Social class

Social class differences in leisure have been exaggerated, but differences in income, car ownership, educational qualifications, and working hours mean that middle- and working-class people often follow different leisure activities. For example, they are likely to read different books, magazines and newspapers, watch different TV programmes and films at the cinema, join different organizations, eat and drink in different pubs, wine bars and restaurants, and travel to different holiday destinations. Some leisure activities are denied to the working class simply because of the high costs involved. For example, the high membership fees of private golf clubs, and the expense of activities such as flying and motor racing, effectively bar such activities to the working class, and much of the middle class.

Age

Age has an obvious influence on the choice of leisure activities. The leisure of young single people tends to be spent outside the home in the company of their peer group. They may gain some economic independence from either a wage packet or benefits obtained on Youth Training, but lack the financial commitments and responsibilities of household bills, children, and the burden of a mortgage. This means young people are more leisure centred than perhaps any other age group except the retired. The most common

Figure 14.11 Influences on the choice of leisure activity

leisure activities among the young are going to the cinema, pubs, and discos, as well as listening to music.

Young couples tend to be more home based, as they have little spare money for leisure, after buying or renting a home, buying furniture, and starting a family. DIY, home and car maintenance, and watching the TV or video are likely to be typical activities.

Middle-aged people tend to have the most money available for leisure. Children have grown up, the mortgage is nearly paid off and there is more disposable income to spend on leisure activities like holidays and eating out.

Older retired people are more likely to be home based than any other group, through either choice, ill-health, pressure of declining income, or poverty. Reading, gardening, television, and other inexpensive pursuits are likely to be typical activities.

Sex

A person's sex has an important influence on the choice of leisure activity. As a result of gender role socialization, men and women show different leisure interests and some leisure activities are more associated with one sex than another. For example, knitting, dancing, horse-riding, aerobics and keep-fit are more likely to be pursued by women; car maintenance, DIY, watching or playing football, and weight-training by men. As table 14.4 shows, women in full-time employment generally have less time available for leisure activities than men.

Activity

Table 14.4 Time use in a typical week: by economic status and sex, Great Britain, 1989

	Full-time employees	
	Males	*Females*
Weekly hours spent on:		
Employment and travel[a]	48.9	43.6
Essential activities[b]	25.9	42.2
Sleep[c]	49.0	49.0
Free time	44.2	33.2
Free time per weekday	4.7	3.2
Free time per weekend day	10.4	8.5

[a]Travel to and from place of work
[b]Essential domestic work and personal care Including essential shopping, childcare, cooking, washing, and getting up and going to bed
[c]An average of 7 hours sleep per night is assumed.

Source: Adapted from *Social Trends 21* (HMSO 1991).

Study table 14.4 and answer the following questions:

1. How many hours a week did females in full-time employment spend on essential activities?
2. Who spent the most time each week on employment and travel to and from work?
3. Which category of time use showed the greatest difference between males and females?
4. What evidence is there in the table to back up the view that women in paid employment have two jobs while men only have one?
5. List all the explanations you can think of for the differences between male and female full-time employees shown in the table.
6. What restrictions are there on the leisure activities of women which men don't usually face? Think about things like women going alone into pubs or discos, going home alone at night, and responsibilities for elderly relatives, husbands, and children.

Occupation and work experience

A person's occupation can have important effects on leisure activities. The hours worked, how much overtime has to be worked, and the amount of shift-work and nightwork can all restrict leisure opportunities.

The experience of work is perhaps one of the most important factors influencing non-work behaviour and leisure, as discussed earlier in this chapter when Parker's research on the opposition, neutrality, and extension patterns was considered (see table 14.1).

Chapter Summary

After studying this chapter, you should be able to:

- Describe and explain the importance of work, and the range of ways it can affect a person's life.
- Explain the difference between an instrumental and an intrinsic attitude to work.
- Describe and explain a range of causes and consequences of unemployment.
- Describe and explain the groups most at risk of unemployment.
- Suggest ways unemployment might be reduced.
- Describe the main features of an industrial society.
- Explain what is meant by craft production, mechanization, assembly line production, and automation.
- Explain what is meant by job satisfaction and alienation, and outline Marx's and Blauner's views of alienation.
- Describe and explain a range of factors which might influence the amount of job satisfaction a worker enjoys.
- Describe how workers respond to alienation.
- Describe attempts to increase job satisfaction.
- Describe and explain the possible effects of changing technology on society.
- Describe and explain how the occupational structure has changed in Britain this century.
- Explain what trade unions are and why individuals join them.
- Describe the methods unions use to protect their members' interests.
- Explain why the influence of trade unions has declined in recent years.
- Explain what is meant by leisure, and why it is sometimes difficult to make the distinction between work and leisure activities.
- Describe how leisure has changed this century.
- Outline a range of factors which influence the choice of leisure activity.

Project Suggestions

1. Interview a sample of people in different types of work, or in the same work, asking them about the kinds of thing they like or dislike about their job. Try to draw conclusions about the factors influencing job satisfaction and alienation.
2. Carry out a survey among some unemployed people, asking about how they spend their time, the problems they encounter, whom they feel is to blame for their unemployment, etc.
3. Using secondary sources (see chapter 16), carry out a study of the pattern of unemployment in your area, such as the age, sex, and ethnic background of the unemployed.
4. Carry out a study of the introduction of new technology into a workplace, its advantages and disadvantages and workers' attitudes towards it. You could study the introduction of bar-code checkouts in supermarkets, computers into district nursing, or word processors into office work.
5. Carry out a study of the structure and activities of a local trade union branch.

Key Terms

alienation
automation
craft production
division of labour
mechanization
work

15 Population

The study of population is known as **demography**. Evidence about the size and composition of Britain's population is obtained mainly through the census. This is a survey which asks questions of the entire population of a country. Censuses have been carried out every ten years since 1801, with the exception of 1941, when the Second World War made it impractical to hold one. Censuses are carried out by the Office of Population Censuses and Surveys, which is directed by the Registrar-General.

The last census was carried out in 1991 at a cost of £135 million, and asked questions about age, sex, marital status, ethnic group, country of birth, relationships within the household, housing, change of address within the last year, employment, higher qualifications, having the use of a car, and long-term illness. Questions about ethnic group, long-term illness, and central heating were asked for the first time in 1991.

Other information on population is obtained through the compulsory registration of births, marriages, and deaths at local Registry Offices, and through the General Household Survey.

In this chapter, the main changes in the population of Britain this century will be considered, together with some of the social consequences of these changes.

The Importance of Information on Population

In order for a government to plan its policies with regard to social policy, the allocation of scarce resources, land, housing, education, and finance, it is necessary to have accurate information and estimates of future trends in population size and distribution. It is important to know, for example, whether the population is increasing or decreasing, and what proportion of the population will be at school, working (or possibly unemployed), and retired in fifteen or twenty years' time. Such information will influence, for example, the number of schools, hospitals, and houses that will need to be built, the number of teachers, doctors, and nurses to be trained, the number of jobs that will be required, and the number of welfare benefits to be paid out. Details about employment help government and businesses to plan jobs and training, and transport information makes possible future planning on road building and public transport. Details on ethnic groups help to identify racial disadvantage, and allocate resources and plan programmes to meet the needs of minority groups. Health information enables health authorities to plan services and facilities for long-term sick and elderly people. These changes cannot be made overnight, and so governments need this information to plan for the future.

Key Terms Used in the Study of Population

- The **birth rate** is the number of live births per 1000 of the population per year.
- The **general fertility rate** is the number of live births per 1000 women of child-bearing age (15–44) per year.
- The **death rate** (or mortality rate) is the number of deaths per 1000 of the population per year.
- The **infant mortality rate** is the number of babies who die in their first year of life per 1000 live births per year.
- **Life expectation** is an estimate made about the number of years the average person can be expected to live. It is based on information about existing patterns of infant mortality and death. Estimates of life expectation can be based on any age, but the most common are life expectation at birth and at one year. Generally, the older you get, the more life expectation increases, as early childhood diseases and accidents of youth are overcome.
- **Migration** is the term used to describe the movement of people from one area to another. **Emigration** is movement out of a country or area on a permanent basis, and **immigration** is movement into a country or area on a permanent basis. **Net migration** is the term used to describe the *difference* between immigration and emigration, and therefore whether the population of a country or area has gone up or gone down when both

emigration and immigration are taken into account. Net migration is usually expressed in terms of a net gain(+) or a net loss(−) of population. For example, in 1986 in Britain there were about 250 000 immigrants and 213 000 emigrants. The net migration figure is obtained by subtracting the number of emigrants (213 000) from the number of immigrants (250 000), giving a net migration figure of +37 000 (a net gain or increase in population through migration).

- A *natural increase(+)* or *decrease(−)* in population is the term used to describe changes in the size of a population due to changes in the number of births and deaths, but it excludes migration. A *net natural change* is the term used to describe the difference in population size after both births and deaths are taken into account. Like net migration, a *net natural increase* should be preceded by a + sign, and a *net natural decrease* by a − sign. For example, in 1901 there were 1 091 000 births and 624 000 deaths. The net natural change in population size was therefore +467 000 (the difference between the 1 091 000 births and the 624 000 deaths).

- **Population projections** are attempts to predict future changes in population size. These involve complex calculations based on past and present trends in the fertility rate, the birth rate, the infant mortality rate, the death rate, average life expectation, and migration patterns. Accurate population projections are very difficult to make because of the wide range of economic, social, and political factors which might influence future developments in any of these areas.

- The **dependent population** is that section of the population which is not in work and is supported by others. This includes the under-16s (who are still at school); the over-60/65s (who have retired); housewives; many single-parent families; the unemployed; the chronically sick and handicapped; prisoners; and students in full-time education.

- The **dependency ratio** is the proportion of those working compared to those who are dependent.

- *Age distribution* refers to the percentage of the population which falls into the various age groups.

- The **dependent age groups** are those under age 16 and over retirement age (60 for women and 65 for men). These have increased this century because of the raising of the school leaving age and more people reaching old age.

- *Sex distribution* refers to the proportion of males and females in the population. The **sex ratio** of a population is the proportion of males to females, expressed as the number of males per 1000 females in the population.

- *Regional distribution* is the percentage of the population which lives in different geographical areas (such as urban and rural areas).

- *Occupational distribution* is the percentage of the population working in different occupations.

Activity

In 1975 the population of the United Kingdom was approximately 55 928 000. There were 736 000 births compared with 666 000 deaths. The population gained 186 600 people from outside the United Kingdom, and lost 207 700 who left the United Kingdom.

By 1989, the population had risen to 57 065 000. There were 778 000 births in that year, compared with 639 000 deaths, and 232 100 immigrants and 208 000 emigrants. (*Source*: Based on OPCS data.)

Use the information above to complete a copy of the following table:

Year	Total Population	Births	Deaths	Net natural change	Immigrants	Emigrants	Net migration	Total population change
1975								
1989								

Population Size

There are three main factors which can affect the size of a population, and whether it increases or decreases. These factors are the birth rate, the death rate, and migration.

Population trends are often derived from natural changes in population size (changes in the number of births and deaths) as migration patterns are quite difficult to predict. The basic rules for interpreting figures and graphs showing natural changes in population size are:

- Whenever the birth rate *equals* the death rate, there will be no natural change in population size: for every baby born, someone dies.
- Whenever the birth rate is *higher* than the death rate, there will be a natural increase in population size: more babies are being born than there are people dying. This means that even if there is a falling death rate and a falling birth rate, but the birth rate still remains higher than the death rate, the size of the population will continue to increase.
- When the birth rate is *lower* than the death rate, there will be a natural decrease in population size: the number of births is simply not enough to replace the numbers who die.

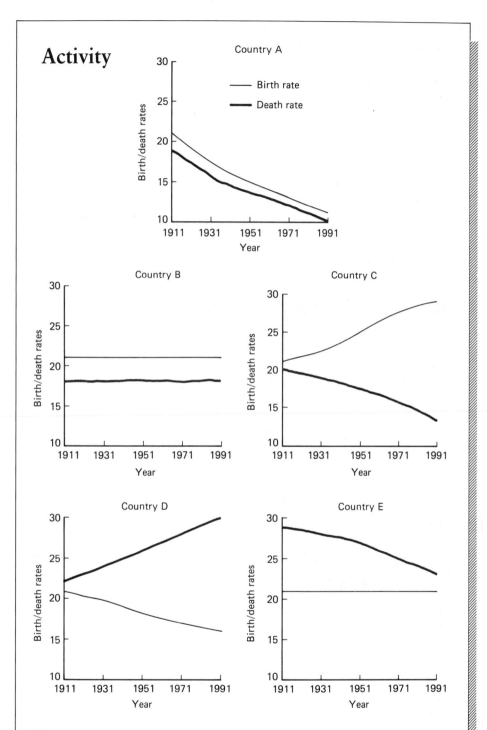

Figure 15.1 Examples of natural changes in population size

Study figure 15.1 on the previous page and answer the following questions, assuming there is no migration:

1. What is happening to the population size of country A?
2. What is happening to the population size of country B?
3. In which countries is there a natural decrease in population size?
4. In which country is population size increasing the fastest? Explain your answer.
5. In which country is population size decreasing the fastest?
6. Suggest two possible reasons for both the rising death rate and the falling birth rate in country D.
7. Suggest three possible consequences for society of a falling birth rate.

Population Change in Britain

The population of the United Kingdom has risen from about 10.5 million in 1801 (the first census) to an estimated 57.3 million in 1990. This increase has not been a gradual process. Between 1801 and 1851, for example, the population doubled from 10.5 million to 22.3 million, and nearly doubled again in the second half of the nineteenth century, to 38.3 million by 1901.

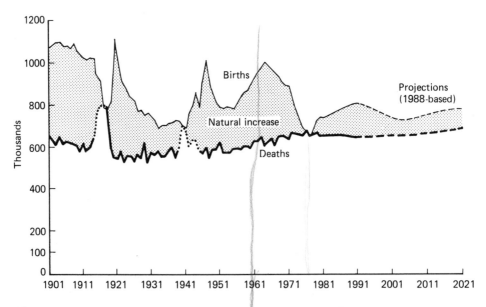

Figure 15.2 Population changes and projections, United Kingdom, 1901–2021

Source: Adapted from *Social Trends 16, 20* (HMSO 1986 and 1990).

The major reasons for this growth were the falling death and infant mortality Newly,
rates, while the birth rate remained relatively unchanged. This century, a
continuing fall in the death rate as well as a falling birth rate has slowed
down population growth, and there is greatly improved life expectancy.

Figure 15.2 illustrates the main changes in population this century, with
projected changes for the twenty-first century.

Activity

Study figure 15.2 and answer the following questions:

1. Approximately how many births were there in 1921?
2. In what year was there the lowest number of deaths?
3. Between what years was there the largest natural increase in
   population size?
4. What trend is shown in the number of births between 1921 and
   1941?
5. How many deaths are there projected to be in 2001?
6. Suggest three social factors which might make the population
   projections for births and deaths made in 1988 inaccurate.

Changes in the Death Rate, Infant Mortality Rate, and Average Life Expectation

The overall increase in the population of the UK since 1870 has been caused
by the gradual decline in the death rate. A century ago it was 22 per 1000; in
1902 it was 18 per 1000; and in 1990 it was around 11.5 per 1000. The
infant mortality rate has also fallen, from around 142 per 1000 live births in
1902 to about 9.3 per 1000 in 1990. Average life expectation has consequently risen, as shown in figure 15.3.

Activity

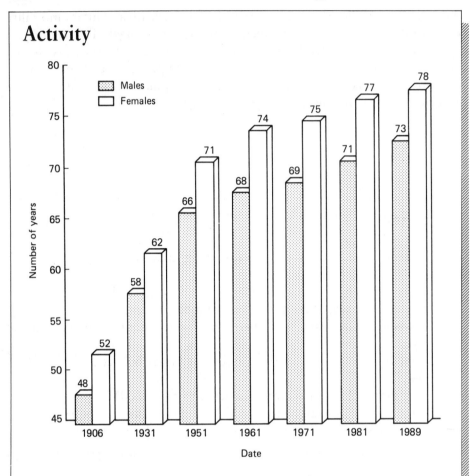

Figure 15.3 Life expectation at birth: by sex, United Kingdom, 1906–89

Source: OPCS.

Study figure 15.3 and answer the following questions:

1. What was the life expectation of females in 1931?
2. What was the difference between the life expectation of males and females in 1961?
3. Identify three trends shown in figure 15.3 between 1906 and 1971.
4. Using the data given in figure 15.3, draw a graph to show the same information.
5. Suggest three reasons why women live longer than men.

Explanations for changes in the death rate, infant mortality rate, and life expectation

Improved hygiene, sanitation, and medicine

Public hygiene and sanitation have improved enormously since the early nineteenth century, with the construction of public sewer systems and the provision of clean running water. These changes, together with improved public awareness of hygiene and the causes of infection, have contributed to the elimination in Britain of the great epidemic killer diseases of the past, such as cholera, diphtheria, and typhoid, which were spread through infected water and food. These improvements in environmental conditions were more important than medical advances in wiping out the epidemic diseases. The importance of these changes is shown by the scale of death caused by epidemic diseases in the past. For example, between 1337 and 1351 the Black Death, a plague carried by black rats, is estimated to have wiped out about one-quarter of the British population, and in 1918 flu killed about 250 000 people.

Advances in medicine and science, such as vaccines and the development of penicillin, antibiotics, and other life-saving drugs, and advances in surgery and medical technology, such as transplant surgery, have further contributed to the decline in the death rate. More sophisticated medical care means that people now survive illnesses that would have killed them even in the recent past. Before this century, the highest mortality rates were among babies and young children, but today death rates rise the older you get. The major causes of death today in Britain are from the non-infectious degenerative diseases, such as cancer and heart disease.

Higher living standards

Rising standards of living have further assisted in reducing death rates. Higher wages, better food, more amenities and appliances in the home, and greatly improved housing conditions, with less damp, inside toilets, and running hot water, have all assisted in improving the health and life expectation of the population. Because of improved transportation and food technology, a wider range of more nutritious food is available, with improved storage techniques (such as freezing), making possible the import of a range of foodstuffs, including fresh fruit and vegetables all the year round.

Public health and welfare

There has been a steep rise of state intervention in public welfare, particularly since the establishment of the welfare state in 1945. The National Health Service has provided free and comprehensive health care, and there is much better ante-natal and post-natal care for mothers and babies. More women have children in hospitals today, and there are health visitors to check on young babies, which helps to explain the decrease in the infant mortality rate. The wide range of welfare benefits available helps to maintain standards of health in times of hardship, and old people in particular are cared for better today, with pensions and a range of services like home helps, social workers, and old people's homes.

Health education

Coupled with these changes has been a growing awareness of nutrition and its importance to health. Improved educational standards generally, and particularly in health education, have led to a much better informed public, who demand better hygiene and public health, and welfare legislation and social reforms to improve health. Bodies like the Health Education Authority seek to improve the health of the public by education, such as emphasizing the benefits of exercise, giving up smoking, and eating a balanced diet. The public outcries in 1989–90 over risks of food poisoning, such as salmonella in eggs, 'mad cow disease' in beef, and listeria in cook-chill foods, are all evidence of this growing health awareness, particularly in recent years.

Improved working conditions

Working conditions have improved dramatically this century. Technology has taken over some of the more arduous, health-damaging tasks, and factory machinery is often safer than it was last century. Higher standards of health and safety at work, shorter working hours, more leisure time, and earlier retirement ages have all made work physically less demanding and therefore have reduced risks to health.

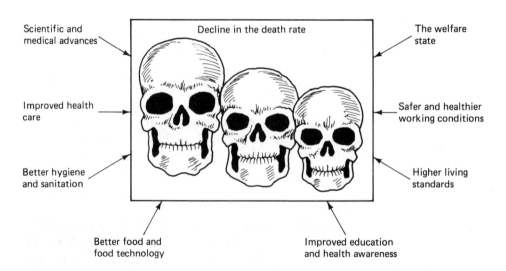

Figure 15.4 Reasons for the decline in the death rate

Sex differences in life expectation

In chapter 3, major social class differences in health and life expectation were discussed, but such differences also exist between men and women.

In most younger age groups, the population is roughly evenly divided between the sexes, but in the older age groups there are far more women than men. There are therefore slightly more women than men in the population as a whole. This is because there is a higher death rate among men and life expectation for women is longer: in 1989, average life expectation was 78 for women, but only 73 years for men. Figure 15.3 shows these differences in life expectation between 1906 and 1989.

Why do women live longer than men?

- Evidence suggests that boys are the weaker sex at birth, with a higher infant mortality rate, and women seem to have a better genetic resistance to heart disease than men.
- The process of gender role socialization means men are more likely to be brought up to shrug off illnesses, they drink and smoke more (with all the consequences for health), they are more aggressive and take more risks, are less careful in what they eat, and are not socialized to show their emotions as much as women and so have less outlet for stress. Women are socialized to 'take care of themselves' more than men, and they are more likely to visit doctors, which may mean they receive better health care.
- Men generally live more hazardous lives than women. The more dangerous occupations are more likely to be done by men, such as construction work, and they are therefore more at risk of industrial accidents and diseases. In the home, men are more likely to do the dangerous and risky jobs, such as jobs using ladders and climbing on the roof. Men also make up the majority of car drivers and motor-cyclists (63 per cent in 1990), and are therefore more at risk of death through road accidents.
- Men are more likely to work full-time and to work longer and more unsociable hours, such as overtime working and shift-work, which can be harmful to health.
- Jobs carrying high levels of responsibility are more commonly done by men, which may cause higher levels of health-damaging stress.
- Men retire later than women (age 65 compared to 60). Evidence suggests that the later retirement age of men could be an important factor in reducing their life expectation.

Activity/Discussion

1. Which of the reasons given for women living longer than men do you think is most important? Give your reasons.
2. Do you think that men's 'macho' behaviour is an important factor in shortening their lives? Suggest evidence for this from your own experiences.
3. 'The growing equality of women with men is a threat to women's health'. Explain this statement. Do you agree? How might this situation be avoided (apart from stopping women becoming more equal!)?

Changes in the Birth Rate

Over the last century, the birth rate has been declining in the UK, from 28 per 1000 in 1902 to about 13.6 per 1000 in 1990. The only major exceptions to this trend were the post-war 'baby booms' of 1920 and 1947, as men and women started families delayed by separation during the war. There was a further baby boom in the late 1950s and 1960s, when increases in the standard of living and low unemployment meant some parents felt they could afford more children, and improved welfare services and payments made having extra children less of a hardship. However, with increasing unemployment and hardship in the 1970s and 1980s, birth rates have declined once again. A decline in the birth rate has meant that the average family has been getting smaller, from about 6 children per family in the 1870s to about 1.8 in 1990. Despite the declining birth rate, the population has continued to grow slowly, because the birth rate has remained slightly higher than the death rate.

Explanations for the falling birth rate and smaller family size

Contraception
More effective and cheaper methods of contraception have been developed this century, and society's attitudes to the use of contraception have changed from disapproval to acceptance. This is partly because of growing seculariza-

tion, and the declining influence of the church and religion on people's behaviour. The availability of safe and legal abortion since 1967 has also helped in terminating unwanted pregnancies. Family planning is therefore easier.

Activity/Discussion

1. What sort of pressures might influence governments either to promote or restrict the use of contraceptive devices?
2. What are the social pressures which influence whether or not individuals choose to use contraception?

The compulsory education of children

Since children were barred from employment, and education became compulsory in 1880, children have ceased to be an economic asset that can contribute to family income through working at an early age. Children have therefore become an economic liability and a drain on the resources of parents, as they have to be supported for a prolonged period in compulsory education. Parents have therefore begun to limit the size of their families, to secure for themselves and their children a higher standard of living. The move to a more child-centred society has assisted in this restriction of family size, as smaller families mean parents can spend more money and time on and with each child.

The changing position of women

The changing position of women, particularly this century, has involved more equal status with men and greater employment opportunities. Women today have less desire to spend long years of their lives bearing and rearing children, and many wish to pursue a career of their own. In 1990, it was estimated that 21 per cent of 25-year-old women would have no children at all.

The declining infant mortality rate

In the nineteenth century, the absence of a welfare state meant many parents relied on their children to care for them in old age. However, many babies failed to survive infancy, and it was often uncertain whether children would outlive their parents. Parents therefore often had many children as a safeguard against some of them dying. The decline in the infant mortality rate and death rate has meant less children are dying before adulthood and old age, so parents need no longer have many children as security against only a few surviving. In addition, the range of agencies which exist to help the elderly today mean people are less reliant on care by their children when they reach old age.

A geographically mobile labour force

Industrial societies generally require a geographically mobile workforce, which means a workforce that can easily move to other areas for work or promotion. This may have been a factor in encouraging smaller families, as they can more easily pack up and move elsewhere.

Figure 15.5 Reasons for the decline in the birth rate

The Ageing Population

Britain, like most Western industrialized countries, today has an ageing population. This simply means the average age of the population is getting higher, with a greater proportion of the population over retirement age, and a smaller proportion of young people.

The high birth and death rates of the nineteenth century meant that the majority of the population was young – people didn't live long enough to grow old! The decline in the death rate and increased life expectation has meant that more people are living longer, and more are reaching old age.

However, the decline in the birth rate has meant that fewer children are being born as well, and this has changed the overall age structure of the population. For example, in 1901, about 33 per cent of the population were under age 15, 63 per cent were between the ages of 15 and 65, and only about 4 per cent were over 65. In 1989, about 19 per cent were under 15, 65 per cent were between 15 and 65, and 16 per cent were over 65. This changing age structure of the population is shown in the pyramids in figure 15.6, and figure 15.7 shows the growing numbers of the elderly.

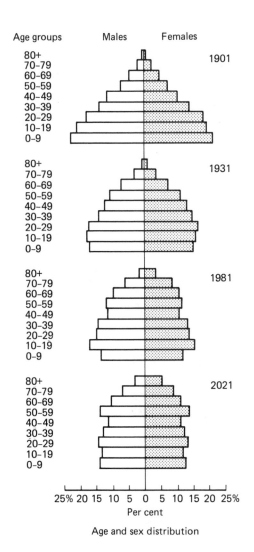

Figure 15.6 The ageing population of Great Britain, 1901–2021

Source: *Social Studies Review*, vol. 1, no. 3, January 1986.

Activity

Look at figure 15.6 on the previous page.

1. About what percentage of females were in the 80+ age group in 1931?
2. About what percentage of males were aged between 20 and 29 in 1981?
3. By approximately how much has the percentage of females in the 70–9 age group increased between 1901 and 1981?
4. What evidence is there in figure 15.6 that women live longer than men?
5. Explain briefly how figure 15.6 shows that Britain has an ageing population.

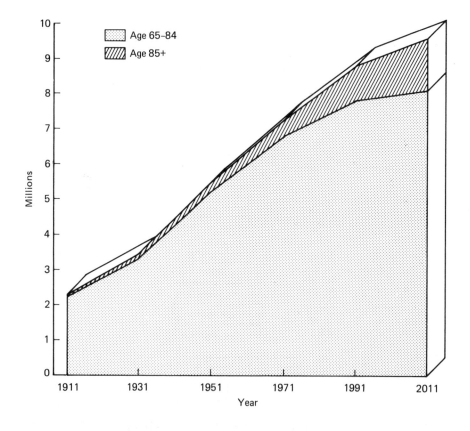

Figure 15.7 The growing numbers of the elderly, United Kingdom, 1901–2011

Source: OPCS.

The growing proportion of old people in the population creates a growing 'burden of dependence', or an increasing dependency ratio. This simply means that an increasing number of old people have to be supported by a decreasing proportion of the working population. This could mean higher taxes on those working to pay the cost of benefits for the elderly, such as the costs of income support payments for board and lodging of elderly people in residential and nursing homes. Some of the consequences of the ageing population are summarized in figure 15.8. Figure 15.8A shows the results of a survey about how elderly people themselves felt about ageing in 1991.

Activity

Study figures 15.8 and 15.8A.

1. Explain fully two problems for society of an ageing population, and the possible consequences of these problems.
2. When elderly and infirm relatives move in with their adult children, it is usually the female who gives up paid work. Why do you think this is?
3. Look at figure 15.8A.
   (a) What percentage of retired people thought there was nothing good about getting older?
   (b) What was the main problem most retired people faced in getting older?
   (c) What percentage of retired people thought lack of respect from society was a main problem of getting older?
4. Why do many of the elderly live in poverty?
5. What welfare services are available to help the elderly? List all those you can think of, explaining in each case the kind of help provided.
6. If you have, or were to have, an elderly parent, grandparent, or great-grandparent living with you, what advantages and problems are or might be created for family life? Discuss these with others if you are in a group.

Migration: Immigration and Emigration

A further influence on Britain's population size and composition has been migration. Migration to and from Britain has usually occurred because of 'push' factors, such as poverty, unemployment, or persecution, and 'pull' factors, such as the search for jobs and a higher standard of living, more political freedom, and joining relatives.

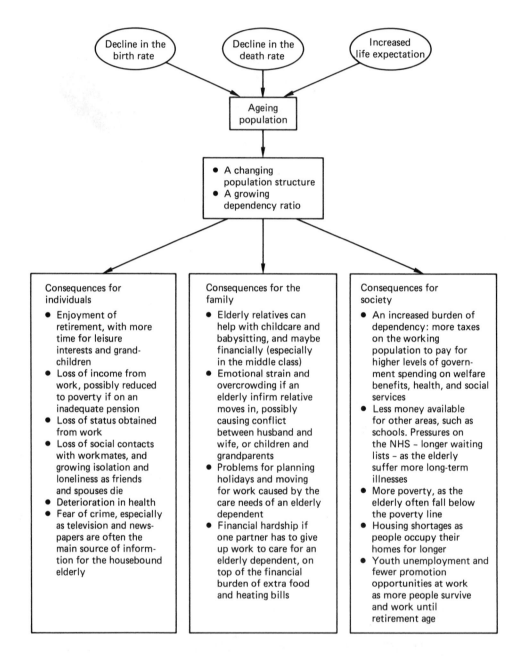

Figure 15.8 The causes and some possible consequences of an ageing population

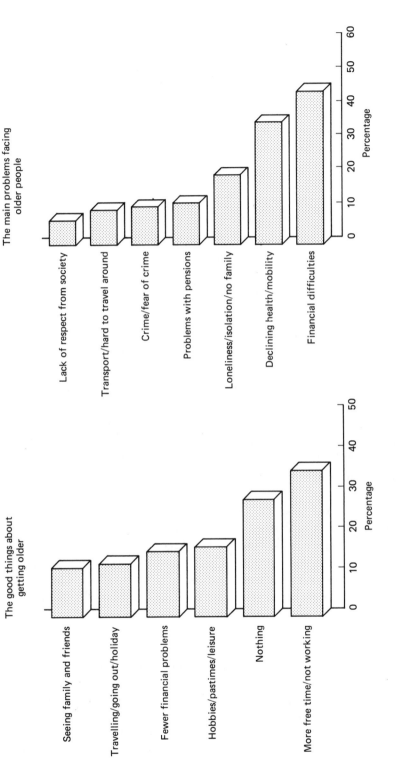

Figure 15.8A Growing older in Britain in the 1990s: the good and the bad. A British Gas Report on ageing in Britain in 1991 asked a representative sample of retired people over the age of 55 about what they thought were the good things about getting older in Britain in 1991, and what they thought were the main problems facing older people.

Source: Adapted from The British Gas Report on Attitudes to Ageing 1991.

The pattern of migration

The peak period of immigration in the nineteenth century was in the 1830s and 1840s, when over half a million Irish fled the effects of the potato famine in Ireland. The Irish still remain the single largest immigrant group in Britain. The peak periods of emigration from Britain were in the 1880s and the first quarter of the twentieth century, when many left to go to places in the British Empire.

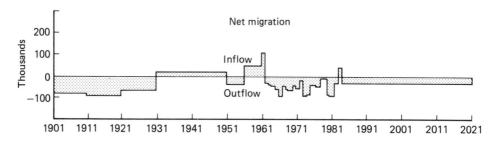

Figure 15.9 Net migration, United Kingdom, 1901–2021

Source: Adapted from *Social Trends 16* (HMSO 1986).

In the twentieth century, there have been two peak periods of immigration. During the 1930s and up until about 1945, several hundred thousand refugees fled to Britain from Europe to escape the effects of Nazi occupation and persecution. In the late 1950s and 1960s, widespread immigration from the black Commonwealth (mainly India, Pakistan, and the West Indies) was actively encouraged by the British government, which sent out recruiting teams to these countries to solve labour shortages in unskilled and poorly paid occupations in Britain. Large-scale black immigration has been effectively ended by a series of racist Immigration Acts since 1962. These have taken away many of the rights to residence in Britain of black British people living in former British colonies, while at the same time preserving those of white people.

Overall, the pattern of net migration shows that from about 1870 to the 1930s there were more emigrants than immigrants; that is, a net loss of population through migration. In the periods between about 1931 and 1951, and 1955 and 1962, immigration exceeded emigration (that is, a net gain). Since 1962 more people have left the country each year than have entered it, with the exception of a brief period in the early 1980s. Figure 15.10 shows the overall origins and destinations of migrants between 1974 and 1988.

Figure 15.10 International migration into and out of the United Kingdom, 1974–88

The Ethnic Minorities

An **ethnic group** is a group of people who share a common culture. An **ethnic minority group** is a group which shares a cultural identity which is different from that of the majority population of a society.

There is a wide range of ethnic groups who have emigrated to Britain over the years, such as the Irish, the Chinese, the Jews, the Poles, and more recently the Asians and Afro-Caribbeans (West Indians). However, when most people think of 'immigration' they think of people of a different racial origin – of a different skin colour – mainly those of Afro-Caribbean or Asian origin. Only about 6 per cent of the population of Britain are non-white, and these make up a small minority of all immigrants. Asians and Afro-Caribbeans together make up about 4 per cent of the population of Britain. About 40 per cent of the Asian population and 55 per cent of the Afro-Caribbean population in Britain were actually born here, so it is misleading to regard them as immigrants at all.

Table 15.1 Ethnic origins of the British population 1988

Ethnic group	Total (thousands)	% of the population
White	51 470	94.0
West Indian/Guyanese	495	1.0
Indian	787	1.5
Pakistani	428	0.75
Bangladeshi	108	0.2
Chinese	125	0.2
African	112	0.2
Arab	73	0.1
Mixed	287	0.5
Others	163	0.3
Not stated	472	1.0
All ethnic groups	54 519	100.0

Source: OPCS.

The Problems of Ethnic Minority Groups

People of Asian (especially Pakistani and Bangladeshi) and Afro-Caribbean origin in particular face a series of disadvantages in Britain compared to the white majority, although there are differences within each group. Some of these disadvantages are discussed in chapters 8 and 12, but they also exist in a range of other areas.

Employment and unemployment

- People of Afro-Caribbean, Pakistani, and Bangladeshi origin are less likely than white people to secure the best jobs. These groups are under-represented in non-manual occupations, particularly in managerial

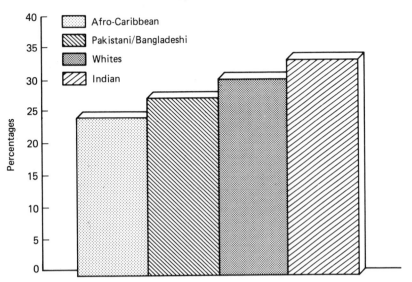

Figure 15.11 Percentage of workers in professional and managerial occupations: by ethnic group, Great Britain, 1989

Source: Department of Employment Labour Force Surveys, 1987–9.

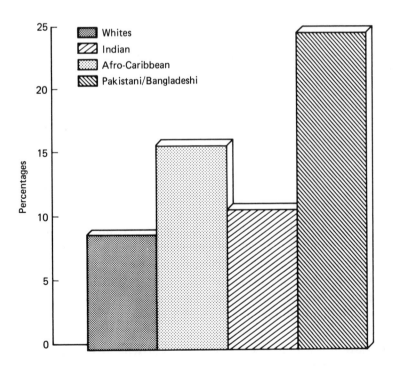

Figure 15.12 Unemployment rates: by ethnic group, Great Britain, 1987–9

Source: Department of Employment Labour Force Survey.

Figure 15.13 Percentage of households living with more than one person per room: by ethnic group, England, 1988

Source: Social Trends 20 (HMSO 1990).

and professional work (see figure 15.11). They are also over-represented in semi-skilled and unskilled manual occupations, and often work longer and more unsociable hours (shift-work and nightwork) than white people.

- Black people are less likely to get employed when competing with white people with the same qualifications for the same job.
- Black people are more likely to face unemployment, especially those of Pakistani/Bangladeshi origin (as figure 15.12 shows).

Housing

- Black people tend to live in inferior housing to white people and in the 'less desirable' areas of towns and cities.
- They tend to live in older properties than white people, and are more likely to live in a terraced house or flat.
- They face more overcrowding, with fewer rooms in the house and more people per room (as shown in figure 15.13)
- People of Afro-Caribbean origin are more likely to live in rented accommodation, particularly council housing where they are often allocated the least desirable homes. People of Asian origin, however, are more likely to be owner-occupiers than white people, although their homes still tend to be in 'poorer areas'.

Explaining racial disadvantage in employment and housing

The following explanations for racial disadvantage should be considered together, as they are cumulative, in that one aspect of discrimination or disadvantage can lead to further disadvantage in other areas.

Many of the black population are working class, and therefore face the problems encountered by all working-class people, regardless of their ethnic origin. This would explain their relative disadvantage compared to the population as a whole. However, there is also evidence of additional racial prejudice and racial discrimination.

Racial prejudice and discrimination

Racial prejudice is a set of assumptions about a racial group which people are reluctant to change even when they receive information which undermines those assumptions. **Racial discrimination** happens when people's racial prejudices cause them to act unfairly against a racial group. For example, a racially prejudiced police officer might use his or her power to 'pick on' black people more than white people; for example stopping them in the street and asking what they're up to.

The 1965 Race Relations Act made it illegal to discriminate on the grounds of race in employment and housing, and to 'incite racial hatred', and this was strengthened by the establishment of the Commission for Racial Equality in 1976. However, there is widespread evidence that racial discrimination in employment, housing, and other areas continues. Part of the problem is that it is difficult to prove racial discrimination. For example, a black person who is turned down for promotion at work in favour of a white person may be told the white person was simply more suited to the job in some way.

Underachievement in education, which was discussed in chapter 12, may partly explain why black people are under-represented in managerial and professional work, and more likely to be found in unskilled and semi-skilled occupations. These occupations tend to be those most at risk in times of recession, which helps to explain the higher levels of unemployment among black people. However, discrimination might well mean that they are more likely to be singled out for redundancy when the axe falls.

The generally lower pay of Asian and Afro-Caribbean minorities which follows from these explanations might explain their inferior housing. However, there is evidence of discrimination among landlords and council officials in allocating housing to black people.

FIGHT RACISM

Discrimination is part of the black experience.
It happens with jobs. It happens with housing.
You see it in pubs, in clubs and in restaurants.

Many people think it's just part of life.
But it needn't be. You have rights and you should use them.
The law says that everyone must have equal treatment
and if someone tries to hold you back because of your colour
you can take them to Court.
Maybe it will never happen to you, but if it does, talk to us.
We're the Commission for Racial Equality
and we can tell you how the law works.
We can tell you if we think you can win.
And we may be able to represent you in Court.

Racism won't just go away. We must fight it.
If you want help, contact us.

Commission for Racial Equality
Elliot House 10/12 Allington Street
London SW1E 5EH

Reproduced with permission of the Commission for Racial Equality.

Policing and the law

The way the police go about their work – what they look out for – is guided by their ideas about who 'trouble-makers' or criminals are. Black people (especially black youth) fit the police stereotype of 'trouble-makers'. Black areas are therefore subject to heavier policing. Black people are more likely to be stopped and searched than white people, and charged with offences such as obstruction or breach of the peace – offences which the police themselves can decide have been committed or not. Evidence suggests that black people are more likely to be arrested than white people for the same offence. That they are more heavily policed and stopped and searched means that the police are likely to discover more crime among black than white offenders. In some cases, resentment at this treatment may actually provoke trouble and cause offences to be committed.

A 1991 study by the National Association for the Care and Resettlement of Offenders (Nacro), *Black People's Experience of Criminal Justice*, suggested there was evidence of police misconduct towards black people, with black people facing more unnecessarily rough treatment and abusive language than white offenders. Black people were far more likely than white people to be detained after being charged, and less likely to be allowed to make contact with friends, relatives, or a lawyer.

Black people are therefore more likely to get caught, arrested, and charged, and the original police stereotype is confirmed by the activities of the police themselves. Judges and magistrates hold similar stereotypes, and the evidence suggests that they 'crack down' harder on black people than white, giving them heavier fines and sentences than white offenders committing similar offences. The 1991 Nacro study found black offenders were more likely than white to be given prison sentences rather than probation.

Racial attacks

Black people are the victims of more crimes of violence than white people, usually motivated by racism and organized by fascist groups like the National Front. In some areas with high concentrations of ethnic minorities, such as Brick Lane in the East End of London, these racial attacks are reaching almost epidemic proportions. A report published in 1991 by the European Parliament's Committee of Inquiry on Racism and Xenophobia (*xenophobia* means an intense dislike or even hatred of foreigners) reported an estimated 70,000 racist incidents in Greater London in 1989. The

1988 British Crime Survey found that people of both Afro-Caribbean and Asian origin were more likely to be victims of assault than white people. Asian victims were particularly vulnerable to random attacks and harassment by passing groups of strangers unknown to the victim. This means black people often live in fear of being attacked in the streets or in their homes.

Activity

1. Suggest all the explanations you can think of why people from ethnic minorities, particularly Afro-Caribbean and Asian minorities, often face racial prejudice and discrimination.
2. For each explanation, suggest ways in which the causes of the prejudice and discrimination might be removed.

Urbanization

Urbanization is the process of the movement of people from rural (country) areas to urban areas (towns and cities), with the corresponding growth in towns and cities which become the major centres of population in a society. An urbanized society is one where most of its population live in towns and cities.

In Britain, urbanization really began with the beginnings of industrialization in the late eighteenth and early nineteenth centuries. For example, in 1800 about 15 per cent of the population lived in towns and cities, and by 1900 this had increased to about 77 per cent of the population of England and Wales. In 1991, about 76 per cent of the population of Britain lived in urban areas, with about one-third of the population concentrated in seven large conurbations (large, densely populated urban areas including a number of towns). These conurbations are Greater London, Greater Manchester, Merseyside (around Liverpool), Strathclyde (around Glasgow), Tyne and Wear (around Newcastle upon Tyne), the West Midlands (around Birmingham), and West Yorkshire (around Leeds).

Figure 15.14 The urban/rural population, England and Wales, 1851–1981

Source: OPCS census data.

The Reasons for Urbanization

Urbanization is linked to two basic factors: the mechanization of agriculture and the industrialization process. The movement to larger farms and the increasing mechanization of agriculture reduced the number of farm workers required. In the absence of any form of social welfare, these rural unemployed generally had no alternative but to seek work in the towns and cities. Industrialization in the nineteenth century led to the development of industrial centres in urban areas, and people moved to these centres for employment.

De-urbanization

Since the 1960s, there has been a gradual reversal of the process of urbanization, with a decline in the population living in cities. Between 1961 and 1981, for example, the population of the six largest conurbations fell by about two million. This movement of people away from living in cities towards the suburbs and new towns (like Milton Keynes) is known as **de-urbanization**, or urban dispersal.

Why has de-urbanization occurred?

- Industrial firms have moved from the cities. This is because land prices, rent, and rates tend to be higher in city areas, and firms can cut costs by moving out. This has been assisted by government incentives in terms of rent and rate concessions for firms which relocate in rural areas or in new towns. *and technology*
- Improved road networks and fast rail services have enabled industry to operate just as efficiently outside the cities, and have also enabled people to commute to work rather than having to live within walking or cycling distance. The increase in private and company car ownership has helped in this.
- People have moved to get a better environment and cheaper housing. Often life in the suburbs and in new towns is generally more pleasant than in the cities. With the move towards more home-ownership, house prices in the more pleasant areas of cities are often too expensive for many people, and housing is more modern and generally cheaper in the suburbs and new towns. Often there are more parks and open spaces, newer leisure facilities, and less noise and pollution. General costs of living are lower, and there also tend to be less social problems like crime, vandalism and violence in these areas.
- As firms have left the cities, employees following these firms can cut down travelling time and costs in getting to work.
- Many inner-city slum areas have been redeveloped, and this has often meant the people living there have been rehoused in large new council housing estates in the suburbs or in new towns.

Activity

There is often today much movement of people around the country, and there may be people in your school or college class, your neighbourhood or workplace, who have recently moved to your area. Do a small survey of these people, finding out:

1. Why they *left* the area they came from.
2. Why they chose to move *to* your area.
3. On the basis of your findings, what seem to be the principal factors influencing the movement of people around the country?

The Inner Cities

kensington, hoxherl

The inner cities have undergone a rapid decline in recent years as firms either close down or move out to the suburbs and new towns. Often the only people left in the inner cities are those who can't afford to move out, such as the old, the unemployed, and low-paid unskilled and semi-skilled workers. Inner-city residents are among the most deprived sections of the population in Britain. These areas have proven to be 'flashpoints' of social conflict, with riots breaking out in the 1980s in the St Paul's area of Bristol, the Toxteth area of Liverpool, in the Southall, Brixton, and Tottenham areas of London, the Handsworth area of Birmingham, and other inner-city areas.

The inner cities have become centres of deprivation and 'flashpoints' of conflict for a number of reasons.

Poverty and unemployment

Unemployment is particularly high in the inner cities. Many of the sorts of work which are available for inner-city residents without paying expensive travelling costs have been declining. Traditional industries such as docking, shipbuilding, textiles, and clothing have been disappearing, partly because of cheaper foreign competition, and new firms have not opened up in these areas. The demand for semi-skilled and unskilled labour has in any case been declining with increasing mechanization. A lack of government investment in these areas has meant that little has been done to halt this decline.

Poor housing

The inner cities are likely to have the worst and oldest housing, with fewer facilities, more overcrowding, and a higher level of rented accommodation (often at exorbitantly high rents) than other areas. Tenants often can't afford to look after their homes properly, and private landlords frequently refuse to do so. Even owner-occupiers may have few extra resources to maintain their homes properly.

Crime

Those who can afford to move out of the inner cities have done so, and only the poor are left. Petty crime is more likely as a necessity for surviving daily life. The redevelopment and slum clearance that has gone on has broken up extended kin networks and traditional communities, and this has weakened informal social controls. The anonymity this creates means delinquency and 'street crime' is therefore more common, as people can get away with it. This is frequently fuelled by police activity, as the inhabitants of inner-city areas fit their stereotype of potential criminals. Policing is therefore heavier in these areas, which may cause resentment among those living there, and consequently more confrontations with the police.

Racism and racial tension

Some inner-city areas have high concentrations of ethnic minorities, since they are often among the poorer sections of the population and live where they can best afford. The white population in such areas may scapegoat these ethnic minorities by blaming them for their problems of housing and unemployment, which may create racial tension. There is also evidence of racism in the police force, especially in the Metropolitan Police in London, and this often generates hostility and resentment among black people against the police for harassing them, for example by stopping and searching them without good cause.

Poor schools

Schools are often in dilapidated buildings in inner cities. There is frequently a high turnover of teachers in such schools because of the stress caused by having to deal with the complex social problems they encounter in the classroom. Parents do not have the money to provide support for the schools, which happens in many middle-class areas.

General social problems

The inner cities are more likely to have a concentration of other general social problems, as a result of the stresses and strains caused by the accumulation of the points mentioned above. For example, the inner cities have higher levels of family breakdown and single-parent families, drug addiction, drug abuse, and prostitution than found in other areas.

Some attempts have been made to redevelop and improve the inner cities recently, but often these have not resolved the underlying problems. For example, the redevelopment of London's Docklands in the late 1980s simply meant a massive increase in property prices, and a takeover of the area by highly-paid 'yuppies' (young, upwardly-mobile professionals). Such redevelopment means life for the remaining local residents is made ever more expensive and difficult to cope with. Often these residents are forced to move out by such circumstances, and the 'problem' simply moves elsewhere.

Chapter Summary

After studying this chapter, you should be able to:

- Explain why governments need to collect information on population trends.
- Define the key terms used in the study of population.
- Explain the factors which influence the size of a country's population.
- Explain why the death and infant mortality rates have fallen in Britain, and why life expectation has increased.
- Explain sex differences in life expectation.
- Explain why the birth rate has fallen in Britain.
- Describe and explain the causes and consequences of an ageing population.
- Explain briefly the reasons for immigration and emigration.
- Identify and explain a range of problems experienced by some ethnic minorities.
- Explain why urbanization and de-urbanization have occurred in Britain.
- Identify and explain the major problems of the inner cities.

Project Suggestions

1. Using secondary sources – such as the census – give an account of the major features of the population of your area, including the balance of the sexes, age distribution, ethnic origins, and occupational composition.
2. Interview a sample of elderly people (over retirement age) asking them about the advantages and disadvantages/problems of being elderly. Figure 15.8A earlier in this chapter may give you some ideas for a questionnaire. Compare your findings with those in figure 15.8A.
3. Investigate the forms of discrimination faced by an ethnic minority group.

Key Terms

birth rate
death rate
demography
dependency ratio
dependent age groups
dependent population
de-urbanization
emigration
ethnic group
ethnic minority group
general fertility rate
immigration
infant mortality rate
life expectation
migration
net migration
population projections
racial discrimination
racial prejudice
sex ratio
urbanization

16 Doing Sociological Research

As has been seen throughout this book, sociology is concerned with a wide range of issues in social life, spanning the continuing existence of poverty, the influence of the mass media on our views about the world, the things that make work interesting or not, and how the very centre of our personalities is constructed through socialization into gender roles. The interests and concerns of sociologists are not that different from those of most people in society. However, what makes the views of sociologists different from those likely to be aired in a pub, in the canteen at work, or in other daily situations where views get exchanged, is that sociologists try to provide evidence to back up what they say. This evidence is collected from a variety of sources and through the use of a number of research methods. In this section, we will examine the types of data (or information) sociologists collect, the range of sources used, and the methods sociologists use to collect their own information.

Quantitative and Qualitative Data

Quantitative data is anything that can be expressed in statistical or number form or can be 'measured' in some way, such as age, qualifications, or income. Such data is usually presented in the form of statistical tables, graphs, pie charts and bar charts. There is more about interpreting statistical data in the appendix.

Qualitative data is concerned with people's feelings about some issue or event, and tries to get at the way they see things. Such data is normally in the form of the sociologist describing and interpreting people's feelings and lifestyles, often using direct quotations from the people studied.

This data may be gathered from either primary sources or secondary sources.

Primary and Secondary Sources

Secondary sources of data are those which already exist. **Secondary data** has already been collected by others. Figure 16.1 shows a range of secondary sources which might be used by sociologists in carrying out research.

Because the existing data required for research may be unreliable or may simply not have been collected, sociologists often have to collect their own data from primary sources. **Primary data** is that which is collected by sociologists themselves – it only exists because the sociologist has collected it. Such information is usually obtained by carrying out a social survey or by participant observation (these will be discussed shortly).

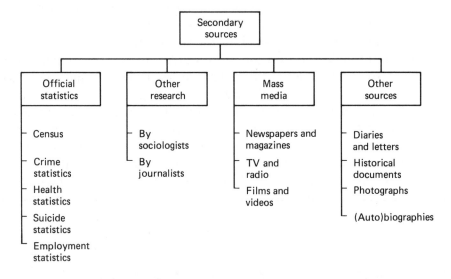

Figure 16.1 Secondary sources of data

The Advantages of Secondary Sources

Secondary sources have the main advantage that the material is readily available and so is cheap and easy to use. There is no need to spend time and money collecting data, and some data, such as that provided by the census, would be impossible for an individual to collect. In some cases, secondary sources may be the only sources of information available in an area, such as in historical research, and sociologists may therefore have no alternative but to use them.

The Problems of Secondary Sources

Secondary sources do present problems for use in sociological research. The information may be unrepresentative, and therefore may not apply to the whole population. For example, before the beginning of compulsory education in Britain in 1880, it was mainly only the well-off who could read and write, and so it was mainly they who left documents behind them.

The information may be inaccurate in some way and therefore unreliable or misleading. It may be forged or biased, contain errors or be exaggerated. Newspaper reports, for example, are notoriously unreliable as sources of evidence, as discussed in chapter 8.

Official statistics

Sociologists very often use official statistics, which are those produced by the government, in their research, such as those on crime, unemployment, and health. Such statistics must be treated very cautiously by sociologists. Chapter 9 showed the problems involved in using the official crime statistics as evidence of the real extent of crime. Two further examples of the possible inaccuracies of official statistics are shown by those on unemployment and health.

Unemployment statistics
Unemployment statistics have a number of limitations. According to the Unemployment Unit, the method of calculating unemployment statistics has been changed thirty times since 1982, with each change creating a drop in the numbers counted as unemployed. Unemployment figures only include those signing on at job centres and eligible for benefit. They therefore exclude married women, people who have retired early, those reluctantly staying on at school or college because there are no jobs, those on government training schemes and those working part-time because there are not enough full-time jobs. This problem of the inaccuracy of unemployment figures was shown by the 1971 census, in which about 40 per cent more people reported themselves as unemployed than official unemployment figures showed.

Health statistics
A further example of the problem of using official statistics is shown by health statistics. These can be inaccurate because they depend on people

persuading doctors they are ill, and are therefore simply a record of doctors' decision-making. Doctors may diagnose illnesses incorrectly, and therefore recorded illnesses may not be accurate. For example, there may have been many AIDS deaths recorded as pneumonia or another illness before doctors 'discovered' AIDS. Recent research has suggested that deaths from AIDS may have occurred in the 1950s in Britain, although the disease was not really 'discovered' until the 1980s. Finally, of course, not all sick people go to the doctor.

The above discussion of unemployment and health statistics, and the discussion in chapter 9 of crime statistics, shows that when sociologists use such secondary data, they must be very aware of its limitations, and approach it with care.

Activity

Read the following passage and then answer the questions.

Suicide is, by definition, the death of a person who intended to kill him- or herself. The problem for coroners is they can't ask dead people if they meant to kill themselves, so they can only guess at the truth by looking for 'clues' in the circumstances surrounding the death. Atkinson has suggested (in 'Societal Reactions to Suicide: The Role of Coroners' Definitions', in Stanley Cohen, ed., *Images of Deviance* (Penguin 1971)) there are four main factors which coroners take into account when deciding whether a death was a suicide or not:

- Whether there was a suicide note.
- The way the person died, for example by hanging, drowning, or a drug overdose. Death in a road accident rarely results in a suicide verdict.
- The place the death occurred and the circumstances surrounding it; for example, a drug overdose in a remote wood would be more likely to be seen as a suicide than if it occurred at home in bed. A coroner might also consider circumstances such as whether the person had been drinking before taking the drugs, and whether the drugs had been hoarded or not.
- The life history and mental state of the dead person, such as her or his state of health, and whether the victim was in debt, had just failed exams, lost her or his job, got divorced, and was depressed or not.

Coroners do not always agree on the way they interpret these clues. For example, Atkinson found one coroner believed a death by drowning was likely to be a suicide if the clothes were left neatly folded on the beach, but another coroner might attach little importance to this.

1. How is suicide defined in the passage?
2. Why do you think coroners attach such importance to suicide notes?
3. Suggest two reasons why the presence or absence of a suicide note might be an unreliable 'clue' to a dead person's intention to die.
4. Suggest ways relatives and friends might try to persuade a coroner that a death was not a suicide but an accident.
5. On the basis of the evidence in the passage, suggest reasons why:
   (a) Some deaths classified as suicides may have been accidental.
   (b) Some deaths classified as accidents may in fact have been suicides.
6. With reference to the evidence in the passage, suggest reasons why a sociologist should be very careful about using official statistics on suicide as a record of the real number of suicides in society.

Social Surveys

Surveys involve the sociologist in systematically gathering information about some group of people. This is done by questioning them using questionnaires and interviews.

The Survey Population

One of the first steps in any social survey is the selection of the group of people to be studied. This group is called the **survey population**. The choice of survey population will depend on the *hypothesis* which the sociologist is investigating. For example, a hypothesis like 'teachers treat males more favourably than females' might mean the survey population would include all pupils and teachers in a particular school.

> A **hypothesis** is an idea which the sociologist guesses might be true, but which has not yet been tested against the evidence.

If the survey population is small, such as a class of college students, it may be possible to interview everyone in the survey population. In some cases, because the organization doing the research has enough time and money, it may be possible to investigate everyone even in a very large survey population. For example, the government has the resources to survey the entire population of Britain in the census every ten years – at a cost of £135 million in 1991. Such costs are way beyond the reach of most sociologists and market research organizations, and because of cost and time, most surveys are limited to studying a **sample** of the survey population.

Sampling

A sample is simply a small group drawn from the survey population. It is a way of making general statements about the whole survey population based on the responses of only a small percentage of the total survey population.

If the results obtained from the sample are to be used to make generalizations about the whole survey population, it is important that the sample is *representative*. Sociologists obtain representative samples by using various sampling methods.

A Representative Sample

A representative sample is one that contains a good cross-section of the survey population, such as the right proportions of people of different ethnic origins, ages, social classes, and sexes. The information obtained from a representative sample should provide roughly the same results as if the whole survey population had been questioned.

Methods of Obtaining a Representative Sample

1 Drawing up a sampling frame

A **sampling frame** is simply a list of names of all those included in the survey population from which the sample will eventually be selected; for example, the names of all schoolchildren in a school taken from registers, or doctors in a town. A commonly used sampling frame is the Electoral Register, which includes the names and addresses of all adults over the age of 18 in Britain who are eligible to vote in elections. Doctors' lists of patients are also commonly used as sampling frames, as most people are registered with a doctor.

The choice and completeness of the sampling frame is very important if the results obtained are to be generalized to the whole survey population. For example, a telephone directory would be a poor sampling frame if we wanted to select a sample which was representative of the entire adult population, as it only contains those on the telephone and excludes those who may not be able to afford or want a telephone.

2 Deciding on the sample size

The size of the sample will depend on the amount of time and money available. However, if the sample is too small the results obtained may not be representative of the whole survey population. The ideal size of a sample is that at which the results obtained won't be made much more accurate by increasing the size of the sample.

3 Deciding on a sampling method

A sampling method is the process by which the sociologist selects representative individuals from the sampling frame to question. There are a number of sampling methods used by sociologists to try to gain a representative sample.

Simple random sampling

Simple random sampling means that every individual in the survey population has an equal chance of being picked out for questioning. For example, all names are put in a hat and enough names picked out to make up the required sample size. This is most commonly done by numbering all the names in the sampling frame and then getting a computer to select enough numbers at random to make up the size of sample required.

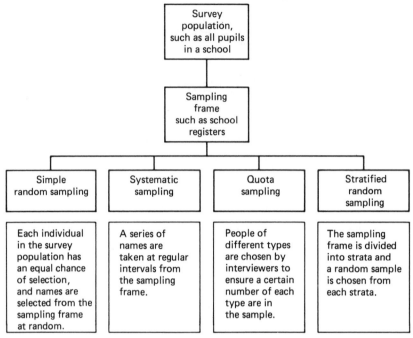

N.B. The sample must be *representative* of the survey population.

Figure 16.2 Sampling methods

The problem with this method is that, purely by chance, the random sample may not be representative of the survey population. For example, there may be too many people of one sex, of one age group, or who live in the same area.

Systematic sampling

Systematic sampling is a method where names are selected from the survey population at regular intervals until the size of sample is reached. For example, every tenth name in the sampling frame is selected.

Quota sampling

Quota sampling is a method where interviewers are told to go and select people who fit into certain categories according to their proportion in the survey population as a whole. For example, an interviewer may be asked to question thirty men and women over the age of 45. The choice of the actual individuals chosen is left to the honesty of the interviewer (unlike other sampling methods where actual named individuals are identified).

Stratified random sampling

Stratified random sampling is a way of attempting to avoid the possible errors caused by simple random sampling. In this case, the sampling frame is divided into strata (layers) or sub-groups, such as groups of a similar age, sex, ethnic group, or social class, and a random sample is then taken from each sub-group. For example, in a survey of doctors, we may know from earlier research that 8 per cent of all doctors are Asian, and so the sociologist must make sure 8 per cent of the sample are Asian. To do this, the sociologist will separate out the Asian doctors from the sampling frame of all doctors, and then take a random sample from this list of Asian doctors to make up the 8 per cent of the sample of all doctors. In this way, the final sample is more likely to be representative of all doctors in the survey population. Stratified random sampling has the advantage over simple random sampling of being much more representative, because all the characteristics of the survey population are more certain to be represented in the sample.

By using one of the above sampling methods, the information provided by the sample can be generalized with great accuracy to the whole survey population. For example, opinion polls on the voting intentions of electors often produce extremely accurate predictions of the outcome of general elections from questioning only about two thousand voters.

Examples of simple random, systematic, and stratified random sampling

Survey population   400 students in a school
50 per cent are male and 50 per cent are female.
This information would be known from earlier research, such as school records.
In each group, 75 per cent are white and 25 percent are black.

Sample size   10 per cent (40)

A simple random sample
To obtain a simple random sample:

1. Draw up a sampling frame: a list of the names of the 400 students in the survey population.
2. Pick out 40 names at random.

A systematic sample
To obtain a systematic sample:

Pick out every tenth name from the sampling frame until 40 names are collected.

The possible problem with these random and systematic samples is that, purely by chance, they might consist of too many males or females or too many black or white students. If this happened, the sample would be unrepresentative of the survey population, and therefore the survey results would give biased, inaccurate, and unrepresentative results. Stratifying the sample can avoid this problem.

A stratified random sample.
To obtain a stratified random sample:

1. Draw up a sampling frame (list of names) of the 400 students in the survey population.
2. Divide this sampling frame according to the way the survey population is made up. We know 50 per cent are male and 50 per cent are female, so divide the sampling frame into two:

   200 males
   200 females

3. We know that 25 per cent of males and females are black, and 75 per cent are white, so divide *each* of these sampling frames into two:

   50 black males
   150 white males
   50 black females
   150 white females

4. From each of these *four* sampling frames take a 10 per cent random sample, by picking out names at random. This produces a sample made up as follows:

   5 black males
   15 white males
   5 black females
   15 white females
   = 40 (the 10 per cent sample required)

This stratified random sample should be representative of the sex and ethnic characteristics of the entire school population, as these features of the survey population are now certain to be included in the 10 per cent sample.

Activity

1. In each of the following cases, suggest both a hypothesis you might wish to test and how you might obtain your sampling frame.

   - The attitudes of family doctors (GPs) to changes in the National Health Service.
   - The attitudes of football supporters to soccer hooliganism.
   - The reasons why few female school-leavers in a town go on computer courses at a local college.
   - A survey of young mothers.
   - A survey of old age pensioners.
   - The opinions of adults in your neighbourhood about how they will vote in the next election.

2. Buneaton College has 3000 full-time students, and 6000 part-time students. Half of the full-time students are women, and three-quarters of the part-time students are men. You want to do a survey among students at Buneaton College. You haven't the time or the money to question every student, so you need to take a 10 per cent sample. In order to make this as representative as possible, you have decided to use a stratified random sampling method.
   (a) Explain how you would select this 10 per cent sample.
   (b) Give the actual numbers of the different groups in the survey population which will be included in your sample.

Research Methods Used in Surveys

There are two main methods which are used in social surveys to collect data: questionnaires and interviews.

Questionnaires

Most surveys involve the use of a questionnaire of some kind. A questionnaire is a printed list of questions to be filled in either personally by the *respondent* (the person answering the questions) or by an interviewer. All respondents answer exactly the same questions.

There are two main types of questionnaire: the pre-coded questionnaire and the open-ended questionnaire

The pre-coded questionnaire

The pre-coded questionnaire involves the individual being asked a number of pre-set questions with a limited number of multiple choice answers. The person filling in the questionnaire will tick off the answer. A typical question might be 'Do you think wages should be paid for housework?' with available answers being Yes/No/Don't know. The problem with this type of questionnaire is that it does not allow respondents to explain their views fully or to develop their answers. An example of a pre-coded questionnaire (to be carried out by an interviewer) is shown in figure 16.3.

The open-ended questionnaire

Like the pre-coded questionnaire, the open-ended questionnaire usually has a number of pre-set questions, but there is no pre-set choice of answers. This allows respondents to write their own answer or dictate it to an interviewer.

Newspaper survey

Conduct the interview politely. Ask questions clearly. Do not give extra emphasis to any words. Use only the words that are underlined. Mark the answer given by putting a circle round the appropriate code number.

Good morning/afternoon/evening. I am conducting a survey on newspapers and I would be grateful if you would help me by answering some questions.

		Code
A.	Sex of respondent: Male Female	1 2
B.	Estimated age of respondent 16 or under 17–21 22–40 41–60 61 or over	1 2 3 4 5
C.	Would you please tell me which of the following categories best describes your occupation: (show list) Professional/senior manager Manager in business Administrator/clerical Self-employed/business owner Manual Housewife Student Retired Unemployed Other	 1 2 3 4 5 6 7 8 9 10

Question		Code	Route

Q.1	Do you read a daily morning newspaper
	   every day
	   4–5 times a week
	   2–3 times a week
	   once a week
	   less than once a week
	   never?
		1
		2
		3
		4
		5
		6
			Q.2
			Q.2
			Q.2
			Q.2
			Q.2
			Classify

Q.2	Do you usually read:
	   all the newspaper
	   most of it
	   part of it
	   or just glance through it?
		1
		2
		3
		4
			Q.3
			Q.3
			Q.3
			Q.3

Q.3	Which newspaper or newspapers do you read?
	  Sun Star Today
	  Mirror Telegraph Independent
	  Mail Guardian Financial Times
	  Express Times Others (please
	                 write in)
		1 5 9
		2 6 10
		3 7 11
		4 8 12
			Q.4
			Q.4
			Q.4
			Q.4

Q.4	Where do you usually get most of your news about
	what's going on in Britain today? Is it from:
	   Newspapers
	   Television
	   Radio
	   Other (specify)
	   Don't know
		1
		2
		3
		4
		5
			Q.5
			Q.5
			Q.5
			Q.5
			Q.5

Q.5	Which of the following do you think gives the
	most truthful account of the news:
	   Newspapers
	   Television
	   Radio
	   Don't know
		1
		2
		3
		4
			Q.6
			Q.6
			Q.6
			Q.6

Figure 16.3 An example of a pre-coded questionnaire conducted by an interviewer
Note the instructions given to the interviewer at the top of the questionnaire. These seek to ensure objectivity and consistency between different interviewers.

An example of an open-ended question is 'What is your opinion of the present government?'. Such questions give respondents scope to express their own views. Such a questionnaire may form the basis for an unstructured interview (see below).

In a survey, both pre-coded and open-ended questions may be combined in the same questionnaire.

Designing a questionnaire

To be successful, the following rules should be followed when designing a questionnaire:

- It should be clearly laid out and well printed, and instructions for completing it should be easily understood by the respondent. The questionnaire should be easy to follow and complete.
- Questions should only be asked which the respondents are likely to be able to answer accurately. For example, people can only give opinions on things they know about and can remember accurately.
- The number of questions should be kept to the minimum required to produce the information. Respondents may be unwilling to spend a long time answering questions, or might stop answering the questions seriously.
- Questions should be simple and direct, and able to be answered briefly.
- Questions should be phrased in simple, everyday language so they are easily understood by the respondent. Technical words and 'jargon' should be avoided as the respondents may not understand the question. For example, a question about 'marital status' should be avoided – it is better to ask if someone is married, single, or divorced.
- Questions should be unambiguous, and their meaning quite clear. For example, a question like 'Do you watch television often?' is a bad question because people might interpret 'often' in different ways – it is better to specify actual time periods such as 1–2 hours a day, 3–4 hours a day, and so on.
- 'Leading' questions which encourage people to give particular answers should be avoided – otherwise the respondent might feel he or she is expected to give a particular answer. This might then produce invalid (or untruthful) answers.
- Pre-coded questionnaires should provide enough alternative answers to apply to all the respondents. There should be an opportunity for the respondents to give a 'Don't know' answer.

Activity

1. The following questions, which are intended to be filled in by the respondent, all have at least one thing wrong with them. In each case, describe what is wrong with the question and re-write the question in a more correct or more appropriate way.

(a) Do you watch television: 1–2 hours a night?
2–4 hours a night?
4–6 hours a night?

(b) Don't you agree sex before marriage is wrong? YES/NO

(c) Don't you think you should vote Labour if there were a General Election tomorrow? YES/NO/ DON'T KNOW

(d) Which recommendation of the Government Road Safety Committee regarding the change in the upper speed limit on class A roads and motorways do you support?

(e) Are you happy with your washing machine? YES/NO/ DON'T KNOW

(f) Do you have joint conjugal roles in your household? YES/NO/ DON'T KNOW

(g) Which social class do you belong to?

(h) Do you bonk with your partner a lot? YES/NO

(i) Are you a good driver? YES/NO/ DON'T KNOW

(j) Do you read newspapers: A LOT?
QUITE A LOT?
OFTEN?
SOMETIMES?
A BIT?
NOT MUCH?
NEVER?

2. Do you think any of the questions above in their present form would be either unlikely to be answered or answered dishonestly? Give reasons for your answer.

Questionnaires should be
phrased in straightforward
everyday language.

The postal questionnaire

A postal questionnaire is one which is sent to the respondents through the post with a pre-paid envelope for the reply. The respondents fill in the form themselves.

A key problem with postal questionnaires is that often people don't bother to return them. The percentage returning them may sometimes be only 20 per cent to 50 per cent of the sample, and this may mean the results obtained may be inaccurate, biased, and unrepresentative. For example, those not replying may have answered differently from those who did reply, and those replying may be more educated, interested in the topic being investigated, or have some 'axe to grind'.

To try to overcome the problem of non-response, postal questionnaires often have covering letters from well-known individuals or organizations, or offer free gifts, and other rewards. A reply-paid envelope is essential if the questionnaire is not to be dropped into the nearest waste-paper basket!

Interviews

Questionnaires are often carried out by an interviewer. There are two main types of interview: the structured or formal interview and the unstructured or informal interview.

The structured or formal interview

The structured interview is based on a pre-coded questionnaire. The interviewer asks the questions and does not probe beyond the basic answers received. It is a formal question-and-answer session.

The unstructured or informal interview

This type of interview is based on an open-ended questionnaire, or simply a list of topics the interviewer wishes to discuss. The interviewer will ask the respondent open-ended questions which may trigger off discussions or further questions. The interviewer will try to put the respondent at ease in a relaxed, informal situation and encourage him or her to express his or her feelings and opinions. This means the interviewer can obtain much greater depth of information than is possible in a structured interview or in a postal questionnaire. It is a bit like a TV chat show.

Interviewer bias

A major problem with interviews, particularly unstructured interviews, is the problem of **interviewer bias**. Interviewer bias is the way in which the presence or behaviour of the interviewer may influence in some way the answers given by the respondent. There is always the possibility that the respondent might adapt his or her answer according to the status, class, ethnicity, age, sex, speech, accent or tone of voice, style of dress, or behaviour of the interviewer. The interviewer may give the impression of wanting to hear a certain answer, and the respondent may try to impress the interviewer by giving answers she or he thinks the interviewer wants to hear and would approve of, rather than giving her or his real opinions.

Interviewer bias is a serious problem, as it could mean that respondents do not give answers which they really believe, and therefore the results of the survey may be unreliable. To overcome interviewer bias, interviewers are trained to avoid giving any impression of approval or disapproval based on their own opinions and feelings about the answers they receive. They should give the impression of polite indifference to the answers received.

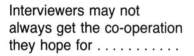

Interviewers may not always get the co-operation they hope for . . . .

. . . . especially if they choose the wrong moment!!!!

Activity

Consider the following situations, and in each case:

1. Suggest possible ways in which interviewer bias might occur.
2. Suggest what might be done to help remove the bias.

- A white person being questioned by a black interviewer about his or her racial attitudes.
- An adult interviewing pupils in a school.
- A British person interviewing a French person about her or his attitudes towards the English.
- An adult interviewer asking teenagers about their attitudes to glue-sniffing or other drug abuse.
- A well-dressed, middle-class sociologist asking gypsies questions about their lifestyle.
- A middle-class interviewer asking lower-working-class people about their attitudes to social welfare payments.
- A female interviewer asking a married or cohabiting couple about how household tasks are divided between them.

- An interviewer asking questions on birth control techniques.
- An older woman asking questions of a young mother about the way children should be brought up.
- An interviewer who is a committed Christian asking questions about religious belief.

The strengths and limitations of postal questionnaires and interviews

Strengths	*Limitations*

Postal questionnaires

Strengths	Limitations
• Fairly cheap compared to paying interviewers.	• Non-response, leading to un-representative, biased results.
• Large numbers of people over a wide geographical area can be questioned.	• Extra questions cannot be asked or added, to get the respondents to expand or explain themselves more fully. The depth of information is therefore limited.
• Results are obtained quickly.	
• People have more time to reply than when an interviewer is present, so more accurate answers may be obtained.	• With pre-coded questionnaires, the limited range of questions and answers may mean the researcher isn't getting at what the respondent really thinks.
• Questions on personal, controversial, or embarrassing subjects are more likely to be answered than if they are asked by an interviewer.	• The wording may be confusing to the respondent, and the questions therefore misunderstood. There is no interviewer present to explain the question if necessary.
• The problem of interviewer bias is avoided.	
• Answers are easy to compare and put into statistical form (numbers and percentages) – for example, '87 per cent of housewives questioned said they had to do all the housework.'	

Strengths	*Limitations*

Interviews

- It is the best way of getting questionnaires completed – the problem of non-response found with postal questionnaires is much rarer. Skilled interviewers can persuade people to answer questions.

- There is more flexibility than with postal questionnaires – questions may be explained and, except with pre-coded questionnaires, extra questions can be asked and more detail obtained.

- Unstructured interviews allow the respondent to be more open and honest, and therefore more accurate information about the respondents' attitudes, values, and opinions can be obtained.

- Unstructured interviews enable the ideas of the sociologist to develop during the interview, and the interviewer can adjust questions and change direction as the interview is taking place if new ideas and insights emerge. By contrast, structured interviews have already decided the important questions.

- Interviews are more time-consuming and costly than postal questionnaires – interviews are often slow and interviewers have to be paid. Many more people can be questioned with a postal questionnaire for the same cost.

- Because interviews tend to be slow and expensive, often only a small number can take place – this means the sample size is often small, and therefore risks being unrepresentative of the survey population.

- Interviews tend to be artificial situations, and there is no way of knowing whether what people say in an interview is what they really believe or how they behave in real life.

- The success of interviews depends heavily on the skill and personality of the interviewer, especially in unstructured interviews; for example, in getting people to answer questions that produce useful information and in keeping the conversation going.

- There is a risk of interviewer bias, leading to inaccurate results.

The Stages of a Survey

Before carrying out a large-scale survey, it is important to carry out a **pilot survey**. This is a trial run of the final survey, using fewer people than the final sample. Its purpose is to iron out any problems which the researcher might have overlooked. For example, some questions may be unclear, some of the sample may have died or moved away, or there may be problems with non-response or non-cooperation by respondents.

After the pilot survey is completed, the results are reviewed, any necessary changes are made, and the main survey can then proceed. The stages of a survey are shown in figure 16.4.

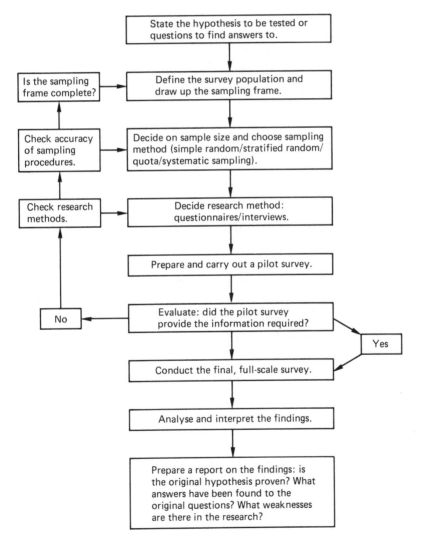

Figure 16.4 The stages of a survey

Observation

Apart from surveys, sociologists also collect data by observation. There are two main kinds of observation: non-participant observation (or direct observation) and participant observation.

Non-participant Observation

The researcher observes a group or situation without taking part in any way. This has the advantage that the sociologist can study people in their 'natural setting' without their behaviour being influenced and changed by the presence of the researcher. For example, a researcher may observe people queuing in a supermarket to see how impatient they get. However, observation without involvement in the group means it is often not possible to understand what is really happening, or to find out more by asking questions. Therefore sociologists more often join in with a group to observe it. This is known as participant observation.

Participant Observation

Participant observation is a very commonly used observation technique. In this method, the researcher actually joins in the group or community she or he is studying. The researcher tries to become an accepted part of the group. For example, the sociologist may spend time as a mental patient in a hospital, join a gang, live as a gypsy or as a 'down and out', spend time in prison, or teach in a school.

The strengths and limitations of participant observation

Strengths	Limitations
• The sociologist gains first-hand knowledge of the group being studied. This provides much more detail and depth than other methods like questionnaires and interviews.	• It is very time-consuming and expensive compared to other methods, as it involves the sociologist participating in a group for long periods.

- Questionnaires and interviews tend to provide information only at one point in time. Participant observation takes place over a long period and can therefore give a much fuller account of a group's behaviour.

- With other methods, the sociologist has already decided on a hypothesis, which affects what questions are asked and therefore what is found out. With participant observation, interesting new ideas to explore may emerge during the research itself.

- Participant observation may be the only possible method of research. For example, a criminal gang is hardly likely to answer questionnaires or do interviews for fear of the consequences, and a group like gypsies may well see an interviewer as 'official' and prying, and may fear harassment by councils, police, and other official bodies. By adopting a *covert* role – keeping her or his identity secret – the researcher may be able to investigate such groups. Even if the group knows who the researcher is (this is known as an *overt* role), the researcher may, after a time, win the trust of the group.

- Because only a small group is studied, it is difficult to make generalizations.

- It depends a great deal on the personality of the investigator and his or her ability to fit in with the group.

- There is a danger of the researcher becoming so involved with the group and developing such loyalty to it that he or she may find it difficult to stand back and report his or her observations in a neutral way.

- There is no real way of checking the findings of a participant observation study. There is no real evidence apart from the observations of the researcher, and what one researcher might regard as important may be missed or seen as unimportant by another.

- There may be a problem of gaining the group's confidence (getting into the group) and maintaining it (staying in), especially if criminal and other deviant activities are involved. What does the researcher do if a group involves itself in criminal activities like theft, drug-dealing, or acts of violence? Failure to take part may result in the group's loss of confidence and trust, and the effective end of the research.

- The presence of the researcher, if she or he is known to the group as a researcher, may change the group's behaviour simply because they know they are being studied.

Activity

1. What does the cartoon above suggest might be some of the difficulties involved in a participant observation study of a gang?
2. Many participant observation studies have been concerned with the study of various forms of deviance, such as homosexual groups or drug users. Suggest ways you might get in touch with and accepted by such a group to study it, and outline any difficulties you might have with staying in the group.

In an actual piece of research, sociologists will probably use a variety of methods to collect the data they require. The methods chosen will be influenced by the questions or hypothesis being investigated, the information required (whether quantitative or qualitative), the scale of the research, and the time and money available to complete it. Figure 16.5 illustrates the relationship between some of these factors.

Activity

1. According to figure 16.5, which method of data collection involves the largest number of respondents?
2. Which method has the highest level of personal involvement of the researcher with the respondents?
3. Which method, apart from observational methods, provides the most qualitative data?

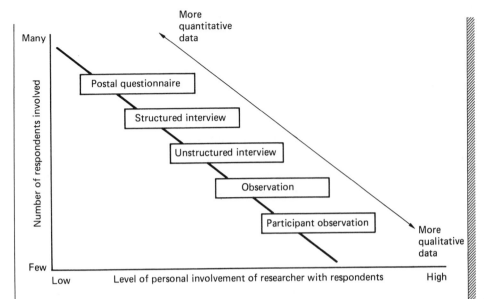

Figure 16.5 Methods of data collection

4. Imagine you have three months to carry out a small-scale research project on one of the following issues, using both primary and secondary sources:

- The difficulties facing the elderly.
- The opinions of adults in your neighbourhood about how they will vote in the next election.
- How household tasks are divided between men and women in the home.
- Gender stereotyping in a school or college.
- The attitudes of people towards religion.
- The lifestyle of teenagers.

Select one of the issues above, and:

(a) Suggest a hypothesis you might wish to test or questions you want to find answers to.
(b) Identify at least one secondary source of information you might use, and explain what information you would expect to obtain from it.
(c) Explain how you might select the group of people to be studied.
(d) Explain carefully what research method or methods you would use to collect your primary data.
(e) Identify three problems or difficulties you might face in carrying out your research, and in each case suggest how you might overcome these problems.

Doing Your Own Research: Coursework

As part of GCSE and many other introductory sociology courses, some form of coursework or project work has to be carried out. This coursework component is usually a small-scale piece of research into an area of sociology related to the syllabus.

One of the most important factors in successfully completing coursework is to keep research small-scale and manageable, to choose a topic you're interested in, and to recognize the limited time and resources available. Marks are awarded for the quality of the research and not simply quantity – a short (but not too short!), well-executed project is far better than a long rambling one.

Planning a Project

In planning and carrying out a project, the sampling techniques and research methods discussed in this chapter should be applied. A successful project should follow the stages of research shown in figure 16.6.

You should also follow these guidelines:

- If information was collected from a sample of people, you should explain how you selected your sample. Was it representative? (It usually won't matter if it is unrepresentative, so long as this limitation of the research is explained in the conclusion.)
- You should give convincing reasons for the method(s) you chose, explain why they were particularly suited to the aims of your research, and give a clear description of how the information was collected.
- Your report should include:
  (a) A table of contents.
  (b) Clearly marked chapters.
  (c) Good layout.
  (d) Clear language.
  (e) The use of relevant diagrams and illustrations, with any pie charts, graphs, tables, photographs, or cassette or video tapes being clearly labelled and referred to in the text.
  (f) A list of books and sources you used – this is known as a bibliography.

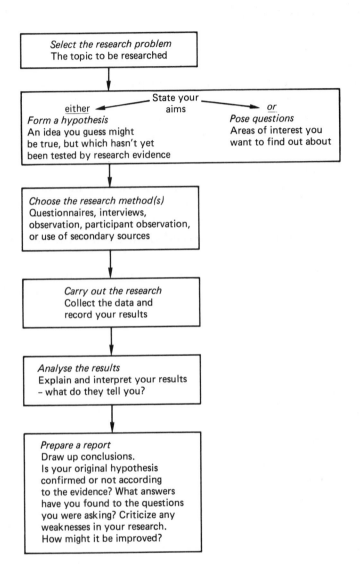

Figure 16.6 The stages of research

Suggestions for possible projects are included at the end of each chapter in this book, except chapter 1 and this chapter, but you can usually choose any topic which interests you, so long as it is relevant in some way to the syllabus you are following.

Chapter Summary

After studying this chapter, you should be able to:

- Explain the difference between quantitative and qualitative data.
- Explain, with examples, the difference between primary and secondary sources of data, and their advantages and disadvantages.
- Explain the various methods sociologists use to obtain representative samples.
- Outline the stages of a survey.
- Describe and explain the use of questionnaires, interviews, and non-participant and participant observation in sociological research, and explain their various strengths and limitations.
- Outline the stages a sociologist would go through in carrying out a piece of research.
- Carry out a small-scale piece of research of your own, using the various sources, sampling techniques, and research methods covered in this chapter.

Key Terms

hypothesis
interviewer bias
pilot survey
primary data
qualitative data
quantitative data
sample
sampling frame
secondary data
survey
survey population

Appendix: Reading Statistical Data

The evidence that sociologists use in their research comes in a variety of forms, but often consists of statistical data presented in the form of tables, pie charts, graphs, bar charts, and various combinations of these. These often prove difficult for newcomers to sociology to understand. This appendix is designed to introduce you to the use and interpretation of these forms of data, and give you practice in doing so. This should make it easier to read the tables and figures appearing in this book, and construct your own should you wish.

Statistical Tables

When confronted with a statistical table, you should first read carefully the heading of the table – this will tell you what subject the statistics refer to. Tables generally show the relationship between two or more factors, and the key thing to note is what the statistics refer to – whether they are in actual numbers or percentages and what units the numbers are in. For example, the numbers might be in thousands or millions or they might be in the form of numbers per thousand of the population.

Table A1 is taken from a major source of official government statistics, *Social Trends*, which is published annually. The data in this table will be used to show the variety of ways in which statistical evidence can be presented.

Table A1 on divorce shows the relationship between a number of factors (shown in the left-hand column) and how these have changed over time (the dates shown along the top row). Notice that:

Table A1 Divorce

	1961	1971	1976	1981	1984	1985	1986	1987	1988	1989
Petitions[a] filed (thousands)										
England and Wales										
By husband	14	44	43	47	49	52	50	50	49	50
By wife	18	67	101	123	131	139	131	133	134	135
Total	32	111	145	170	180	191	180	183	183	185
Decrees nisi[b] granted (thousands)										
England and Wales	27	89	132	148	148	162	153	150	155	152
Decrees absolute[c] granted (thousands)										
England and Wales	25	74	127	146	145	160	154	151	153	151
Scotland	2	5	9	10	12	13	13	12	11	12
Northern Ireland	–	–	1	1	2	2	2	2	2	2
United Kingdom	27	80	136	157	158	175	168	165	166	164
Persons divorcing per thousand married people										
England and Wales	2.1	6.0	10.1	11.9	12.0	13.4	12.9	12.7	12.8	12.7
Percentage of divorces where one or both partners had been divorced in an immediately previous marriage										
England and Wales	9.3	8.8	11.6	17.1	21.0	23.0	23.2	23.5	24.0	24.7
Estimated numbers of divorced people who had not remarried (thousands)										
Great Britain										
Men	101	200	405	653	847	918	990	1047	–	–
Women	184	317	564	890	1105	1178	1258	1327	–	–
Total	285	517	969	1543	1952	2096	2248	2374	–	–

[a]A petition is a request to a court to grant a divorce.
[b]A decree nisi is the stage before the divorce is finalized.
[c]A decree absolute is the final divorce, representing the legal termination of the marriage.

Source: Social Trends 21 (HMSO 1991).

- The table refers to the different countries making up the United Kingdom. There are references to England and Wales, Scotland, Northern Ireland, Great Britain, and the United Kingdom.
- There are three ways in which the figures are expressed:

(a) 'Petitions filed', 'decrees nisi granted', 'decrees absolute granted', and 'estimated numbers of divorced people who had not remarried' are expressed in *thousands*.
(b) 'Divorces where one or both partners had been divorced in an immediately previous marriage' are expressed in *percentages*.
(c) 'Persons divorcing' are expressed as *'per thousand* married people' (this is known as the divorce rate).

Activity

Study table A1 carefully and answer the following questions to check whether you are reading the table correctly:

1. How many divorce petitions were filed by husbands in England and Wales in 1985?
2. How many divorced women in Great Britain in 1971 were estimated not to have remarried?
3. How many decrees absolute were granted in Scotland in 1976?
4. By how many had the number of decrees absolute granted in the United Kingdom increased between 1961 and 1987?
5. How many divorce petitions were filed by wives in England and Wales in 1984?
6. How many persons were divorcing per thousand married people in England and Wales in 1986?
7. What percentage of divorces in England and Wales in 1987 involved at least one partner who had been divorced in an immediately previous marriage?
8. What was the total number of decrees absolute granted in the United Kingdom in 1987?

Describing a Trend

When interpreting statistical data, you will often be expected to describe a trend, or how the pattern shown changes over time. In describing a trend, you should normally give the starting figure and date and the finishing figure and date, and state whether the figure has increased or decreased, and by how much.

For example, with table A1 you might be asked: 'What trend is shown in the number of decrees absolute granted in the United Kingdom between 1961 and 1989?'. Your answer might take the form: 'The number of decrees absolute has increased by 137 000, from 27 000 in 1961 to 164 000 in 1989' (the figure of 137 000 being obtained by subtracting the figure of 27 000 in 1961 from 164 000 in 1989).

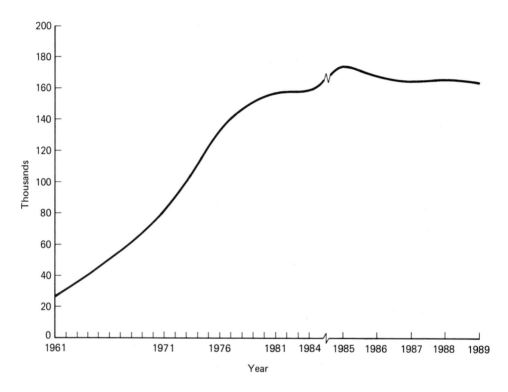

Figure A1 Decrees absolute granted, United Kingdom, 1961–89

Activity

Using table A1, practise describing the following trends:

1. What trend is shown in the number of persons divorcing per thousand married people in England and Wales between 1961 and 1989?
2. What trend does the table show in the number of decrees nisi granted in England and Wales in the period covered by the table?
3. Comparing the number of petitions filed by husbands and wives in England and Wales between 1961 and 1989, what *three* trends are shown?

Graphs

Statistics are commonly presented in the form of graphs. These show the relationship between two factors and how they change over time. These are shown on the vertical and horizontal axes, which are labelled to show what they represent. Trends can be immediately spotted by studying whether the line rises or falls between two dates. It is always important to note what the figures on the axes refer to – numbers, percentages, dates, and so on.

Figure A1, using the data given in table A1, illustrates how the number of decrees absolute granted in the United Kingdom has changed over time. Notice how the horizontal axis gives the date and the vertical axis gives the number of divorces (in thousands)

Activity

Using figure A1:

1. How many decrees absolute were granted in 1971?
2. About how many decrees absolute were granted in 1985?
3. What trend is shown in the graph?
4. Using the data given in table A1, practise drawing your own graph to illustrate the changing number of persons divorcing per thousand married people in England and Wales between 1961 and 1987. Make sure you label the axes correctly and put a title on your graph.

Graphs may have more than one curve on them to show more information, and this is useful for making comparisons. For example, figure A2 shows that both the number of petitions filed for divorce and the decrees absolute granted (in thousands) have increased over time, and it is easy to see at a glance that there are large differences between them.

Activity

What does figure A2 on the next page show about the number of divorce petitions compared to the number of decrees absolute granted over the period covered by the graph? How might you explain this difference?

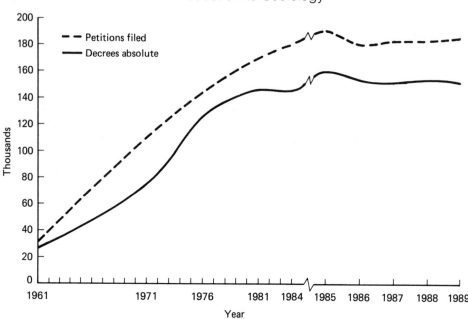

Figure A2 Divorce in England and Wales, 1961–89

Cumulative Graphs

Sometimes graphs may show how a total figure is made up by adding one set of figures to another. This is called a cumulative graph, as the figures 'build up' to the total. This is illustrated in figure A3, using the data from table A1 on 'petitions filed for divorce by husbands and wives in England and Wales'.
    In figure A3:

- The top line shows the total number of petitions filed for divorce.
- The bottom line shows the number of husbands filing petitions.
- The space between the two lines represents the number of wives filing petitions.

By subtracting the number of husbands (the bottom line) from the total (the top line), it is possible to calculate the number of wives filing petitions. For example, in 1981, there was a total of about 170 000 petitions filed (point A), with 47 000 by husbands (point B). The number of wives petitioning for divorce is therefore about 123 000 (A minus B).

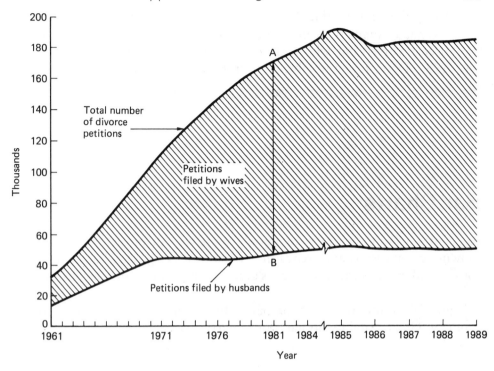

Figure A3 Petitions filed for divorce by husbands and wives, England and Wales, 1961–89

It is immediately obvious from looking at the graph that:

- Far more wives petition for divorce than husbands, as the gap between the top line and the bottom line is much wider than the gap between the bottom line and the horizontal axis.
- The gap between the curves widens over time, showing that the number of wives petitioning for divorce has grown at a faster rate than that of husbands seeking divorce.

Activity

Referring to figure A3:

1. About how many wives were petitioning for divorce in 1961?
2. Identify three trends that are shown in the graph.

3. Using the data in table A1, draw a cumulative graph showing the estimated numbers of men and women in Great Britain who had been divorced but who had not remarried in the period 1961 to 1987. Don't forget to label your graph correctly and give it a title.

Bar Charts

Bar charts are another very commonly used way of presenting data and showing comparisons and trends in a visually striking way. Bar charts are constructed in much the same way as graphs, but columns are used instead of lines.

Figure A4 shows a bar chart comparing the estimated numbers of divorced people in Great Britain who had not remarried between 1961 and 1987.

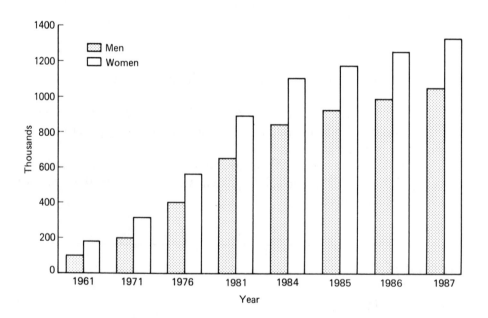

Figure A4 Estimated numbers of divorced people who had not remarried, Great Britain, 1961–87

Activity

Referring to figure A4, answer the following questions:

1. About how many divorced women were estimated not to have remarried in 1985?
2. About how many divorced men were estimated not to have remarried in 1971?
3. Identify two trends shown in the chart.

Cumulative Bar Charts

Bar charts may, like graphs, be cumulative and show how totals are made up. Compare figure A4 with figure A5, in which exactly the same information is presented in a different form (note, however, that the scales on the vertical axes differ between the two).

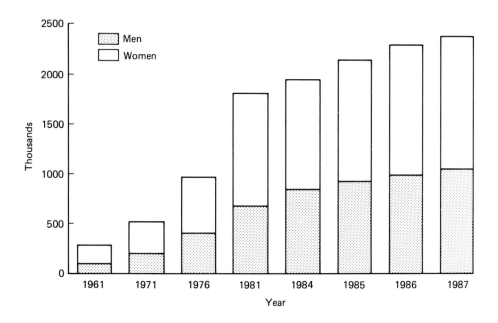

Figure A5 Estimated numbers of divorced people who had not remarried, Great Britain, 1961–87

> ## Activity
>
> Using the data in table A1, construct a bar chart comparing the petitions filed for divorce in England and Wales by husbands and wives for the years 1961, 1971, 1981, and 1989.

Pie Charts

Pie charts present data by dividing a circle into sectors, with each sector being of the same size as the item it represents. Pie charts are very effective in showing statistics in an easily digestible and striking way. For example, using the data given in table A1, the number of divorce petitions filed by husbands and wives in England and Wales in 1989 might be presented as in figure A6:

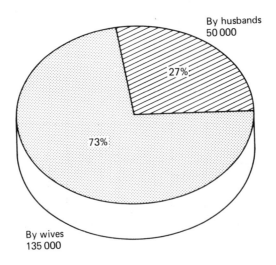

Figure A6 Petitions filed for divorce by husbands and wives, England and Wales, 1989

Activity

Draw a pie chart illustrating the way your 24-hour day is divided up between school/college work or paid employment, travelling to and from work, leisure activities, domestic jobs in the home, and sleeping and eating.

Throughout this book there are many examples of statistics presented in a variety of forms, often with activities to develop your understanding of them. You should not simply ignore them, but try to read and interpret them. They often contain important information which will help you to understand the text better.

Glossary

Words in **bold type** within entries refer to terms found elsewhere in the glossary.

Absolute poverty. Poverty defined as lacking the minimum requirements necessary to maintain human health.

Affluent worker. Well-paid manual worker.

Agenda-setting. The list of subjects which the mass media choose to report and bring to public attention.

Alienation. A lack of power and satisfaction at **work**.

Anomie. Confusion and uncertainty over social **norms**.

Anti-school sub-culture. A set of **values**, attitudes, and behaviour in opposition to the main aims of a school.

Arranged marriage. A marriage which is arranged by the parents of the marriage partners, with a view to background and status. More a union between two families than two people, and romantic love between the marriage partners is not necessarily present.

Authority. Power which is accepted as fair and just.

Automation. Production of goods by self-controlling machines with little human supervision.

Bigamy. Where **monogamy** is the only legal form of marriage, the offence of marrying a second partner without first getting divorced.

Birth rate. The number of live births per 1000 of the population per year.

Blue-collar workers. Manual workers.

Bourgeoisie. Class of owners of the **means of production**.

Caste system. A stratification system (see **social stratification**) based on Hindu religious beliefs, where an individual's position is fixed at birth and cannot be changed.

Class consciousness. An awareness in members of a **social class** of their real interests.

Classic extended family. A family where three or more generations of kin live in the same house, street, or area.

Closed society. A stratification system (see **social stratification**) where **social mobility** is not possible.

Coercion. Rule by violence or the threat of violence.

Communes. Self-contained and self-supporting communities, where all members of the community share property, childcare, household tasks, and living accommodation.

Communism. An equal society, without **social classes** or conflict, in which the **means of production** are the common property of all.

Compensatory education. Extra educational help for those coming from disadvantaged groups to help them overcome the disadvantages they face in the education system and the wider society.

Conjugal roles. The **roles** played by a male and female partner in marriage or in a cohabiting couple.

Consumption property. Property for use by the owner which doesn't produce any **income**, such as owning your own car.

Craft production. The production of goods by hand tools.

Culture. The language, beliefs, **values** and **norms**, **customs**, **roles**, knowledge, and skills which combine to make up the 'way of life' of any society.

Culture of poverty. A set of beliefs and **values** thought to exist among the poor which prevents them escaping from poverty.

Customs. **Norms** which have existed for a long time.

Death rate. The number of deaths per 1000 of the population per year.

Democracy. A form of government where the people participate in political decision-making, usually by electing individuals to represent their views.

Demography. The study of population.

Dependency ratio. The proportion of the population which is dependent (see **dependent population**) compared to those who are working.

Dependent age groups. The under 16s, who are at school, and the over 60s (women) and 65s (men), who are retired.

Dependent population. That section of the population which is not in **work** and is supported by others, such as those in full-time education, pensioners and the unemployed.

Deskilling. The removal of skills from **work** by the application of new machinery which simplifies tasks.

De-urbanization. The movement of people away from towns and cities.

Deviance. Failure to conform to social **norms**.

Deviancy amplification. The process by which the mass media, through exaggeration and distortion, actually create more crime and **deviance**.

Deviant career. Where people who have been **labelled** as deviant (see **deviance**) find conventional opportunities blocked to them, and so they are pushed into committing further deviant acts.

Deviant voter. Someone voting against the **political party** representing the interests of her or his **social class**.

Dictatorship. A form of **totalitarianism** where **power** is concentrated in the hands of one person.

Division of labour. The division of **work** into a large number of specialized tasks, each of which is carried out by one worker or group of workers.

Divorce rate. The number of divorces per 1000 married people per year.

Domestic labour. Unpaid housework, including cooking, cleaning, childcare, and looking after the sick and elderly.

Ecumenical movement. A movement which seeks to achieve greater unity between different Christian churches.

Educational Priority Areas. Areas which face a range of social problems, such as poverty and unemployment, in which schools are given extra money and teachers to help children overcome difficulties at school arising from their home backgrounds.

Elaborated code. A form of language use involving careful explanation and detail. It is the language used by strangers and individuals in some formal context, like a job interview, writing a business letter, or in a school lesson or textbook. (See also **restricted code**.)

Elite. A small group holding great **power** and influence in society.

Embourgeoisement. The idea that, with higher wages, the working class are becoming part of the middle class. The opposite of **proletarianization**.

Emigration. The movement of people out of a country or area on a permanent basis.

Endogamy. Where marriage must be to a partner of the same **kinship** or social group.

Equality of educational opportunity. The principle that every child should have an equal chance of doing as well in education as his or her ability will allow.

Ethnic group. A group of people who share a common **culture**.

Ethnic minority group. A social group which shares a cultural identity (see **culture**) which is different from that of the majority population of a society.

Ethnocentrism. A view of the world in which other **cultures** are seen through the eyes of one's own culture, with a devaluing of the others. For example, school subjects may concentrate on white British society and culture rather than recognizing and taking into account the cultures of different ethnic communities (see **ethnic groups**).

Evangelicalism. A form of Christianity involving a fundamentalist (see **fundamentalism**) belief in the Bible and a commitment to preaching the Christian gospel.

False consciousness. A failure by members of a **social class** to recognize their real interests.

Feminist. Someone who believes that women are disadvantaged in society, and should have equal rights with men.

Feudalism. A closed (see **closed society**) system of stratification (see **social stratification**) based on land ownership and legal inequalities.

Floating voter. A voter with no fixed political opinion, nor a committed supporter of any **political party**.

Folk devils. Individuals or groups posing an imagined or exaggerated threat to society.

Fundamentalism. A return to the literal meaning of religious texts.

Gate-keeping. The media's refusal to cover some issues.

Gender. The culturally created differences between men and women which are learnt through **socialization**.

Gender role. The pattern of behaviour which society expects from a man or woman.

General fertility rate. The number of live births per 1000 women of child-bearing age (15–44) per year.

Hidden curriculum. Attitudes and behaviour which are taught through the school's organization and teachers' attitudes but which are not part of the formal timetable.

Hypothesis. An idea which a researcher guesses might be true, but which has not yet been tested against the evidence.

Immigration. The movement of people into a country or area on a permanent basis.

Income. The flow of money which people obtain from **work**, from their investments, or from the state.

Infant mortality. The death of babies in the first year of life.

Infant mortality rate. The number of deaths of babies in the first year of life per 1000 live births per year.

Integrated conjugal roles. Roles in marriage or in a cohabiting couple where male and female partners share domestic tasks, childcare, decision-making, and income earning.

Inter-generational social mobility. A way of measuring **social mobility** by comparing an adult's present occupation with that of the family she or he was born into (usually measured against the father's occupation). It therefore shows how much **social class** mobility there has been between two generations.

Interviewer bias. The answers given in an interview being influenced or distorted in some way by the presence or behaviour of the interviewer.

Intra-generational social mobility. A way of measuring **social mobility** by comparing a person's present occupation with her or his first occupation. It therefore shows how much mobility an individual has achieved within her or his lifetime.

Kibbutz. A community established in Israel, with the emphasis on equality, collective ownership of property, and collective child rearing.

Kinship. Relations of blood, marriage, or adoption.

Labelling. Defining a person or group in a certain way – as a particular 'type' of person or group.

Laws. Official legal rules, formally enforced by the police, courts, and prison, involving legal punishment if they are broken.

Liberation theology. A Christian doctrine mixing **Communism** and Catholicism, and supporting the poor and oppressed in their fight for freedom.

Life chances. The chances of obtaining those things defined as desirable and of avoiding those things defined as undesirable in a society.

Life expectation. An estimate of how long people can be expected to live from a certain age.

Master status. The dominant status of an individual which over-rides all other characteristics of that person, such as that of an 'ex-con'.

Matriarchy. Power and **authority** held by women.

Matrilineal descent. Property or title passing through the female side of the family.

Matrilocal residence. Where, on marriage, the husband is expected to live with or near his wife's family.

Means of production. The key resources necessary for producing society's goods, such as factories and land.

Mechanization. The process where production of goods by hand is replaced by machinery.

Meritocracy. A society where social positions are achieved by merit, such as educational qualifications, talent, and skill.

Migration. The movement of people from one country or area to another.

Modified extended family. A family type where related **nuclear families,** although living apart geographically, nevertheless maintain regular contact and mutual support through visiting, the phone, and letters.

Monogamy. A form of marriage in which a person can only be legally married to one partner at a time.

Moral panic. A wave of public concern about some exaggerated or imaginary threat to society, stirred up by exaggerated and sensationalized reporting in the mass media.

Neo-local residence. Where, on marriage, the couple are expected to live away from both sets of parents.

Net migration. The difference between the number of people entering a country (immigrants) and the number leaving (emigrants) in a given period.

News values. The values and assumptions held by journalists which guide them in choosing what to report and what to leave out, and how what they choose to report should be presented.

Norms. Social rules which define correct behaviour in a society or group.

Norm-setting. The process whereby the mass media emphasize and reinforce conformity to social **norms,** and seek to isolate those who don't conform by making them the victims of unfavourable public opinion.

Nuclear family. A family with two generations, of parents and children, living together in one household.

Objectivity. This means approaching topics with an open mind, avoiding bias, and being prepared to submit research evidence to scrutiny by other researchers.

Open society. A stratification system (see **social stratification**) in which **social mobility** is possible.

Parity of esteem. The intention that the three types of school in the **tripartite system** should be of equal status.

Patriarchy. Power and **authority** held by men.

Patrilineal descent. Property or title passing through the male side of the family.

Patrilocal residence. Where, on marriage, the wife is expected to live with or near her husband's family.

Peer group. A group of people of similar age and status with whom a person mixes socially.

Perinatal death. Still-births and deaths within the first week of life.

Pilot survey. A small-scale practice **survey** carried out before the final survey to check for any possible problems.

Political party. A group of people organized with the aim of forming the government in a society.

Politics. The struggle to gain **power** and control in society, by getting in a position to make decisions and implement policies.

Polyandry. A form of marriage in which a woman may have two or more husbands at the same time.

Polygamy. A form of marriage in which a member of one sex can be married to two or more members of the opposite sex at the same time.

Polygyny. A form of marriage in which a man may have two or more wives at the same time.

Population projections. Predictions of future changes in population size based on past and present population trends.

Positive discrimination. Giving disadvantaged groups more favourable treatment than others to make up for the disadvantages they face.

Poverty line. The dividing point between those who are poor and those who are not. There is no official poverty line in Britain today, but income support/supplementary benefit level and 50 per cent of average income are both used.

Power. The ability of people or groups to exert their will over others and get their own way.

Pressure groups. Organizations which try to put pressure on those with **power** in society to implement policies which they favour.

Primary data. Information which sociologists have collected themselves.

Privatized nuclear family. A **nuclear family** unit which is separated and isolated from wider kin and the community, with members spending time together in home-centred activities.

Productive property. Property which provides an unearned **income** for its owner, such as factories, land, and stocks and shares.

Proletarianization. The process of decline in the pay and conditions of sections of the middle class, so they become more like the working class. The opposite of **embourgeoisement.**

Proletariat. The class of workers, who have to work for wages as they do not own the **means of production.**

Proportional representation. A voting system where the number of representatives elected accurately reflects the proportion of the votes received.

Qualitative data. Information concerned with the meanings and interpretations people have about some issue or event.

Quantitative data. Information that can be expressed in statistical or number form.

Racial discrimination. When **racial prejudice** causes people to act unfairly against a racial group.

Racial prejudice. A set of assumptions about a racial group which people are reluctant to change even when they receive information which undermines those assumptions.

Racism. Believing or acting as though an individual or group is superior or inferior on the grounds of their racial or ethnic origins.

Reconstituted family. A family where one or both partners have been previously married, and they bring with them children of a previous marriage.

Relative poverty. Poverty defined in relation to a generally accepted standard of living in a specific society at a particular time.

Restricted code. A form of language use which takes for granted shared understandings between people. It is colloquial, everyday language used between friends, with limited explanation and use of vocabulary. (See also **elaborated code.**)

Role conflict. The conflict between the successful performance of two or more **roles** at the same time, such as worker and mother.

Role model. Patterns of behaviour which others copy and model their own behaviour on.

Roles. The patterns of behaviour which are expected from individuals in society.

Sample. A small representative group drawn from the **survey population** for questioning or interviewing.

Sampling frame. A list of names of all those in the **survey population** from which a representative **sample** is selected.

Sanction. A reward or punishment to encourage social conformity.

Scapegoats. Individuals or groups blamed for something which is not their fault.

Secondary data. Data which already exists and which the researcher hasn't collected her or himself.

Secularization. The process whereby religious thinking, practice, and institutions lose social significance.

Segregated conjugal roles. A clear division and separation between the **roles** of male and female partner in marriage or in a cohabiting couple.

Self-fulfilling prophecy. People acting in response to behaviour which has been predicted of them, thereby making the prediction come true. Often applied to the effects of streaming in schools.

Serial monogamy. A form of marriage where a person keeps marrying and divorcing a series of different partners, but is only married to one person at a time.

Sex. The biological differences between men and women.

Sexism. Prejudice or discrimination against people (especially women) because of their sex.

Sex ratio. The proportion of males to females in the population, expressed as the number of males per 1000 females.

Sexual division of labour. The division of **work** into 'men's jobs' and 'women's jobs'.

Social class. An open (see **open society**) system of stratification consisting of broad groups of people (classes) who share a similar economic situation, such as occupation, **income**, and ownership of **wealth**.

Social control. The process of persuading or forcing individuals to conform to **values** and **norms**.

Social institutions. The organized social arrangements which are found in all societies.

Socialization. The process of learning the **culture** of any society.

Social mobility. Movement of groups or individuals up or down the social hierarchy.

Social stratification. The division of society into a hierarchy of unequal social groups.

Sociology. The systematic (or planned and organized) study of human groups and social life in modern societies.

Status. The amount of prestige or social importance a person has in the eyes of other members of a group or society. *Ascribed status* is status which is given to an individual at birth and usually can't be changed. *Achieved status* is status which is achieved through an individual's own efforts.

Status frustration. A sense of frustration arising in individuals or groups because they are denied status in society.

Status group. A group of people sharing a similar social standing and lifestyle.

Stereotype. A generalized, over-simplified view of the features of a social group, allowing for few individual differences between members of the group.

Sub-culture. A smaller **culture** held by a group of people within the main culture of a society, in some ways different from the main culture, but with many aspects in common.

Survey. A method of gathering information about some group of people by questioning them using questionnaires and interviews.

Survey population. The section of the population which is of interest in a survey.

Symmetrical family. A family where the **roles** of husband and wife have become more alike (symmetrical) and equal.

Totalitarianism. A system of government where society is controlled by a small powerful group or an individual, and ordinary people lack any control over government decision-making.

Tripartite system. The system of secondary education established in 1944 in which pupils were selected for one of three types of secondary school according to their performance in the 11+ exam.

Underachievement. The failure of people to achieve as much as they are capable of.

Urbanization. The movement of population from rural (country) areas to urban areas (towns and cities), which become the major centres of population in a society.

Value freedom. The idea that the beliefs and prejudices of the sociologist should not be allowed to influence the way research is carried out and evidence interpreted.

Values. General beliefs about what is right or wrong, and the important standards which are worth maintaining and achieving in any society.

Wealth. Property which can be sold and turned into cash for the benefit of the owner.

White-collar workers. Non-manual clerical workers, sales personnel, and other office workers, whose work is non-professional and non-managerial.

Work. The production of goods or services that usually earns a wage or salary, though housework remains unpaid.

Index

Using the index
If you are looking for general topics, it is probably best to refer first to the detailed contents pages at the beginning of this book. If you want to find particular items of information, look them up in this index. If the item is not listed, then think of other headings it might be given under: the same information is often included several times under different headings. This index only includes the main references found in the book, rather than every single occurrence of the theme, and it is sensible to check the largest references first, such as pages 128–40 before 37, 38, and 97. The chances are that what you're looking for will be in the largest entry, and save you time wading through a lot of smaller references.

Page numbers in bold refer to items in the glossary.